How Real Estate Developers Think

THE CITY IN THE TWENTY-FIRST CENTURY

Eugenie L. Birch and Susan M. Wachter, Series Editors

How Real Estate Developers Think

Design, Profits, and Community

Peter Hendee Brown

UNIVERSITY OF PENNSYLVANIA PRESS

PHILADELPHIA

Published by
University of Pennsylvania Press
Philadelphia, Pennsylvania 19104-4112
www.upenn.edu/pennpress

Printed in the United States of America
on acid-free paper

10 9 8 7 6 5 4 3 2 1

Library of Congress Cataloging-in-Publication Data
Brown, Peter Hendee, author.
   How real estate developers think : design, profits, and community / Peter Hendee
Brown.
      pages cm — (The city in the twenty-first century)
   ISBN 978-0-8122-4705-3
   1. Real estate development—United States. 2. City planning—United States. I. Title.
II. Series: City in the twenty-first century book series.
HD255.B758 2015
333.73'150973—dc23
                                                                    2014040780

*For Anna
and for our children,
Magnus and Astrid*

Contents

A Brick Wall in Evanston

> We used to call them our town founders and we honored them by
> erecting their statues in our town squares. Today we just call them
> "developers."
> —Andrés Duany, Miami architect and planner[1]

The Costs of Opposition

In 2002 a Chicago developer named Neil Ornoff hired the architect David
Haymes and his firm, Pappageorge Haymes, to design a twenty-unit residential project on a corner site at 525 Kedzie Street, in Evanston, Illinois,
a northern suburb of Chicago. "The alderman—the city councilman—was
really fearful of the people who lived in the adjacent building and were concerned about losing views they had across the vacant parcel, so he asked the
developer to work with them," recalled Haymes. "We designed a beautiful
building," but the design required a small portion of the building to be a little
bit taller than what the height limits in the code allowed. The site plan also
required the developer to seek relief on a parking rule that required a twenty-
foot setback from the street to the building face to allow for on-street parking
for the property, even though all of the parking for the building was going
to be accommodated onsite, within the building, and concealed from view.
These were routine and modest variance requests but, as Haymes recalls,
"The neighbors simply said no, we are going to oppose the project."[2]

So Haymes went back to the drawing board and redesigned the façade
on the side of the building that faced the neighbors, adding articulation and

setbacks that made the building look better from the neighboring property but increased project costs. This time the neighbors said, "No, that is a very nice design, but we are still going to oppose it." So the developer said, "That's it—we will build it 'as-of-right,'" which means per the letter of the code and without any variances. Haymes redesigned the building, eliminating the small portion that was to be taller and changing the site plan to accommodate the required twenty-foot setback. He stripped off all of the articulation and setbacks on the side facing the neighboring building because there wasn't room and the developer no longer felt the need to incur the costs required to curry favor with the neighbors. "We gave them an unadorned brick wall facing their building because we had to push our own building so far back on the property." In the end, it took the developer and his team more than two years to obtain the approvals required to build a small, twenty-unit condominium project and by then it was late to market. The project opened in 2007, just as the housing bubble burst. The condominium units failed to sell out at pro forma prices so the developer was unable to fully repay the construction loan. The bank foreclosed on the property and sold it to another developer, who converted it to apartments.

In addition to providing architectural design services to developers, David Haymes and his partner have done some small development projects themselves and Haymes is also the head of his own community organization, so he has seen development from those viewpoints too. "There are still some in my community group who harbor those really harsh feelings about developers; they just don't want change. They don't trust developers because anything a developer does is going to be a change, and so they hammer any developer who comes in. Fortunately," says Haymes, "over time, my community group has become more sensitive and understanding of what development is. We have also come to understand that we are better off having a say than not being involved at all, because if you take the attitude that you don't want to talk to somebody then you are going to have to live with the consequences."

Haymes sympathizes with how the public views developers but at the same time he finds that the whole process is far too distrustful to be productive. When Haymes presents at a public meeting, his job is to support his client by positively representing the project, but Haymes says he almost always fully backs and believes in what he is doing for that client. "That is why it is disturbing for us when the developer really is making an honest and forthright effort but he's being abused and we are being called liars and

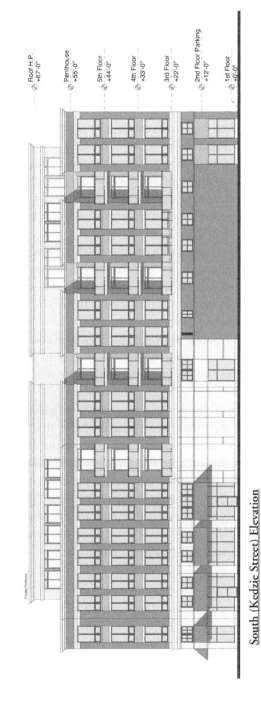

Roof H.P. +67'-0"

Penthouse +55'-0"

5th Floor +44'-0"

4th Floor +33'-0"

3rd Floor +22'-0"

2nd Floor Parking +12'-0"

1st Floor +0'-0"

South (Kedzie Street) Elevation

Figure 1. The improved design for the Kedzie project, Evanston, Illinois. Courtesy of Pappageorge Haymes Partners.

whores." Haymes is disturbed not only because the developer's efforts are being minimized, but also because good things for communities are being passed up—like what happened in Evanston.

In what became a lose-lose outcome, the developer spent extra time and money in a costly and fruitless effort to secure the support of the neighbors. But at the same time, in overplaying their hand the neighbors failed to stop the project and also still lost their views across the vacant parcel, views that were not really theirs to begin with. In giving up their leverage they also gave up views of a more handsome façade from their own windows in exchange for a plain brick wall. By forcing the developer into an as-of-right design, the neighbors forfeited the opportunity to let the developer of the adjacent property increase the value of their own property by building a more attractive building next door.

Unfortunately, for everyone involved, the neighbors misunderstood that the developer had rights and options too. Indeed, his best option was to give up trying to do a more creative design that required minor variances and settle for an as-of-right design that complied with all codes and regulations and could be administratively approved without the need for zoning commission review and a public hearing. The developer could no longer bear the carrying costs on the property, the uncertainty of the approvals process, and the related risk of being late to market. He needed to regain control of the project.

More important, the developer understood the neighbors' strategic position better than they did themselves—certainly better than they understood his position and particularly his property rights. If the neighbors had only been able to see the project from the developer's viewpoint, they may have realized that taking an absolute position—opposition—was a risky strategy that was not necessarily in their own best interests. Then they may have been more open to a collaborative approach and the ability to influence the design in a way that would have maximized the benefits flowing from the project to them and to the larger community.

A Common Story

Unfortunately, this is a common story and anyone who lived in an urban neighborhood in the 2000s and since can probably remember attending a meeting of the neighborhood organization and hearing a contentious

Figure 2. The completed building, an as-of-right design. Could it have been better? Photo by Daniel Kieckhefer/Phorio.

debate over a similar project. Nearby neighbors of development projects deserve consideration, and savvy developers know that they will gain public support and attract more potential buyers and tenants if they listen and adjust their designs to reflect the community's feedback and concerns. But how can community members most effectively use their influence to improve the design of a project? Which things can a developer change, which are nonnegotiable, and how can the neighbors tell the difference? How can the neighbors even tell the difference between a good project and a bad one? What powers do members of the community have to influence private business decisions through the public regulatory review process? And what should the neighbors do when a developer walks through the door with a proposal for a project?

The most common strategies are apathy or opposition. Apathy means de facto support and forfeiture of the opportunity to become engaged and to contribute useful local knowledge to improving the project for all parties. Blanket opposition, on the other hand, signals the end of a discussion rather than the beginning of one, and, again, it turns away from the opportunity to positively influence a project. When community members stop talking to developers, they give up whatever voice they do have in shaping projects in their community. Worse, as in Haymes's story, successful opposition may kill a good and creative proposal only to pave the way for something of lesser quality. The answer lies somewhere between the simple extremes of apathy and opposition—in conversation, compromise, and understanding. Before neighbors and community members can effectively participate in this kind of conversation, they must come to a better understanding of developers and, before that, they must first acknowledge their own motives, interests, and fears.

Fear of Change

Buildings made of glass, stone, and metal make us think of permanence. But cities are fluid and ever-changing places where, over time, streets, infrastructure, public spaces, and buildings are constantly being built, improved, demolished, and replaced. For the people who live next door to a potential development site, such as a vacant lot or an old obsolete building, this means something new will be built on that property sooner or later and it is not a question of if but of when. Yet change is frightening and many people are more comfortable with the familiar, in part because they have difficulty visualizing how a proposed project might actually look and fit into their community. Fear of the unknown begins with rumors of a potential development and increases when community members see the first images of the proposed project at the neighborhood meeting. For people who are not in the development business, it can be difficult to know what to focus on, what to worry about, and how to try to influence the project. Neighbors also have a relatively brief period of time to review the proposal and offer their feedback to the developer and city officials in community meetings and at public hearings. And if the project is approved they know that the inconvenience and aggravation of construction will soon follow.

For a typical project all of this may take less than two years but in the heat of the moment some community members will be unable to pull back and take the long view of this relatively brief period of stress and discomfort. They will have difficulty imagining how the completed development might improve their own lives and make their community a better place—for years, decades, and even centuries to come. It can bring new benefits to the community, including more neighbors, businesses, services, bars, restaurants, retail shops, and perhaps even a grocery store. The development will also increase the tax base and cause the city to increase spending on infrastructure, parks, and other public facilities. And a real estate development project represents a significant and concentrated investment in the community that usually increases surrounding property values. But well before any of these good things will happen, those community members must attend that first public meeting where they learn that change is coming—and that the person who is delivering that change is the real estate developer.

The Stereotypical Developer

Each year, on the first day of the real estate development class that I teach, I ask my students, "What words come to mind when I say 'real estate developer'?" Their answers include "rip-off artists," "greedy," "bloodsuckers," "bulldozers," "used-car salesmen," "devils," "rich white men," "opportunists," and so on. They pile it on and I have difficulty writing everything on the board fast enough. Then, after most of the class has exhausted itself, someone nervously chirps, "entrepreneur" or "creative" or "visionary" or "risk taker," and a more positive, if shorter, list emerges.

Like my students, I suspect that many people believe that developers are rich, greedy, and driven by profits alone; that they know little about planning or design; that they are egotistical if not arrogant and often untrustworthy; and that they neither understand nor care about the impacts of their projects on nearby residents and the larger community. But developers are not all the same and as in any other business or industry, while there may be some "bad" ones, there are many others who have made and continue to make important contributions to cities and communities. As with other industries and government agencies, sensational media accounts of the antics of a few often overshadow the good efforts of many others who quietly go about doing their work. Many people have never met a developer and they know of only the famous and larger-than-life Donald Trump. Some have met developers at neighborhood meetings and others through the experience of buying a new home or condo. And then there are those pervasive stories and sometimes all-too-personal experiences with developers that reinforce the stereotypes listed above.

To the people who buy or rent units or space in their finished buildings, developers can be known to overpromise and underdeliver, hyping their projects in the beginning but cheapening them in the end. To architects, contractors, and other members of the project team, developers are seen as risky clients to work for, because they are known for squeezing their team members' fees when they are negotiating contracts at the beginning and then withholding payments for completed work, particularly when times get tough. And many members of the broader community, particularly architects, think developers either do not know or do not care about good design. Rather, they think developers always take the cheapest route by dumbing down design and reducing material quality to maximize profits. Many people conclude that cities are not as good as they could be because of the work of developers. So when community members make suggestions in neighborhood meetings like "can't you just make it shorter, give it more articulation, use better materials, put the parking underground," and so on, their suspicions are reinforced when the developer's answer is more often "no" than "yes."

And developers seem so different from the rest of us. They appear to enjoy great wealth, dress well, drive fancy cars, own several homes, take exotic vacations, go cruising on their yachts, fly around in private planes, and live in a world that is completely different from our own. They can also be charming, charismatic, bright, knowledgeable, and fun to be around and talk to. They hobnob with local politicians and business leaders, are often viewed as local celebrities and important civic leaders, and can seem bigger than life in person. So when they come to neighborhood meetings they generate feelings of ambivalence from community members who find themselves attracted to these important and alluring people while also feeling distrustful of their motives and methods and, in some cases, jealous of their lifestyles.

But stereotypes can be misleading: While they are often rooted in truths, these generalizations fuel the public's distrust by painting all developers with the same brush. In the near term, distrust and misunderstanding reduce the potential for collaboration between developers and members of the community and the chances for developing the best and most creative projects for communities and cities over the long run. And stereotypes are often one-sided and do not reflect other important truths.

For developers to remain in business they must finance and sell a product in advance, for a price that is greater than its costs. Their projects can take years to complete so inflation and unforeseeable market forces make cost control more difficult and increase uncertainty. They must walk a fine line with their buyers, attracting them with a compelling vision while managing expectations for perfection within the limits of reality. They want happy buyers but they cannot earn a profit if they capitulate to requests for things they are not contractually obligated to provide. They must also be tough negotiators with their team members because the sum of the costs of their work—design services, construction materials and labor, and other products and services—must be less than the final sale price. They often do care about good design, because good design sells, but it is good design in the eye of the average potential buyer, rather than those of the elite design professional. And often the buyer's idea of good design can lead to projects that make for good communities in the long run. More important, the neighbors' seemingly reasonable questions and suggestions for improving the design by reducing height and density and adding setbacks don't reflect the increase in costs—and decrease in profits—that those changes often cause. And despite the impressions of wealth that they may project, many developers are just one bad deal away from serious financial hardship and there is no guarantee of endless riches or that the next project will be a success. Development is a very risky and complex business, which is why more people don't do it.

For many community members, real estate developers remain a mystery, and because we don't really understand who they are, what they do, and why they do it, we are in a difficult position when it comes to working with them. And that's why we need to come to a better understanding of developers, because they are going to keep on developing, and their buildings will remain with us long after the construction dust has settled. The purpose of this book is to begin building that deeper understanding.

Understanding Developers

This book takes the position that developers are people whose interests, motives, and actions can be easily understood and that a more complete understanding will lead to better outcomes for neighbors, communities, and cities, as well as for developers. This new understanding will help everyone from academicians who study urban development and public policy to elected officials, city planners, architects, and others who work with developers. Most important, it will help community members—like those neighbors in Evanston—when they find themselves sitting across the table from a developer who is planning to bring change to their neighborhood.

This book is based on interviews with more than one hundred people involved in the real estate development business in Chicago; Miami; Portland, Oregon; and the Twin Cities of Minneapolis and Saint Paul, Minnesota, although the emphasis is on development in those first three cities. Together, the stories of these developers and their projects paint a vivid picture of what is common to the real estate development process. They also offer vivid contrasts that illustrate how development is a distinctly local activity that is influenced by climate and geography as well as by the unique social, political, and economic cultures of different cities. An understanding of what is common and what is different will help community members, elected officials, and others participate more productively in the development process in their own communities.

Chicago has a very large population and dense urban development patterns that were created before the proliferation of the automobile and suburbanization. Despite being located on the open prairie, it grew up on and is bounded on the east by the edge of Lake Michigan, where density is at its greatest. Chicago is also the birthplace of the modern skyscraper, so for these and other reasons, urban living—high-density as well as high-rise—is well established. Housing in Chicago is designed for people who live and work in a city where commuting from the suburbs can take an hour or more.

Portland's adoption of an Urban Growth Boundary in the 1970s led to the more recent and rapid development of that city's urban core. Development in Portland was also stimulated by significant public investment in transit and public realm infrastructure. The city is dense, efficient, and filled with buildings and places characterized by consistently high-quality architecture and urban design. And Portland's location in the environmentally conscious Pacific Northwest has cultivated an ethic of sustainable development that has been integrated into public policy, design practice, and construction industry standards.

Miami is the product of a major speculative real estate boom in the early twentieth century, and it has seen numerous booms and busts since. It is also a global city, the gateway to Latin America, and an economic powerhouse. Miami experienced incredible growth in the 2000s as people from around the world bought condos not for housing but as speculative investments. Many of those buyers never intended to live in their own units, so layout and function were secondary considerations. More important were striking ocean views, exotic amenities, image, hype, and the seemingly endless potential for big profits from increased appreciation that drove repeated resales and "flipping." To attract these potential buyers, developers relied increasingly on star architects and famous interior designers not just for their design skills but also for their marketing value. This speculation led to overproduction and by 2008, after the bursting of the housing bubble, there were estimated to be more than forty thousand empty condominium units standing on the market.[3]

By highlighting the projects and personal career stories of developers from these three different areas, this book illustrates differences in approach that reflect both individual backgrounds and the influence of local cultures on real estate markets. At the same time, this approach illuminates those traits and characteristics that are common to developers almost everywhere. Understanding both common traits and regional variations is the first big step toward being able to predict what developers working in other communities and cities are likely to do.

The developers profiled here were selected by consulting media accounts; articles in real estate, design, planning, and construction trade periodicals; and industry experts as well as local elected officials, academics, journalists, community members, and other developers. The emphasis was on successful, productive, career developers who had done interesting or important projects; on independent developers of all sizes rather than larger corporate developers; and on developers who worked primarily in urban areas and particularly in city centers. This approach led to a group of developers with diverse backgrounds and portfolios and who operated at different scales, ranging from very small to very large. Many of these developers had experience with several product types but most of them also developed condominiums during the 2000s because cheap and plentiful financing was available for for-sale housing so everyone was doing it. All are career developers who have completed numerous projects, are experienced, and have been generally successful over time. And while most have experienced losses at some point in their careers, when the housing bubble burst in the late 2000s they all stayed in the development business and were hard at work getting new projects off the ground by the end of the decade. By the early 2010s many were back in business developing apartments, senior housing facilities, condos, and other types of products. Importantly, while many of these developers are considered to be "good developers" by their peers and elected officials, city staff, architects, and some members of the community, none are without detractors. Few developers have completed a single project that has satisfied everyone, and criticism has come from various places: the local architectural critic, the district council member, nearby residents of a certain building, the neighboring property owner, or a disappointed buyer. Developers create buildings that change communities, and they construct products that may not meet everyone's standards, so success in one realm does not mean that they are beloved by everybody. Political and community opposition, negative media coverage, harsh architectural criticism, financial difficulties, and lawsuits are part of doing business for all developers, even the "good" ones.

Why It Matters: There Will Be More Development— and More Potential for Conflict

During the first decade of the twenty-first century, an unprecedented amount of money—what the real estate economist Anthony Downs called a "Niagara of capital"—flowed into the U.S. real estate market, fueling the overproduction of for-sale housing that led to the bursting of the housing bubble in 2008.[4] That bubble was caused by developers, homebuilders, banks, and all of the people who bought and sold homes hoping to make a huge profit from what appeared to be rapid and never-ending appreciation in home values. Three years later, by 2011, America was still recovering from a protracted recession, investors were still sitting on the sidelines, banks were still not making loans, and many developers were struggling to initiate projects in the face of scarce capital and a dead market. Glum developers, architects, contractors, lenders, and many other industry professionals said things like "we will never see a boom like that again," "we will not see any high-leverage deals again for a long time," and "we have seen the end of urban redevelopment as we know it." But despite their dire predictions, by 2014 we were seeing all of those things again as the new boom in apartments that roared to life in 2012 was still going strong.

Real estate boom-and-bust cycles play havoc with people's confidence and emotions in the short run but they obscure important long-term trends. Three major forces have historically driven and will continue to drive new development in the United States over the long term. First, there is a constant need to replace aged building stock. Second, we must house a continuously growing population—projected to increase by 86 million, from 314 million to 400 million, between 2012 and 2050. Third, a constantly changing demand for new product types reflects shifting demographics and tastes—from "lifestyle" retail centers in the suburbs and luxury apartments in the city to senior housing everywhere to accommodate the huge and growing segment of the population that is sixty-five and over. But in addition to these three drivers, the beginning of the twenty-first century ushered in a fourth—"the flight to the city."[5]

By the 2010s it had become clear that a massive demographic rearrangement of American cities, what Alan Ehrenhalt called "the great inversion," was under way.[6] For the first time in history, new immigrants were moving straight to immigrant communities in the suburbs rather than to their traditional enclaves in city centers. At the same time, unlike previous generations, young middle-class millennials—people born between 1981 and 2000—chose not to move back to the suburbs where they were raised but to move to urban centers instead. Also, unlike previous generations, many of the baby boomer parents of those millennials—people born between 1946 and 1964—chose to abandon their empty suburban nests, follow their children, and move to the city too. These boomers, their children, and other people with the financial means had discovered something important: City living is good for you. In *Triumph of the City: How Our Greatest Invention Makes Us Richer, Smarter, Greener, Healthier, and Happier*, Edward Glaeser cites numerous studies that show that people who live in cities experience a higher quality of life than those who live in suburbs and rural areas.[7]

These four major trends will ensure that development continues in our communities for the foreseeable future—we simply cannot put our heads in the sand, stop the clock, or pull up the drawbridge. We live in a society with a market economy and in a democracy that values personal rights, including property rights. A real estate development is a business venture financed by private investors and lenders who take serious risks with the objective of earning significant profits. Developers are therefore reluctant to let community members have much influence over costs, design, marketability, and profits when they have no financial stake in the project. On the other hand, development affects everything from home values and views to the use and enjoyment of public streets so members of the community feel they should play a stronger role in shaping projects. The underlying source of conflict is that a real estate development is a private enterprise that is acted out on a very public stage. A primary purpose of this book is to help community members understand how they can maximize their influence on that private enterprise by seeing the project from the developer's perspective.

Selling Dreams and Building Communities

I used to work for a developer named Bob Lux who would say, "We don't sell real estate, we sell dreams." What he meant was that it is often easier to sell an idea—by appealing to people's inner idea or image of themselves—than it is to sell an actual piece of real estate. Sales agents know that it is often easier to sell a home before it has been built than after, and the reason is because reality is rarely as good as our dreams. In our dreams, we do not see marred paint, dented appliances, or poorly located light switches nor do we see low ceilings, small rooms, and even smaller windows. But when we walk through an actual home, these and countless other flaws become apparent, even in the best-designed and highest-quality projects. Unlike mass-produced products such as automobiles, buildings are custom-built every time with human hands so it is much more difficult to ensure a consistently high level of quality. Even if one could it would not matter because nothing is perfect except dreams, so that is what developers try to create when they first begin to envision new projects. As they refine and adapt their vision, they must bring everyone else along with them—local politicians, city planners, architects, neighbors, lenders, investors, sales agents, tenants, and potential buyers—and make it their vision too.

If developers succeed in getting those visions built and sold, they may live to see them transformed by time and use from speculative projects into accepted or even beloved parts of a neighborhood or community. But we seem to have forgotten that developers have always played a central role in the creation of home and community, as underscored by Andrés Duany's comment at the beginning of this prologue. People are often wary of "developers" when they are starting a new project, but over the years completed projects blend into and create the fabric of neighborhoods. Indeed, developers have always built our cities, using private capital, and if you look around any city, most of what you see was once a developer's vision. So a second purpose of this book is to place that short, stressful period—community review, city approval, and construction—into a broader context that recognizes the positive impacts that developers and their projects can have on our communities.

Blueprint for the Book

Each chapter of the book begins with an outline of ideas related to development and is followed by stories of developers, their careers, and their projects that illustrate those ideas. This approach provides a theoretical framework through which to view developers while at the same time it takes the reader inside the minds of developers to show how they think. This approach also begins to demystify developers by revealing them—through their own words and stories—as people whose motives and actions can be understood. The chapters build on one another, beginning with what developers do and how they think about opportunities, process, design, sales, risk and reward, reputation, the creation of place and experience, and their role in the community. The book concludes with suggestions for how to think more objectively about developers and how to work more effectively with them. The emphasis throughout is on revealing what motivates developers so that members of the community can better understand how and where they can best exert their influence to achieve the maximum positive effect. Based on a simple variation of the serenity prayer, the objective of this book is to help people who study or work with developers to accept the things they cannot change, identify those things that can be changed, and develop the wisdom to know the difference.

This book focuses primarily on the development of city center sites for multifamily residential projects—for-sale condominiums and rental apartments—and for mixed-use projects that include a combination of housing, commercial office, and retail. This represents just a fraction of the much larger industry of real estate development that encompasses urban commercial and retail development as well as suburban development. Real estate development in the suburbs ranges from subdivisions of for-sale, single-family homes, townhomes, and condominiums to apartments, commercial office parks, industrial warehouse and light assembly buildings, and retail centers. These product types are as important as those developed in central cities and they are produced in great volume in our suburban nation. The risks and rewards for the suburban developer as well as the strategies and aptitudes required for success are somewhat different but the principles are the same, and many of the conclusions in this book apply to all developers. Projects in city centers, however, more directly affect nearby residents, face greater scrutiny, and present greater risks to developers but they are also going to become increasingly prevalent in the future. Chapter 1 explores how development has changed over time and how it has remained the same, beginning with the story of a development that started on a hilly pasture more than two hundred years ago.

Chapter 1

Developer as Visionary

> Buy real estate in areas where the path exists and buy more real estate
> where there is no path, but you can create your own.
> —David Waronker, American real estate investor[1]

Three Hills

In 1625 the Reverend William Blackstone, one of New England's first European settlers, bought a large piece of land in Boston with three hills and pure springs, where he built a small cottage. The area soon began to attract other settlers and Blackstone, a recluse, decamped for Rhode Island in 1630. For the next century and a half, the area, called "Tri-mount" because of its three hills, remained a pastoral grazing common with only a few estates, pastures, and orchards.[2]

In 1795, a group of wealthy businessmen created a private company called Mount Vernon Proprietors for the purpose of developing housing in the area for the growing merchant class. In the same year they bought a south-facing, sloping pasture of eighteen and a half acres from the painter John Singleton Copley, in part because one of their partners, Harrison Gray Otis, had served on the town committee that had settled on the area for the site of a new state house. Copley later protested the sale on the grounds that Otis had inside information about the future value of his land, but Copley lost after a decade-long legal battle. At around the same time the Commonwealth of Massachusetts acquired a six-and-a-half-acre parcel from its first governor, John Hancock, and the new Massachusetts State

House, designed by the architect Charles Bulfinch, was built on the site and completed in 1798.[3]

The Mount Vernon Proprietors got to work soon after, laying out streets in 1799. Next, they began cutting down the three hills and then regrading to create flatter and more developable land. The westernmost hill, Mount Vernon, was cut down first and the spoils were used as fill along the edge of the Charles River, creating more land and increasing the holdings of the Mount Vernon Proprietors. At the top of the steepest of the three hills stood a disused beacon that had been built during the Revolutionary War for the purposes of warning nearby towns in the case of enemy attack. That hill, which then stood sixty feet taller than it does today, was cut down and regraded as well but its name endured and over the coming decades the Mount Vernon Proprietors transformed Reverend Blackstone's pastoral retreat into the area now known as Beacon Hill.[4]

Beacon Hill comprises three districts: the North Slope, the Flat of the Hill, and the South Slope. The North Slope was originally a seedy waterfront area called "Mt. Whoredom," and the Mount Vernon Proprietors purposefully laid out the major streets in an east-west orientation to minimize connections to the area. Over time the North Slope became home to African Americans and abolitionists and then to Irish, Italian, and Eastern European Jewish immigrants. The Flat of the Hill, the filled area along the edge of the Charles River, originally housed both residences and businesses, including the blacksmiths and stables that served the residents of the South Slope. Over time the area grew and a vibrant business and retail district developed along Charles Street.[5]

But the heart of the Mount Vernon Proprietors' plan was to build a new community for Boston's wealthy on the South Slope, so they started with large mansions but soon realized that they could earn a greater return on their investment in the land by developing more densely, building a greater number of smaller homes, and selling in volume. The rest of the streets were laid out to accommodate brick row houses in the Federal style that Bulfinch helped popularize and in the Greek revival style that was also popular at the time.[6]

Few people in the twenty-first century would describe Beacon Hill as a highly speculative "real estate development" but in 1795, that is exactly what it was. A group of wealthy investors with a vision bought land; drafted a plan; completed earth works; platted, subdivided, laid out, and built streets; and built and sold houses designed in broadly popular styles. What

Figure 3. The excavation of Beacon Hill in 1811. Lithograph taken from a watercolor by J. R. Smith. Courtesy Trustees of the Boston Public Library, Print Department.

Figure 4. Beacon Hill in 2006. Photo by Della Huff.

is called Beacon Hill began as a simple land deal and a production housing development, although it took the better part of a century to fill in the entire area. More important, however, is that the vision of the Mount Vernon Proprietors long outlived its creators. Beacon Hill went from being a hilly pasture to becoming the residential heart of Boston, and the South Slope, with its red brick houses that exude class, taste, heritage, permanence, and inevitability, became one of the most desirable and expensive places to live in the United States.

A Brief History of Urban Real Estate Development in America

Real estate development has always meant the investment of capital into improving existing land and property by moving earth, providing infrastructure, subdividing the improved land into smaller parcels or lots, and constructing buildings, typically in order to increase use and density. Urban development in the United States from the seventeenth through the early twentieth centuries more often meant the development of new housing on large tracts of former agricultural land owned by a few individuals close in to the city—land with few neighbors and few problems. Some cities grew organically but in others visionaries with control over large land areas were able to produce grand plans that took centuries to realize. William Penn's seventeenth-century "Greene Country Towne" vision for Philadelphia was based on a gridiron plan and five public squares. A century later Pierre L'Enfant followed with a plan for the new capital city of Washington, DC (at the time, swampland), which was based on a gridiron overlaid with diagonal avenues and circles at their intersections. Much like the Mount Vernon Proprietors, these visionaries first created a plan; they then cut down the trees where the streets would go, built the streets, and subdivided the land. Over time, investment and development followed the path of least resistance: those new streets that provided access to the parcels of land that were for sale.

The industrial era led to urbanization, as people from the countryside made their way into town looking for manufacturing work in the factories that sprang up around the road, rail, and maritime infrastructure that was concentrated within urban areas. Cities filled up with workers who lived in dense housing within walking distance of their factory jobs. At the turn of the twentieth century, public health problems in cities stemming from deplorable housing conditions, overcrowding, inadequate water and sewer systems, and the lack of light, clean air, and public space caused city leaders to begin planning again. The City Beautiful movement that followed resulted in grand plans for urban space and infrastructure. Plans were created for St. Louis by Harland Bartholomew, for San Diego by John Nolen, and for Chicago by Daniel Burnham, who was known for having said: "Make no little plans. They have no magic to stir men's blood and probably will not themselves be realized."[7]

Since the nineteenth century, suburban commuter towns had grown up around train stations but these stations became less important as the invention and improvement of the internal combustion engine led to rapid growth in automobile and truck use, initiating the "rails to rubber" movement. Henry Ford's mass production of cheap automobiles accelerated this movement, opening up the entire countryside to a new form of suburban development while the influence of the railroads on development patterns continued to decline. Automobile use grew throughout the post–World War II era, and the Federal Aid Highway Act of 1956, a $10 billion

-investment in more than forty thousand miles of interstate highways, further fueled this growth. These roads opened up access to the countryside and accelerated the exodus of people and industry to the suburbs, leading to the hollowing out of cities, which were often carved up by the new highways that cut through and isolated urban communities. The flight of the middle class left only low-income immigrants and African Americans in the urban cores of most cities.

In the 1950s and 1960s, the federal government attempted to stimulate private investment in America's struggling inner cities by implementing big plans. While the majority of urban land in the United States is privately owned and developed, the Urban Renewal program of slum clearance and large-scale urban redevelopment projects put the government in the role of a visionary developer by combining federal funding with public planning and private development partners at the local level. Urban Renewal, however, was costly, had mixed results, and dislocated many of the low-income people left behind in the urban core whose homes and communities were bulldozed to make way for new, modern housing projects that generated new social problems of their own. In the 1980s Urban Renewal became a memory, city governments largely ceded responsibility for planning back to the private sector, and few cities possessed enough land, money, or political will to make any plans at all.

At about the same time, many formerly working-class industrial cities, which had suffered from population losses and the depleted tax base that resulted, started to implement a new economic development strategy. Recognizing the permanent loss of industry and blue-collar factory jobs, these cities sought to transform their downtowns and increase private investment and the tax base by attracting the "FIRE" businesses of finance, insurance, real estate, and other businesses that created white-collar professional jobs. These new workplaces, along with improvements to existing arts and culture institutions and tourist infrastructure, initiated the revitalization of the city as a cultural attraction and place to visit, if not a place to live. In addition to these cultural institutions, many higher education and medical institutions with historic roots and large campuses and specialized buildings in the city that could not be easily relocated began to reinvest in their facilities and surrounding communities. Together, arts and culture institutions and the "eds and meds" began to fill some of the gaps in the urban core and began to attract the middle and upper classes back to the city.

But cities still faced a big challenge, because the only property available for large-scale urban development after the 1970s was land abandoned by former industrial uses like factories, railyards, and waterfronts. Many of these sites were in great locations, close to the downtown core, but they often lacked traditional infrastructure and presented significant environmental challenges that together increased costs, risks, and liabilities to cities and private developers alike. Visionary developers and public officials began transforming these kinds of sites into communities in many cities, including Chicago and Portland, Oregon, as we will see. These sites were so large, however, that they took decades of building production and absorption to completely redevelop and in many places they were still being built out in the 2010s. Urban universities, colleges, and major healthcare systems were among the few remaining institutions that could still develop and build according to "master plans" but many of these had become increasingly landlocked too and had to resort to piecemeal infill planning and the replacement of existing facilities with higher-density development.

At a smaller scale, private property owners and developers were no longer converting agricultural land to whole new neighborhoods and commercial and retail districts, as the Mount Vernon Proprietors in Boston had done. Instead, they were replacing aged building stock and infilling smaller vacant parcels, often with new uses and at increasingly higher densities. But many of the parcels that were available came with the same challenges as the larger industrial sites. For example, cities were full of quarter-block parcels that once housed gas stations or laundromats that sat vacant atop contaminated soil that would be costly to clean up and that imposed risks and liabilities on new owners. Efficient development requires an area of minimum size, shape, and dimensions, so parcels that were oddly shaped or too small to accommodate marketable building types presented yet another set of challenges. In these cases a developer would have to buy up and "assemble" one or more adjacent parcels to create a single, large, contiguous parcel of the right size and shape to accommodate an economically viable development. But land assembly requires patience and entails significant transactional risks, because several if not many parties may be involved and a good development idea can be frustrated by a single landowner who does not want to sell, who wants to hold out for a very high price, or who wants to work with a competitor. And for those who control urban property at any scale, private development is no longer as private as it once was since the public has started to directly engage developers and the governments that regulate them after having lost trust in both.

Challenges of Developing in the Twenty-first Century

Developers like the Mount Vernon Proprietors operated with extraordinary freedom because there were few neighbors at the time who would have objected to the development of agricultural land, but cities have changed through urbanization, population growth, and other trends and forces. Four key movements that started in the 1960s increased the public's skepticism of both private- and public-sector development and construction activities and led to the rise of "public participation." First, in 1961, an observant Greenwich Village housewife named Jane Jacobs wrote the classic *Death and Life of Great American Cities*. Jacobs's book was the first significant critique of the Urban Renewal program and the failure of its modernist planning efforts. *Death and Life* marked the turning point in how Americans thought about building their cities, and it has remained a classic and a largely relevant urban planning and design text today. Second, other classics soon followed, including Rachel Carson's *Silent Spring* (serialized in *The New Yorker* and published as a book in 1962), which was widely credited as causing the ban of the pesticide DDT and launching the environmental movement. Third, the mass demolition of blocks of older buildings in city centers by Urban Renewal's "federal bulldozer" culminated in the destruction of New York City's magnificent McKim, Mead, and White–designed Pennsylvania Station. Its replacement with what many considered to be a soulless, modernist monstrosity sparked the birth of the historic preservation movement.[8]

The fourth movement began in 1978 with the passage of the popular ballot initiative Proposition 13 in California. "Prop 13" limited the California state government's ability to increase property taxes in California, initiating a "taxpayer revolt" and ushering in the era of "no new taxes" throughout the United States. One effect of the antitax movement was that cities began to seek alternatives to using general-fund tax revenues for needed public infrastructure projects. The public-private partnership, or PPP project model, an alternative financing method introduced in the early 1980s, quickly proliferated around the United States and the world and has continued to dominate in the twenty-first century. These projects are legal and financial partnerships between private developers and governments—usually city governments—who offer to support a private project financially with public resources such as low-cost land, environmental cleanup grants, low-cost money in the form of tax-exempt debt, and future tax revenues (tax abatement and tax increment financing, or TIF). Policy makers hoped that the use of public resources to reduce the costs and risks for developers working in unproven urban areas would stimulate the market and "prime the pump" for future private development and reinvestment in the city that would not require subsidies. In exchange for these resources, the public would obtain benefits or amenities as a part of the project, ranging from streetscape and sidewalk improvements to public plazas, parks, green roofs, and parking facilities. Often, however, the public benefits seemed sparse or not very public and the subsidies were viewed as payments that lined the pockets of private developers while moving a large share of the risk onto the public partner. At the same time subsidies became a normal expectation from developers in many cities where elected officials wondered when the pump would finally run by itself.

For all of these reasons, by the 1980s, public confidence in local government's ability to fairly represent the public's interests in its regulation of private real estate development was very low. Americans increasingly insisted on having a voice in projects and developments in urban areas that would affect them in the areas of property rights, social equity, and the environment. The public's growing suspicion and distrust of government officials and the private developers they regulated led to ever-increasing scrutiny of development proposals, outright opposition to many, and a general fear of change as exemplified by the term NIMBY, which stands for "not in my backyard," or, worse, BANANA, which means "build absolutely nothing anytime near anything." In this atmosphere of distrust, by the twenty-first century, even traditional private development projects that received no public subsidy had effectively become "public-private" projects in character by the time they had wended their way through long, complex, uncertain, and often-fraught public review and approval or "entitlement" processes. Virtually every urban project required the developer to work with neighbors and the community in addition to the usual approval bodies such as planning, zoning, and heritage preservation commissions as well as the city council. Indeed, by the start of the twenty-first century, being a real estate developer had become more difficult than ever before, in large part because of the public's fear of change and distrust of developers.

By the 2000s and 2010s—and after more than a half-century of residential abandonment—cities had started to become attractive places for middle-class people to live again, as population growth had caused suburban sprawl and congestion while higher gas prices started to make longer commutes increasingly costly in both time and money. These negative push forces, in combination with the pull forces of improved public safety, access to arts and culture, and the rich sense of community that exists in urban areas, began to drive people back toward the core in search of a better quality of life. Demographics played a key role too, as both the baby boomers and their children, the millennials, began to prefer urban living over the suburban single-family homes they were raised in, and this continued to play an increasingly influential role in urban real estate development as the flight to the city took off.

By the 2010s, the question had become how to address this growing demand for new development in cities if each project would be exposed to the kind of opposition that the developer Neil Ornoff had faced in Evanston. The answer lies in coming to a better understanding of developers.

What Are Developers and What Do They Really Do?

There is no one route into the real estate development business. It is not a legally recognized profession like architecture, engineering, or law, which requires specific academic degrees and work experience to obtain licensure. A handful of American universities have offered formal degree programs in real estate in the past and a number of new programs were created during the building boom of the 2000s but even so, relatively few developers are graduates of those programs. The developers profiled in this book who did attend college obtained degrees in everything from architecture, business, and law to art history, music, creative writing, and cooking. States do not license or regulate developers, although many developers are licensed real estate brokers or agents, some are licensed as contractors or homebuilders, and some do hold licenses to practice other professions such as law, architecture, and engineering. Many developers belong to and participate in industry trade organizations such as the Urban Land Institute; NAIOP, the Commercial Real Estate Development Association; and Lambda Alpha International, the honorary society for the advancement of land economics.

The U.S. Bureau of Labor Statistics classifies developers as "land subdividers," because they buy land and increase its value by subdividing it and building higher-density uses on it. There are many different kinds of developers, and they each specialize in different product types, work in different geographic areas and contexts and at different scales, and range in organizational size from solitary individuals to national and multinational corporations.

The one thing all developers have in common, however, is that they make their money by buying a piece of land or a building or a complex of buildings and then increasing its value. They do this by investing in capital improvements such as renovations or the construction of new buildings, by improving operations, or both. If a developer is successful, rents or sale prices can be increased, the final value of the asset will be greater than the cost of acquisition and improvement, and the developer will realize the difference between costs and value as profit.

Land developers, for example, buy suburban or rural land at agricultural prices and then obtain zoning approvals for a subdivision of new homes or an office or industrial park. Once they have received their approvals, they regrade the land and provide the sewer, water, storm water, power, and road infrastructure that will make the land developable. Then they sell the lots or building pads to a homebuilder or to a developer of office or industrial buildings. Land developers make money by selling the improved land for a price that is greater than the combined costs of buying the agricultural land, getting the approvals, and providing the infrastructure. The difference between these costs and the sales price is their profit.

Many commercial office developers and production homebuilders are also land developers who plan for and develop office parks or communities of single-family homes or townhomes on the land they have improved. These developers can also speed up or slow down land development, infrastructure provision, and building production. This flexibility allows developers to match their rate of delivery with market demand and rates of product "absorption"—the speed at which they can sell or lease their buildings. With this incremental approach, these developers can also use anticipated income from the rental of completed offices or proceeds from the sale of completed homes to pay the costs of development related to those buildings or units without having to develop more land than needed at any one time.

Most developers specialize in one of the four traditional rental real estate product types: commercial office space, warehouse and light industrial facilities, retail strip centers and malls, and multifamily housing or apartments. Some developers specialize in variations on these product types, from hotels, casinos, entertainment centers, and mega-malls to senior housing, student housing, and mixed-use development. Finally, some developers specialize in for-sale housing, which includes single-family homes, townhomes, condominiums, and cooperatives.

Developers generally work in either the suburbs or urban areas. Suburban development is typically lower density and less risky in terms of the politics of the approval process. In the suburbs, land is more plentiful, uses are separated, interest group politics are weaker, and people and buildings are farther apart, as are any affected neighbors. At the same time, suburban cities have smaller staffs and less capacity to evaluate development projects. In larger cities, however, there are many more neighbors who are close by and vocal, there are large planning and development staffs, and there are interested politicians who must listen to their constituents as they evaluate proposed projects. And because urban land is scarce and more costly, density is important because it directly influences the value of land. Urban sites also come with more unique constraints from geography and geometry to complex zoning codes and unique local and neighborhood politics. Thus each project is uniquely fitted to its site, unlike a typical template-based suburban subdivision built on agricultural land by a national homebuilder that offers the same ten unit plans across the country. All developers— urban and suburban—innovate constantly at the margins but suburban developers are more able than urban developers to replicate their products. For these reasons, urban development is generally understood to be riskier, more uncertain, more time-consuming, and more costly, so developers who work in cities expect a higher profit margin than they might receive from a relatively simpler office park or subdivision of production homes in the far exurbs.

Developers can be either private, for-profit companies or nonprofit organizations, such as the many community development corporations in the United States that provide affordable rental housing in urban areas. A private developer can be very large or very small, from a single individual with some capital and a good idea to large companies such as Hines Interests, Trammell Crow Company, or the Trump Organization, with many divisions and projects and hundreds or even thousands of employees.

Entrepreneurial people who seek large profits and who have access to capital choose the real estate development business because it can be lucrative and the barriers to entry are low. Smaller and medium-sized private developers—firms of between one and twenty people who are led by one or two visionary and entrepreneurial individuals—undertake an enormous share of the development in cities. Unlike their larger corporate and institutional peers, who often labor under more bureaucratic organizational structures and have less of an equity stake in their projects, these people run efficient organizations and risk their own cash—and that of their investors—on their own creative visions. And while some people go into development during boom times with the hope of earning a quick profit and then getting back out, many others commit their careers to development. These people acknowledge that development can be both rewarding and difficult, that it is risky, and that, like anything else, becoming good at it requires practice. The context within which development occurs has changed since eighteenth-century Boston but developers still conceive and execute grand visions. Some go well beyond being mere "land subdividers," and the most imaginative developers create the world we live in.

City Builders and Creators of Culture

Developers build our cities. Others, from architects, city planners, and elected officials to preservationists, environmentalists, other special interests, community members, and nearby neighbors, play a part in the private development process. Governments build major facilities, public streets, and parks and plazas, and they regulate growth and development through planning and zoning functions and the management of public participation processes. But throughout the history of the United States, where the great majority of land is privately owned, the buildings that make up American cities have been planned, designed, and built almost entirely by developers, using private capital, one project at a time. This incremental process of development—and all of the individual large and small projects that result from it—continues to give shape to cities today.[9]

Developers create the buildings in which we spend much of our lives. We work in their office buildings and we shop at their retail centers, megamalls, and lifestyle centers. Their light assembly, industrial, and distribution centers store the food we eat and the goods we buy, from furniture and electronics to clothes and appliances. When we travel we stay in hotels, eat at restaurants, and visit entertainment and cultural attractions built by developers. Finally, most Americans grow up living in single and multifamily rental properties and for-sale homes that were mass-produced by developers. The work of developers makes up a large share of what we call the "urban fabric" of the city, from the exterior façades of their buildings to the land in between. More important, developers influence our basic conceptions of home, work, and life, from the high-rise office buildings of the early twentieth century, the suburban tracts of the post–World War II era, and the regional malls of the 1960s and 1970s, to the more recent warehouse-to-loft conversions, high-rise condominiums, and luxury apartments of the city.

All new real estate products begin as innovations to existing products. For example, from the downtown department store to the suburban strip center, regional mall, mega-mall, and entertainment center, each grew to become a reality that felt inevitable. But they each began as an untested incremental improvement on a former product. And for each one, a developer had a vision that became a real part of the world and of life for many people. In the next section, a Chicago developer named Gerald Fogelson will explain how vision and several other traits were central to his success in transforming an old railyard into a new urban community.

Seeing What Can Be

In 1988, Gerald Fogelson had a vision of his own. In place of the old, abandoned, sixty-nine-acre Central Station railroad yard on the south side of Chicago that he could see from his office window, Fogelson saw a new and vibrant residential community. He took his vision to Albert Ratner of the Cleveland-based national development company, Forest City, and Ratner agreed to partner with Fogelson on the acquisition and development of the Central Station property.[10]

Fogelson also had tenacity. He first developed townhomes on the land and then other developers saw the promise of his vision and began to partner with him to develop more housing. By the end of the 2000s, the area was home to fourteen million square feet of new real estate and more than five thousand people called the area, now known as Central Station, their neighborhood. In 2014 Fogelson was eighty, the redevelopment of Central

Figure 5. Model showing the Central Station development as of 2010. The dark buildings are part of the Central Station development, which started with low-rise townhomes to the south in the late 1980s (right, in this photo) and then was built up to midrise and high-rise towers on the north, facing Millennium Park. Photo by author.

Figure 6. Central Station in 2010, with the Museum Park towers at the northern end, facing Millennium Park. Photo by author.

Station had been under way for nearly three decades but was still not complete, and he still worked on it from his office on Michigan Avenue, in the heart of the area. But how did it all start?

I Was Hooked

Gerald Fogelson's Russian father came to America in 1908 only to find that the doors to traditional professions and businesses were closed to him. Like many other members of ethnic immigrant communities—Jews, Greeks, Italians, and others—he saw that the barriers to entry were lower in other industries like construction, clothing, movie making, and retailing. So he opened a shoe store in the small town of Dover, New Jersey. Fogelson worked there from the time when he was very young and learned the importance of understanding one's buyer. "One day I said to my father, 'These are the ugliest shoes I have ever seen and I don't know why anyone would buy them.' So my father told me, 'These are not the shoes your mother or sister would wear but a good marketing person—a good buyer—knows his customer, so the reason that I buy and sell these shoes is that I have my customer in mind and I know what they like.' His point," says Fogelson, "was that you have to take your own personal tastes out of the equation, and this has stuck with me. I have always understood my buyer intuitively through all of the many different stages of my life and career even as I have developed different product types."

After graduating high school, Fogelson attended Lehigh University, in Pennsylvania, where he studied business and majored in marketing. When he was a second-semester senior, Xerox and IBM and other companies came recruiting on campus. "I did not think much of the kinds of jobs and salaries they were offering," said Fogelson, "because I had been taught that it is better to make a dime for yourself than to make a dollar for someone else." Then his father came home one day and said, "There is a guy who lives in the next town over who is building houses and doing well, and if he can build houses, you can build houses, because after all, you are graduating from college and you know everything." So in the middle of his senior year, Fogelson and his father went into business together and bought two small lots in Netcong, New Jersey. "We built two small houses and from that point on I was in the business and I was hooked. I knew literally nothing, of course, and in fact, the only subject in school I didn't do well in was shop and to this day I can't draw a straight line. But I had an instinct."

Fogelson sold the first of those two houses for $9,900 in 1955.[11] For that first year everything he touched was a success and he made more money than his parents or anybody else they knew. "I thought I was something special and in hindsight, I became arrogant, because I had a lot of success really soon. But life isn't like that and it all came screeching to a halt in 1956 when I received a two-week notice that I was being drafted into the army for two years." Fogelson went from being "somebody" to being reduced to a buck private who was just another number doing K.P. and guard duty. He also realized that since joining the army his income had stopped, he had no income-producing properties, and he was "like a salaried guy."

Back to School

In the late 1950s a new real estate product—the farmer's market—began to emerge. Developers were buying old mill buildings in New England towns, dividing them up, and renting stalls out for farmers who sold meat, fruit, and vegetables and for other vendors who sold dry goods like linens and sundries. Fogelson thought this idea was going to be the wave of the future so he used his weekend passes to visit a couple of them. Although he could not have known it at the time, Kmart, Wal-Mart, and Target would all be founded in 1962. He was a company clerk in the army, which allowed him to resume his real estate business in his off hours, and by the time he was discharged from the army in 1958 Fogelson, his father, and a cousin had purchased a site outside of Chicago together to build a farmer's market. "And that is what brought me to the middle west—I liked it, got married, and stayed."

The project was successful, but Fogelson did not like the farmer's market business. "I liked building the buildings and leasing up the space, but I did not like the operations side of the business—it was like being a shepherd." More important, Fogelson really wanted to get back into homebuilding but he also knew that he needed to learn the business. He was self-taught and had only built houses in New Jersey—"you know, ten there, five here"—using conventional financing. He didn't know anything about developing large-scale subdivisions or the mortgage programs that were being offered at the time by the Federal Housing Administration and the Veterans' Administration.

So Fogelson applied for a job with a large company in Indianapolis and was hired as a salesman. "I didn't care what they paid me because I was getting paid to learn. I became vice president of sales, then I took over the mortgage department, and within a year sales had increased by 150 percent. I worked seven days a week for a year and that was a cram course in all aspects of subdivisions." When he first took the job, Fogelson told the company that he would stay for one year and that if they didn't give him equity then, he would leave. When that year was up he was not granted equity, so he went out on his own. "And that was the only year in my life when I have worked for somebody else."

Fogelson went on to build garden apartments at a time when there was no alternative minimum tax. "They would throw off cash flow and tax losses and then I would build houses that would throw off tax-sheltered profits, and so I was able to build up equity and cash flow." As his subdivision projects grew larger, "there was always a leftover corner here or there that could be developed for a gas station or shopping center," so over time Fogelson learned these other businesses too. "It was almost like being bilingual because I could talk the talk in retail, office, industrial, for-sale and rental residential, and land development. But what I got really good at was land—property."

"So that is a short version of how I got into the real estate development business—it wasn't some brilliant master plan, that is just the way it evolved. I liked it and I became addicted to it. And the reason that I liked it is because you can see what you have done—those little houses I built back in New Jersey and everything else I have built since. I like it that my children—and now my five grandsons—can see it and I know they get a kick out of driving by $4 billion worth of work and saying 'my grandfather did that.'"

Three Traits of a Developer

Fogelson has been in the real estate business for more than five decades and he has also helped to start up and shape the curriculum for the School of Real Estate at Roosevelt University, in Chicago, where he endowed a professorship. But with all that experience, when asked what the characteristics of a developer are, Fogelson lists just three: vision, tenacity, and the ability to reconcile many voices and make a good decision.

First, developers must have vision. "One of the characteristics that a developer must have is the ability to visualize what can be. If I were to have a self-evaluation that was as objective as I could make it, it would be that I have the ability to visualize things much more so than most people. I understand land and property, how to assemble it, how to buy it, how to sell it, and how to zone it. I can see what can be."

Second, developers must be tenacious. "For example," says Fogelson, "you just can't take a rejection as a flat rejection, because 'no' doesn't necessarily mean 'no,' and sometimes 'no' may mean 'yes.' You have to be persistent and determined, you need to hang in and hang on, and you need to believe in what you are doing, because if you are not persistent and determined, you will get knocked off too many times. McDonalds founder Ray Kroc said it best: 'Persistence and determination are omnipotent.'"

And, third, the developer must be able to reconcile the objective facts of the project—"the pieces of the puzzle"—with the vision or "mystery" of what he or she is going to do with it. "On the one hand, you must consider all of the physical characteristics of the property—the sewer, water, soil capacity, topography, etc. On the other hand, you must be looking at potential uses, product type, absorption rates, and what you would do with the property if you had it. For example, the highest and best use for a piece of property may be retail shops, but you must ask yourself whether there is really a market for that product. When you have those two sets of information on the table then you can make a decision about whether you want to pursue this property or development project or not."

But more important than reconciling these two sets of information is reconciling what Fogelson calls "the subconscious voice and the conscious voice." "You may lay a set of facts on the table, look at them consciously, and it all makes sense and adds up but if it doesn't feel right in your gut—if you instinctively have reservations about it—then don't do it. On the other hand, if your inner voice tells you 'Boy, this is the greatest thing since sliced bread' but you can't make it work with the objective facts, then you shouldn't do it then either. You should not go ahead with any deal until your inner voice and your outer voice are in harmony because if you do, you will decrease your chances of being right." But there is a better reason for waiting until the inner and outer voices are in harmony, says Fogelson. "The chances are, you will run into problems, and when you do, if your inner voice had doubts, then it will say to you, 'See, I told you not to do this,' and, now, when you have got to have that extra conviction required to push through and do it, it won't really be there, because you will be thinking, 'I should have listened in the first place.'"

Like orchestra conductors and movie producers, developers are generalists who bring a lot of other people together to create something. "And at the end of the day," says Fogelson, "when you put together a development you have to think about all of the people who are going to be around the table—the architect, the land planner, the construction people, the marketing people, the finance people, and all of the others. They are all coming at things from their own perspective or point of view, pushing for what they think is going to be best for the project based upon their own role or persuasion. But the developer is the one who is sitting there at the head of the table, and he has to sort through all of the information and all of the voices and make a decision."

Gerald Fogelson's story acts as a bridge between the stories of Beacon Hill and Evanston, showing how long-range vision and tenacity together can shape a place. His summary of the traits required of a developer is just one opinion but in this case, as in all of the stories that follow, his words, views, and ideas closely reflect those of many other developers. Indeed, while each of the stories in this book illustrates specific ideas, in fact the similarities between developers and their stories far eclipse their differences.

Real estate development is an entrepreneurial pursuit, and the qualities that Fogelson describes as being critical to his success—vision, persistence, and tenacity, along with his obvious self-confidence and optimism—are the qualities required of any successful entrepreneur. In the next chapter we will go back to the beginning and look more closely at ideas about the entrepreneur—from the origin of the word itself and the personality traits entrepreneurs have in common to how they think about making money and how they use social and political skills to carry out their work.

Chapter 2

Deal Makers

Entrepreneurs are simply those who understand that there is little
difference between obstacle and opportunity and are able to turn both
to their advantage.
  —Victor Kiam, American entrepreneur[1]

Entrepreneurs and Entrepreneurship

Rather than working for other people and earning a salary in an established
business that makes a marginal profit, real estate developers seek to create
and sell entirely new products in the hopes of earning a much larger entrepreneurial profit. They do this by purchasing property, construction services, and professional services—the project costs—and combining them
together into a new product that can be sold for a price that is greater than
the sum of those costs. The difference between the total cost and the price
is the entrepreneurial profit.

  This is not as simple as it sounds. Not everyone has the risk tolerance to
try it, and of those who do try, not all succeed. Many successful developers,
however, seem to have certain traits in common. People who work closely
with developers often describe them as visionary, creative, open-minded,
optimistic, persistent, tenacious, and charismatic. Developers use these
traits, their ample interpersonal skills, and their social, political, and business connections to structure a series of arrangements with individual land-
owners, consultants, contractors, elected officials, community members,
and other interested parties. Then they assemble these many and varied
arrangements into a single real estate development project or "deal."

Table 1. Profit = Sale Price Less the Sum of Costs

Costs, Price, Profit	Pro Forma		Raise Prices		Lower Prices	
Costs:						
Land	$100,000	10%	$100,000	10%	$100,000	10%
Construction	$650,000	65%	$650,000	65%	$650,000	65%
Fees and Soft Costs	$250,000	25%	$250,000	25%	$250,000	25%
Subtotal Costs	$1,000,000		$1,000,000		$1,000,000	
Sale Price/Value	$1,150,000	115%	$1,300,000	130%	$1,050,000	105%
Entrepreneurial Profit	**$150,000**	**15%**	**$300,000**	**30%**	**$50,000**	**5%**

Note: This table shows how entrepreneurial profit can vary widely. In the first, pro forma version, if everything goes according to plan, the developer can expect to earn a healthy 15 percent profit. If the developer can successfully raise prices 15 percent, then profit doubles to 30 percent. If, on the other hand, prices drop just 10 percent, then the developer's profit drops to 5 percent or just one-third of the original pro forma profit. If prices drop 15 percent or more, profits disappear and the developer's invested capital is at risk.

Because deals are the basic product of entrepreneurial behavior, this chapter will consider how economists, geneticists, and sociologists think about "the entrepreneur" and the field of entrepreneurship. I will discuss their observations about the entrepreneur's role in the economy, why some people are genetically predisposed to entrepreneurial behavior, and what entrepreneurs really do on a day-to-day basis—the social and political work they engage in as a part of doing deals. I summarize these characteristics through a portrait of the entrepreneur and then introduce a Chicago developer whose career story illustrates and brings these ideas to life. First, let's begin with the basic character of the entrepreneur.

The Economist's View

In his 1942 classic *Capitalism, Socialism, and Democracy*, the economist Joseph Schumpeter equated the capitalist entrepreneur with medieval warlords and generals from the Napoleonic era. For these men, "generalship meant leadership, and success meant the personal success of the man in charge, who earned corresponding profits in the form of social prestige." The nature of warfare at the time—before mechanized armies—meant that the individual decision-making ability and driving influence of the leading man, including "his actual presence on a showy horse," were essential to success in the strategic and tactical implementation of warfare. So too for the entrepreneur, says Schumpeter.[2]

This militaristic metaphor may seem extreme but in fact the word "entrepreneur" has military roots. In their book about successful business people, *From Predators to Icons*, the French sociologists Michel Villette and Catherine Vuillermot traced the origins of entrepreneurship to thirteenth-century France. Then, the noun "entreprise" meant a military action and the verb "entreprendre" meant "to attack a person or a castle for pillage or to take prisoners for ransom." By the early eighteenth century, "entrepreneur" had come to mean an individual who engaged in risky economic behavior by relying on a self-interest-based strategy and by using skills and trickery to achieve his objectives. He cared little about social, cultural, and professional norms and was somewhat of a deviant, operating at the margins of society. By the late eighteenth century, however, all reference to pillage and deviance had disappeared as a more positive meaning emerged, and the entrepreneur became "a man of action who achieved something or accomplished a task—an activity that was highly valued in protestant thinking."[3] This new entrepreneur, according to Schumpeter, was someone who used an invention or new technology to create a new product or to revolutionize production methods, or who created a new market, opened a new source of supply of materials, or reorganized an industry. And like his militaristic forebears, say Villette and Vuillermot, he was motivated by a desire for independence, he sought a field that would allow for the full expression of his creativity, and he had a great need for public achievement. The entrepreneur, however, is just one half of the equation, and he cannot realize the full scope of his ambitions without one other key factor—an opportunity.[4]

Enterprising Individuals + Lucrative Opportunities = Profits

In "The Promise of Entrepreneurship as a Field of Research," the economists Scott Shane and Sankaran Venkataraman emphasized that, despite a prevailing "cult of the entrepreneur" that overemphasizes the role of the individual, entrepreneurship actually requires two ingredients: "enterprising individuals and lucrative opportunities." Entrepreneurship involves finding new ways to combine goods, services, materials, and methods in what economists call "joint production." The entrepreneur buys different resources at one set of prices, combines them together, and sells them for a total price that is greater than the sum of their original prices. Success requires making different assumptions about the values of those resources than providers and competitors who would otherwise raise their prices to capture a share of the entrepreneurial profit. Entrepreneurship therefore requires people to value resources differently, and there are two reasons why that might happen. First, estimating the value of individual resources—as well as their final combined value—requires guesswork. People will guess differently, however, so the individual who guesses correctly stands to profit. Second, ongoing technological, political, regulatory, and social changes ensure that all participants have imperfect information and people who possess information earlier than others have an advantage. But while asymmetrical information creates opportunities for some, it rarely lasts. As information and knowledge spread throughout the community of consultants, vendors, and materials suppliers, they will all raise their prices as they try to capture a share of the entrepreneurial profit for themselves. Competitors and imitators will enter the market too, and over time, the diffusion of knowledge will lead to ever-increasing competition between suppliers, competitors, and imitators until the entrepreneurial profit becomes divided among so many actors that the incentive to enter the market is eliminated. This cycle applies to the development of every type of product from condominiums and automobiles to cell phones and personal computers.[5]

How Entrepreneurs Identify and Exploit Lucrative Opportunities

But where do entrepreneurial ideas come from? Usually from very smart people. Each of us possesses different types and amounts of information, say Shane and Venkataraman, and the sum of a person's information and life experience serves as the mental framework through which they view the world. A person who obtains a new piece of information before others do may have a brief advantage but, more important, they are able to fit that piece of information into their thinking in a way that complements their existing mental framework and helps them identify a new entrepreneurial opportunity.[6]

This underscores an important difference between managers, who work at optimizing an existing business, and entrepreneurs, who, according to Shane and Venkataraman, identify new "means-ends relations" and "combine existing information and concepts into new ideas." The latter is more difficult to do, and people who are very intelligent and have the right set of cognitive skills are simply better at it. Intelligence may even influence how different people assess risk. Numerous studies have shown that entrepreneurial people see opportunities in situations where other people see only risks, and this may be because highly intelligent people are better able to accurately assess risk while the average person overvalues the downside risk as compared to the potential upside gain. In other words, according to the behavioral psychologist Daniel Kahneman, for most people, losing a dollar feels twice as bad as winning a dollar feels good. Those who are able to value the upside and the downside equally are better at assessing risk and reward and exploiting entrepreneurial opportunities.[7]

Studies have identified several other attributes common to entrepreneurs. First, they are optimists who perceive their chances of success to be much higher than they really are and much higher than those of their competitors. They are likely to be overly optimistic about the value of the opportunities they discover. This optimism, while driving them forward, can become a disadvantage if taken too far as they undervalue the downside risk. Entrepreneurs must also possess a higher-than-average tolerance for ambiguity because, unlike established businesses, entrepreneurial ventures take shape through a messy, uncertain, and fluid process. Finally, people with a high need for achievement are more likely to engage in entrepreneurial ventures because they offer greater opportunities for wealth creation and public acclaim.[8]

Entrepreneurs make their money by conceiving of new combinations of resources and ideas and creating new products and new markets for those products. They also share certain characteristics—intelligence, optimism, drive, and comfort with ambiguity, to name a few—that are further illuminated by recent research in the area of genetics.

The Geneticist's View

In *Born Entrepreneurs, Born Leaders*, Scott Shane summarizes a growing body of scientific research that proves that our genes influence whether or not we are likely to become entrepreneurs, and that the genetic indicators of our tendency to engage in entrepreneurial behavior fall into three areas.[9]

First, genes influence an individual's predisposition to entrepreneurship through a number of personality traits. Each person falls somewhere on a range of high to low for each of what are called the "big five," or OCEAN, personality traits: "openness to new experience," "conscientiousness," "extroversion," "agreeableness," and "neuroticism." Entrepreneurial people typically rank very high on the first three of these traits and very low on the last two.[10]

Entrepreneurs are more likely to be open to new experience, which is helpful because each entrepreneurial venture is new and different from the last. They are also more likely to be extroverts, and extroverts are also more likely to start their own businesses. Entrepreneurs are usually very conscientious, which translates into determination, discipline, organization, and perseverance in the face of obstacles, challenges, and uncertainty. Entrepreneurs are less likely, however, to be neurotic, to be insecure, or to be worriers. Rather, the entrepreneur must remain emotionally stable, flexible, and positive in the face of stress, financial risk, social isolation, setbacks, and the uncertainty that is inherent to any entrepreneurial activity. Finally, although they can be very charismatic and socially skilled, entrepreneurs are less likely to be agreeable—they do not need to be liked. Indeed, being agreeable—"cheerful, courteous, trusting, cooperative, kind, and altruistic" —is of little benefit to the entrepreneur who must "pursue his own interests, often at the expense of others, and drive hard bargains."[11]

The Influence of Genes on Other Personality Traits and Correlations Between Traits

There are several other personality traits through which genes predispose an individual toward entrepreneurial behavior. The idea of "locus of control" has to do with how much a person believes that he or she can control the world—or that the world controls him or her. A person can have either an internal or an external locus of control but entrepreneurs typically possess a high internal locus of control, which translates into a strong belief in their own ability to influence outcomes through their own behavior. Entrepreneurs must also have a high degree of self-esteem, which translates into high self-efficacy and confidence in one's own ability to achieve goals even in the face of obstacles and uncertainty, and at times when others don't believe in you. Finally, genes influence our predisposition to "novelty seeking," a high "need for autonomy," and "risk-taking propensity," all three of which correlate with entrepreneurial behavior.[12]

There are also correlations between the OCEAN personality traits and these other personality traits that are driven by genes. Extroverts, for example, often also possess the "impulsiveness" and novelty-seeking personality traits that correlate with entrepreneurial behavior. Further, conscientious people often have the persistence, impulsiveness, and novelty-seeking traits. And people who are open to new experiences are also typically imaginative, creative, curious, and inventive.[13]

The Influence of Genes on Intelligence and Energy Levels

Beyond our personalities, genes influence several other important sets of traits that correlate with entrepreneurial behavior. First, genes influence intelligence, and entrepreneurial people are more likely to be highly intelligent. Second, all people are active at some level, ranging between sedentary and hyperactive, and genes influence this "activity level." Entrepreneurial people tend to be more active than others, and people with ADHD (attention-deficit hyperactivity disorder) are more likely to become entrepreneurs than to pursue other professions, in part because, despite their high intelligence, they are less able to focus enough to excel in areas that require hours of reading, study, and concentration, like engineering, law, and medicine. Finally, ADHD and reading disorders such as dyslexia both correlate positively with high intelligence and people with these conditions are also more likely to be entrepreneurs. Many entrepreneurs have neither ADHD nor dyslexia but for those who do have them and who can put these traits to work, the combination can lead to wild success as evidenced by entrepreneurs such as Sir Richard Branson of Virgin Enterprises and David Neeleman, formerly the CEO of JetBlue.[14]

This biological perspective reveals much about the personality of the entrepreneur but genetics is not the only influence on the entrepreneurs' behavior. Environment, upbringing, and life experience play equally important roles in creating and shaping the entrepreneur. Stepping away from the microscope, where do entrepreneurs come from, how do they get their start, what other factors influence their development, and what is it that they actually do all day long?

The Sociologist's View

According to Villette and Vuillermot, the entrepreneur's goal is to identify and exploit a "market imperfection," earning a large, one-time entrepreneurial profit before others involved in the transaction are able to properly value their own contributing resources. This is called a "good deal," which is when "you get a lot for a little" while minimizing your own exposure to risk. Success in exploiting a good deal requires the entrepreneur to use know-how, social position, and reputation to engage in a political pursuit that involves culturing relations with important government representatives, businesspeople, and others who can help him or her succeed. But a good deal happens only once, so the entrepreneur is in a perpetual hunt for the next good deal. Each good deal increases the amount of capital under the entrepreneur's control, paving the way for still larger deals in the future. So for each good deal, the entrepreneur's success depends not on economic or technological innovation but rather on a social framework, "created by real human beings using an informal web of transactions."[15]

Villette and Vuillermot then debunk a handful of common misconceptions about entrepreneurs, most important their attitude toward risk. Rather than taking huge, crazy risks, as is commonly believed, successful entrepreneurs succeed by taking measures to mitigate, minimize, and even eliminate their exposure to risk, sometimes shedding risk onto other partners and providers. They avoid innovation, which is costly on the front end and slow to show returns, and instead they tinker at the margins, producing goods that are rarely very different—or better—than those of their competitors. Rather than making grand plans, entrepreneurs try many things, pursuing those that show promise, abandoning those that do not, and adapting to whatever the market sends their way. And while some entrepreneurs claim to be "self-made," they are often more privileged than others and their backgrounds give them advantages that others lack and that play a central role in their success.[16]

Five Common Characteristics

Indeed, in their study of nearly ninety very wealthy and successful entrepreneurial businesspeople, most of whom were men, Villette and Vuillermot found only five widely shared personal characteristics. First, the entrepreneur was raised in an enterprising environment where parents and other family members were business creators and owners. Second, the entrepreneur benefited from having more education than the average person, and his academic upbringing also provided access to a network of alumni, friends, and family of friends that supplemented family connections. Third, the entrepreneur gained experience in business very early in his career, through experience in sales, negotiations, or the creation of small companies. Fourth, when starting out, the entrepreneur benefited from privileged

financing—access to capital—from family and friends. And fifth, the entrepreneur had the support of a mentor who helped him make his first "good
deal."[17]

Looking through the overlapping lenses of economics, genetics, and
sociology helps to bring into focus how personality traits, background,
upbringing, and lucrative opportunities combine to create the entrepreneur. Throughout the rest of the book we will look at the entrepreneur
through a series of more personal lenses—the career stories of individual
developers. The next is a Chicago developer named Buzz Ruttenberg whose
story brings these ideas to life, from his start in the business and his first
good deal to his approach to risk management through the design of a
condominium project that would soon face a turning market.

Zip-Code Development

David "Buzz" Ruttenberg was born in March 1941 and was raised in a six-
flat walkup in downtown Chicago until he was ten, when his family moved
into a co-op a few blocks away. He attended a private school in the city
that was a short walk from his home and then he enrolled at Cornell University and graduated in 1962. After completing some graduate work at the
London School of Economics, Ruttenberg went on to Northwestern Law
School and graduated with honors in 1966. Ruttenberg initially practiced
law for the renowned Chicago firm of Kirkland and Ellis and then moved
to a family law firm while he was "developing his craft" as a developer. He
left law in the mid-1980s and became a full-time developer in his early
forties. But his career in real estate development really started in the 1950s,
when as a child he would accompany his father on visits to the various
rental properties that his father owned.[18]

Ruttenberg's maternal grandfather was an immigrant from Russia
named David Wolf who came to Chicago in his early teenage years. He
opened a wholesale dry-cleaning business that served hotels and other institutional laundry users. As his business prospered, he became interested in
property. Ruttenberg's parents married in 1940 and his father, David C.
Ruttenberg, was an attorney who "scratched out a living" after the Depres-
sion and then during World War II. But the Ruttenbergs lived relatively
comfortably although they drove old cars and initially lived in a walkup
apartment in the city. By the late 1940s the rush to the suburbs was under

way but Ruttenberg's parents had no interest in moving there, and his mother knew that his father could never ride a train every day, so they stayed downtown.

In the late 1940s, Ruttenberg's father was introduced to a rooming-house operator named Louis Supera. The two men were close in age—born in 1909 and 1910, respectively—and at the time they met they were in their late thirties. "My father had a creative itch and an interest in real estate that he had picked up from his father-in-law, who had since passed away, and Supera knew how to collect rents and maintain B and C class buildings." So the two men bought a nine-flat on Hampton Court, just around the corner from the Ruttenbergs' home at 450 West Wrightwood and two blocks west of Lincoln Park. At the time, says Ruttenberg, "Lincoln Park was green but a little tired and the upscale community now known as 'Lincoln Park' had yet to arrive.

"So they did what I call a 'two-brush rehab,'" says Ruttenberg, "which means they swept it with a broom and repainted it with a brush." David C. Ruttenberg kept on practicing law and Lou Supera kept on running rooming houses, but they collected rent from their nine-flat, and, although it wasn't much, it supplemented the incomes of both families. The Superas and the Ruttenbergs each had two children, all of whom were close in age, and the two families both stayed in the city—the Ruttenbergs in Lincoln Park and the Superas a little to the north, in Rogers Park.

Breaking Rules

About 1950, Ruttenberg and Supera decided that for their next investment they would go farther west and "venture into no-man's land." The two men bought a twenty-unit apartment building two blocks west of Clark Street and four blocks west of Lincoln Park. The area was a little dangerous but there were no gangs, and yet people saw Clark Street as a big psychological barrier. "At the time, going west of Clark Street was like Christopher Columbus in 1492—it was unchartered and you could fall off the edge," says Ruttenberg. "Everyone thought they were crazy but in the end they were right, and they didn't need a market study, it just made sense. After all, in Chicago, east is in the water, which is a real barrier, so any development that is going to happen is going to go west, and if anyone had thought about this it would have been obvious. You start to say, 'Gee, I think I see a pattern here.'"

Figure 7. David C. Ruttenberg (left) and Lou Supera in 1965.
Courtesy of Belgravia Group Ltd.

Ruttenberg and Supera continued to buy and develop properties west of Clark Street. In the 1960s they began to copy what was happening in SoHo in New York City, exposing brick to make things more "cool and hip" for the artist community that was starting to live in Lincoln Park. Ruttenberg and Supera had been working together for about twenty years when, in 1971, two young restaurateurs named Rich Melman and Jerry Orzoff opened a restaurant in Lincoln Park called RJ Grunts. "Everyone told them that they couldn't succeed but RJ Grunts went on to become one of the most successful restaurants in Chicago." By the 2000s, Melman's privately held restaurant company, Lettuce Entertain You Enterprises, owned and operated more than seventy restaurants, mostly in Chicago.

"There was no reason for Clark Street to be a barrier," says Ruttenberg. "It was a psychological barrier. And this is part of what makes the Midwest the Midwest—it is a great place to live but the people are more conservative and risk-averse." Having gone east for school and then to London, however, Ruttenberg had learned that rules are meant to be challenged. "Some of the most successful people in the world today have broken the rules," says Ruttenberg. "Bill Gates did not graduate from Harvard and Steve Jobs dropped out of Reed College but for both of them the old rules did not apply to the new game that they were playing." For Ruttenberg, the lesson was the same: "Here, in Chicago, there are a lot of perceived barriers that really don't make sense. My dad and Lou Supera succeeded by pushing the geographic envelope where it wanted to go, and I have been doing the same thing ever since."

Now I Am a Corporate Raider

"Although I went to law school and practiced law while I was working with my father," says Ruttenberg, "I had always been drawn to entrepreneurial opportunities in real estate and I had a teacher in my dad. We were very fortunate in that we got along well and we found that it was fun to do things together. He had created a base and we had a level of success in the Lincoln Park area and a nice reputation." Then along came an opportunity that Ruttenberg was able to convert into his first good deal.

In 1970, when he was just twenty-nine, Ruttenberg and his father bought a property called Crilly Court, on Wells Street in Old Town, just a little to the north. It was a $2 million purchase, "which was humongous for us at that point," and it comprised about 120 residential units and a dozen stores. "We knew nothing about stores, but it was our neighborhood and we knew that we were experts in our neighborhood, so we said, 'What the hell, let's go for it.'" The seller was a group of investors led by a big Chicago developer named Arthur Rubloff who together owned everything on both sides of Wells Street but who wanted to sell the whole portfolio at once, rather than piecemeal. But to Ruttenberg the seller was Arthur Rubloff, the person. Rubloff had bought up all of this property for the purposes of developing a higher-density project on the east side of Wells Street, closer to the park, but he didn't want the old property on the west side of the street. "So Rubloff signed a contract for all of it and then flipped the old stuff to us."

Rubloff was selling all 108 apartments, 12 rental houses, and 12 stores for an average price of $15,000 per unit but Ruttenberg divided the portfolio into different property types and found hidden opportunities. "We got some homes, some apartments, and some stores, and I took a look at the asset pool and thought, 'Once again, it is a matter of breaking the rules and thinking creatively.' I thought that we could fix up the twelve rental houses and sell them as separate homes, and I knew that the market value for these homes was $70,000. The difference between $15,000 and $70,000 is $55,000 per home, and if you multiply that times twelve homes, it is a lot of money and 30 percent of the deal. On the day I signed the contract the average price was $15,000 but I knew that those twelve houses were worth $70,000, so I said to myself, 'Now I am a corporate raider.'"

Better still, Ruttenberg had a sense that the current tenants of the houses would be ready buyers and indeed they were. "We sold them all as is to the tenants and most of them were thrilled to buy them so it wasn't a big effort. We didn't have to do any renovating or spend any money on marketing so it was the perfect deal."

As for the apartments, there was another reason why Arthur Rubloff and his investor partners did not see what Ruttenberg saw. "They were guilty of living in downtown office buildings but there is no substitute for being the guy in the field with on-the-ground experience." Because they lacked that experience, Rubloff and his partners believed that the rents were maxed out. But Ruttenberg had worked his way through law school as a janitor and property manager: "I knew how to rent buildings, I knew what people wanted, and I knew what they didn't want. I also knew that the problem here was that these owners had never reinvested any money in these properties, so the carpet, hallways, and appliances were all tired and

Table 2. An Example of Entrepreneurial Profit

Arthur's View	No. Units	Value/Unit	Total Value
All Units	132	$15,152	$2,000,000
Sale Price			$2,000,000

Buzz's View	No. Units	Value/Unit	Total Value
For-sale Houses	12	$70,000	$840,000
Apartments	108	$15,152	$1,636,364
Stores	12	$15,152	$181,818
Total Value	132		**$2,658,182**
Less Purchase Price			**($2,000,000)**
Buzz's Profit			**$658,182**
% Gain			33%

Note: Buzz Ruttenberg made a huge profit because when he divided the asset pool, he realized that the twelve houses were worth $70,000 each, whereas Rubloff had not differentiated between units and had priced them all at $15,000 each. Buzz earned a paper profit of more than $600,000 ($55,000 multiplied by twelve houses) in one transaction because he understood the value of the property better than the seller did.

needed to be freshened up." This time, Ruttenberg went up a notch from the two-brush rehab to include some more significant improvements.

Lease turnover dates in Chicago were typically May and October and the closing was going to be in March, which was close to lease renewal time. Rubloff was sensitive to the fact that if the lease renewals did not go out on time it could cause problems for the buyer but because they knew the Ruttenbergs they allowed them to send out the leases one month before the closing. "So we sent out our leases," says Ruttenberg, "and with them we sent a long letter outlining everything we were going to do and informing the tenants that, by the way, your rent is going up 40 percent.

"Well, the tenants wanted it—they were starving for it—and nobody knew. Half of the leases that were up were renewed by the time we got to closing. In the end we looked like we had outsmarted Rubloff, and we had. We closed on March 1, 1971, we made a big paper profit, and I was thirty years old. To this day we still own a part of that asset although we have sliced and diced it a lot of ways, sold off some of the homes, some of the apartments, and kept some of the retail. For us, Crilly Court was the goose that kept laying golden eggs and it gave us a revenue source on refinance and disposition that has been useful ever since."

Cautious Risk Takers

By the late 1960s it had become apparent to the Ruttenbergs that in addition to rehab projects, there were new construction opportunities. There were plenty of vacant lots and the demand for new housing in the city was increasing, so they started by building new six- and eight-unit infill buildings and that gave them the experience they needed to do twenty- and thirty-unit buildings. They continued pushing west and then north, to an area near Wrigley Field. "We thought of ourselves as 'cautious risk takers' and while those areas were rough—there were drugs and gangs—we also knew that Chicago tended to evolve on the basis of contiguity. So if your new neighborhood was contiguous with your old neighborhood, you could generally get people to migrate to the new community. But not if there was a four- or six-block gap—there are plenty of examples of people who went too far west and became isolated and in those cases it took a long time for development to catch up."

In the late 1970s the Ruttenbergs started converting loft buildings into offices in the River North area one mile west of Michigan Avenue. "We could see the activity picking up, there were more people living downtown, and since development is about adaptation rather than innovation, we started looking to New York for inspiration." But by the 1980s they were finished with loft conversions. "Other people started coming in and paying more for loft buildings, so we stopped. We had lived through the run-up but when the office market became supercompetitive in the 1980s we exited, and when we sold our office portfolio it comprised almost one million square feet."

At around the same time, Ruttenberg had come to feel that developing, owning, and managing office space was simply not what they did best. "Apartments are easier—when they turnover, you just paint them. With offices, the new tenant wants more walls, less walls, a different arrangement of space, and so you need to change everything else too—the lights, the heating and cooling, and the sprinklers—and you need to pay brokers all the time. With an apartment you just put a sign on the door and have the janitor show the apartments." So while offices and apartments may look similar, Ruttenberg learned that they are really quite different and he simply

Figure 8. Buzz Ruttenberg (left) and his father, David C. Ruttenberg, in 1993. Courtesy of Belgravia Group, Ltd.

felt that he knew how to do apartments better. He also felt that zip-code development was still the best approach.

"My father and I believed in being in the center of activity and relying on our own judgment. Both of us had always lived in town and we had never hired someone or paid $5,000 or $10,000 for a market study to tell us how to invest $100,000 or more of our own equity. It was our money, we were not syndicators, we were not going anywhere, and certainly not in a hurry. Instead, we were going to creep, crawl, and be cautious risk takers, and this takes incredible discipline that is hard to develop."

Business Transactions Are About "What Is Best for Me"

In the late 1980s the Ruttenbergs started several new construction projects farther west, beginning with one important purchase. A college friend of Ruttenberg's called to let him know that his factory—the old Butternut Bread factory at Clyborn and Webster—in the core of Lincoln Park might be for sale. The Ruttenbergs bought it, demolished it, and redeveloped the site into a retail center. By this time, residential density had increased in the city but retail had not followed, so urban dwellers had to drive to the suburbs to shop at the mall. The importance of being able to park in the city had grown too, and in housing projects the Ruttenbergs were providing off-street parking for one and even two cars per unit. So the Ruttenbergs decided to borrow the model of the suburban shopping mall and bring it downtown. The two-story, 150,000-square-foot Webster Place shopping center was the first new retail center in Lincoln Park. It was anchored by eight movie theaters on the second floor and supported by seven hundred parking spaces. The movie theater was one more case of "breaking the rules."

At the time downtown theater owners had agreements with the movie distributors that gave them exclusive rights to show first-run movies in a zone that included the downtown core and all of the north side, which included Webster Place. The only place downtown to see a first-run movie was at a four-screen theater at Water Tower Place, a seventy-four-story, mixed-use tower on Michigan Avenue, but a moviegoer had to brave congestion and expensive parking to get there.

So the Ruttenbergs gambled that bringing in a new theater in a suburban-style mall on the North Side with free and easy parking would increase the market for first-run movies in the city but they had no guarantee that the movie distributors would create a new zone. "At Webster Place, parking was free and you could tell right away from the parking lot whether the movie you wanted to see was showing, rather than paying for parking and then taking the elevator to the seventh floor of Water Tower Place just to find out what was playing or to find out that the movie you wanted to see was sold out." The theaters at Webster Place opened "with secondary stuff," says Ruttenberg, "but all 1,600 seats were full within a week and the movie distributors realized that two zones might be a good thing after all, since they would ensure more seats and more revenue for first-run movies.

"Business deals are about 'what is best for me,'" says Ruttenberg, "and what was best for the movie distributors was the creation of a new zone. It was a perceived barrier but to me it was obvious." Webster Place went on to become a big hit. "And with the success of Webster Place, our expertise—without any long-term plan—continued to grow, and as it grew, we gained more access to capital."

Value, Value, Value

Since the 1990s, Ruttenberg has done nothing but for-sale housing in the city. "We needed to learn, develop our expertise, and scale up slowly, so we started out doing small townhomes, then small midrises, and then we went bigger." Since 2000, Ruttenberg has developed three condominium towers on Chicago's lakefront, one at 530 Lake Shore Drive and two more across the street at 600 Lake Shore Drive, all adjacent to Navy Pier, Chicago's big waterfront entertainment center. But once again, says Ruttenberg, "Following the business model that I have already described—cautious risk taking—we didn't build condos the way other developers did at the peak."

The property at 600 Lake Shore Drive was about one acre and was the last piece of vacant land on Chicago's lakefront. In the 1980s there had been plans for a ninety-story building but they fell apart when the stock market crashed in 1987. In the 1990s another developer made plans for a massive single tower but it never got off the ground either. As he was finishing 530 Lake Shore Drive, Ruttenberg approached the owner of the property across the street and said, "Your zoning is going to run out soon and the mode in the city these days is downzoning, so if your FAR [floor area ratio, which is the ratio of buildable floor area to site area] gets reduced from 16 to 12, you will lose 25 percent of your value, but if you work with me maybe we can do something." Ruttenberg had a plan that comprised two towers that were perpendicular to the lakefront rather than one big tower that was parallel to it. This scheme offered a number of important benefits.

First, while his competitors developed buildings designed to maximize their buildable area based on zoning, Ruttenberg took a more modest tack. "Instead of building the tallest building with the biggest floor plates, we built the shortest buildings possible based on our land costs, to minimize the risk of having too much product to absorb." Shorter is also better, says Ruttenberg, because "while many people believe that it does not cost more money to go higher, in fact every time a building gets taller it gets more complicated and more expensive." Tall buildings are like sails, and the as they get taller, more must be spent on design and construction to offset the effects of "wind-loading." As a building becomes taller its columns and foundations must become larger to resist the building's tendency to tip, while exterior window and wall systems must be stronger if they are to

Figure 9. Buzz Ruttenberg's two-tower design for 600 Lake Shore Drive, Chicago. Courtesy of Pappageorge Haymes Partners.

resist both positive and negative wind pressure. "But, more important, the taller the building, the longer it takes to complete and the longer it takes to deliver the last units and this is only made worse by having small floor plates at the top." Further, the longer it takes to get to the top the more the market can change in terms of tastes and the more time your competitors have to supply more product and saturate the market.

Second, Ruttenberg's conception for two towers rather than one allowed for smaller floor plates and more exterior perimeter for the same amount of area, which meant more windows in the units. But more important, by placing two towers perpendicular to the lakefront, Ruttenberg's floor plan allowed him to arrange his units so that they all had lake views, whereas a single tower parallel to the Lakefront would have had many units on the back side, facing west, with no lake views. In Ruttenberg's plan, the two-bedroom units were on the southwest and northwest corners, with oblique lake views; the one-bedroom units were in the centers of the long sides of the towers with lake views to the southeast and northeast; and the largest—the three-bedroom units—were on the northeast and southeast corners, where they had panoramic lake views.

Third, Ruttenberg also charged a higher dollar-per-square-foot price for the larger units and a lower price for the smaller units, which is the opposite of typical practice. More often, units are priced so that smaller units cost more per square foot while larger units cost a little less and the difference between the unit prices is not as great. But at 600 Lake Shore, a 1,000-square-foot, one-bedroom unit sold for as little as $400 per square foot, or $400,000, and a 2,500-square-foot, three-bedroom unit sold for $700 per square foot or $1.7 million. Ruttenberg had looked at suburban retirement home models, where larger, better units are sold for a higher dollar-per-square-foot price. He had also learned from the sell-out of his previous project across the street that lake views sell—"what a surprise"—and he was confident that he could charge a significant "view premium" for those three-bedroom corner units facing the lake. "Why pay that premium? Because there is an eighty-mile, no-build zone in front of your unit."

Fourth, building two separate towers also meant that Ruttenberg could manage his risk by building in two phases, giving him more control over construction and market timing. This also allowed him to "prove up" the concept with the smaller first tower, which represented only 40 percent of the project's size. He could then make adjustments to the second tower to

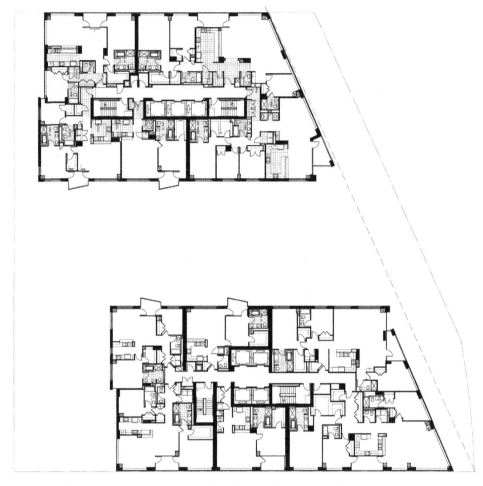

Figure 10. A typical floor plan for 600 Lake Shore Drive. There are six units per floor in each of the two towers, and all units have views of the lake to the east (right, in this plan). Courtesy of Pappageorge Haymes Partners.

best satisfy the market at the time. So the two-tower scheme made sense both economically and in terms of managing risk.

Fifth, Ruttenberg managed his risk by designing reasonably sized units, paying attention to the total sale price of the unit rather than the dollar-per-square-foot price, providing value, and building with an eye toward what inevitably happens—a downturn in the market. At the peak of the

Figure 11. The unobstructed view east, over Lake Michigan, from 600 Lake Shore Drive, with Navy Pier to the right. Courtesy of 600 Lake Shore Drive LLC, a Sandz/Belgravia Group Ltd. Development.

condo boom, many developers were "blowing air" into their floor plans to create larger units that they could sell for higher prices based on dollar-per-square-foot pricing. This has the effect of making larger units look good on paper, but it can lead to difficulty when the market takes a turn for the worse because while home buyers may compare projects based on dollar-per-square-foot prices they buy based on what they can finance—the total price. "So if you provide the same unit as your competitor," says Ruttenberg, "but you blow a little less air into the floor plans and you make them slimmer and a little more efficient, then you are hedging against the day when the market slows down. And if that means as a buyer you are paying $1.7 million to live in a three-bedroom, three-bath unit on the lake but others are paying $2.5 million to $5 million, then that feels pretty good to you."

Ruttenberg concludes that "much has been made of the 'three L's—location, location, location'—but something that is equally as important that gets talked about less is 'value, value, value.' You can have the best location but if it is overpriced then you have to hit the market just right or else you are out of luck. You always have to assume that it is going to go bad," says Ruttenberg, "and so the question becomes, how do I differentiate myself for when that happens? Once again, 'cautious risk taking.' That is how we managed the risk on this project—by designing a product that we could complete and get to market faster and that would be a value even after the market turned down." And when Ruttenberg talks about "we," he is including his main partner on the project, Michael Supera. "Michael is the son of Louis Supera so 600 Lake Shore Drive was like a fifty-year reunion of the Ruttenbergs and Superas working together."

Buzz Ruttenberg's story illustrates how upbringing and background influence a developer's career. His ideas about rule breaking and cautious risk taking offer one view of opportunity, risk, and how "psychological barriers" can cause people to value things differently—and create a good deal for the observant entrepreneur. And with 600 Lake Shore Drive, Ruttenberg explains how he was able to hedge against a downturn in the market by using a more efficient design to differentiate his project from that of his competition. Finally, despite the common misconception of entrepreneurs as crazy risk takers, throughout this story Ruttenberg explains how most developers really think about their business and the products they produce. For those who are successful over time, development is not about taking huge risks on bold, creative, but unproven ideas. Rather, it is about minimizing exposure to risk through a careful process of incremental improvement to traditional product types over time.

"The best Shakespeare plays are based on Greek mythology," says Ruttenberg, "so the question becomes what adaptations can you make and how can you make it better, more interesting, and more current. It is the same for development: You don't want to reinvent the wheel—once they cut the corners off, it rolls." Still, to succeed, a developer must always be improving the product at the margins, so in the next chapter we will look more closely at real estate development as a product-development process and how product types evolve over time.

Chapter 3

The Real Estate Development Process

> There is a reason for everything with each developer and each project is
> a big life story making its way into the building.
> —John Carroll, Portland, Oregon, real estate developer[1]

Real Estate Development as Product Development

Real estate means different things to different people. To most of us it
means the physical homes we live in and the office buildings where we go
to work. To city planners, real estate development is a way to mesh the
economic goals of private developers and their investors with a city's larger
economic and social goals, from business growth to job creation and housing production. Planners may influence the geographic direction of development, for example, by encouraging ground-floor retail in buildings that
will be built on commercial corridors or by encouraging higher-density
and mixed-use development around transit stations. For elected politicians,
development is a way to encourage investment in the city—in ways that are
in concert with policies, plans, and the desires of their constituents—and
as a way to attract and retain businesses, house residents, and expand the
city's tax base. For architects, a real estate development project means the
opportunity to design a building that will generate fees and can lead to
repeat business, allow them to practice their craft, and explore their own
aesthetic ideas. If their peers consider their work important, they may also
win design awards and attract positive media attention. To wealthy investors, real estate development is a way to earn a higher rate of return on
their money than they can earn through the stock market or other less risky

investments. From the developer's viewpoint, real estate is all of these things but first and foremost it is "product" and real estate development is "product development."

In the same way that Apple Computer, Inc., developed the next generation of computers, phones, pods, pads, and other must-have gadgets, real estate developers constantly work to produce the next generation of office spaces, warehouses, retail centers, or housing units. Developers even use the same language as other product manufacturers. They "develop," "design," "produce," "market," and "sell," and they talk about what is in "the pipeline," whether or not they have enough "sales velocity," and the problem of having too much "inventory" or "product on the shelf." Products change over time, however, and if there is one constant to the product-development process—and the real estate development process—it is innovation.

The Role of Innovation in Real Estate Development

In *The Innovator's Dilemma: When New Technologies Cause Great Firms to Fail*, Clayton Christensen differentiates between "sustaining" and "disruptive" innovation. Sustaining innovation is an innovation that does not affect existing markets and can either be "evolutionary" or "revolutionary." An evolutionary innovation is an improvement to an existing product that consumers expect, such as fuel injection for automobile engines. A revolutionary innovation is one that is new and unexpected but that does not affect existing markets. The automobile itself, for example, did not affect the horse-drawn carriage business because it was so costly and out of reach for the average consumer.[2]

Disruptive innovation, however, creates a new market by "applying a different set of values," and it ultimately and sometimes unexpectedly overtakes an existing market. The use of the assembly line to manufacture the Ford Model T at a significantly lower cost is an example of disruptive innovation because it overtook the entire existing automobile industry and made cars cheap for the masses. Products based on disruptive technologies are typically cheaper, simpler, smaller, and more convenient to use.[3] Examples of disruptive innovations and the markets they overtook include over-the-road trucking and railroads, digital photography and chemical photography, and cloud computing and USB flash drives.[4]

Real estate usually falls in the category of sustaining innovation, with evolutionary innovations including incremental improvements to materials and building systems for all product types as in the increasing emphasis on sustainable design and construction. Revolutionary innovations in real estate often take the form of variations on existing product types and locations. Over the past century, revolutionary jumps in retail products, for example, have led from downtown department stores to suburban strip malls, regional shopping centers, mega-malls, entertainment centers, and lifestyle centers. Similarly, revolutionary jumps in residential products have led from dense single-family and multifamily housing in cities to single-family homes and townhomes in the suburbs and then back downtown to loft conversions, new townhomes, high-rise condominiums, senior housing, student housing, and luxury apartments.

Whether evolutionary or revolutionary, different types of products evolve at different rates. In his book about product design and development, *Where Stuff Comes From*, Harvey Molotch points out that the introduction of entirely new products is relatively rare, and most products are based on existing but constantly evolving "type forms." Vacuum cleaners, toasters, and other household goods evolve over time but do not change in terms of their general look and function. Across the spectrum of goods, "quick-turn" type forms like mobile phones evolve rapidly while products such as household appliances, automobiles, and homes that are more costly and expected to last much longer are called "slow-turn" type forms. In product-development terms, real estate is a "slow-turn type form," and there are a number of reasons for this.[5]

First, real estate development is very risky. Every time a developer initiates a project he or she is attempting something that has, in effect, never been done before. Each project represents a unique combination of price, product, location, and market timing. Second, real estate development is very costly. Unlike other entrepreneurial ventures that can be cash-flowed or "bootstrapped," development requires the upfront investment of large amounts of capital. Developers use their own risk capital—cash—and that of their investors to obtain control over a piece of property, complete a conceptual design, seek and obtain key approvals, and test the market for their product. The expenditure of these funds, however, is no guarantee of success and if the project does not get completed those funds are lost. So in order to preserve capital and minimize risk, developers are more inclined to adapt a product slightly rather than strike out into the unknown and try something significantly different. Equity investors and banks take a similarly conservative view—they want their money returned and so they are less inclined to try far-out things. For example, a developer may not think he needs to provide as much parking as a typical project because the site is near a transit line. He may have difficulty, however, obtaining a construction loan because the product does not provide the same basic features as its competitors, so the bank sees increased risk. On the other side, the market's tastes evolve slowly too, so developers are careful not to get too far ahead of their buyers in terms of price, product, or location. There have been plenty of examples of development projects that were too exotic, in the wrong place, mispriced, or simply before their time, which is why, as one saying goes, "pioneering developers are the ones with arrows in their backs."

When compared to the latest cell phone, real estate—housing, office, retail, and industrial—is a product type that evolves slowly, and yet it is always evolving. It takes a long time to get a real estate product to market—years and even decades can go by between the time a developer conceives of a project and the day the last unit is sold or the last lease is signed. During that time many things change, from market tastes and demographic trends to construction costs and the efforts of the competition. How, then, does a developer go about successfully conceiving, producing, and selling a real estate product? What are the steps and who are the actors?

The Five Stages of Development

Concept Stage

The real estate development process can be divided into five basic stages: concept, approvals, design, construction, and sales. First, during the concept development or "pursuit" phase, a developer must have an idea or a vision for a product that will serve a specific market, for which there will be adequate demand, and that can be built at a cost and sold at a price that will yield a minimum profit. This idea may start with a piece of land or a building in a good location, a product type for which there is demand, a real tenant or buyer, or an amount of investment capital under the developer's control. The developer will take into account supply and demand for the product type and local, regional, and national business, technological, and population growth trends.

The developer will also begin assembling a skeletal team, starting with an architect whose job it will be to test what kind of project will fit on the property, including use, numbers of floors, and numbers and types of units. The developer may also ask a contractor to provide a simple cost estimate for the project, based on the architect's preliminary sketches and an antici-pated quality level. This cost estimate will serve as the basis for an economic model of the project or "pro forma" that summarizes project costs, financ-ing, and potential profits based on anticipated prices. The developer will need access to capital to finance the project through to completion so she will begin to court potential investors, lenders, and other individuals and institutions that may be potential sources of funds. The developer rarely has a monopoly opportunity, so she must also scrutinize the marketplace and consider what her competitors are doing, what comparable products are already in the development pipeline, when they will hit the market, and the likely costs and prices of those products.

The developer must then consider the politics of obtaining approvals and whether or not she can generate the good will and support required from local elected officials and government staff, neighbors and members of the community, and other special interests. At the end of the concept phase the developer will have a team, a concept design, a pro forma, poten-tial investors and lenders, a preliminary indication of support from the city and other relevant stakeholders, and a good idea of the market's appetite for the product. The developer's objective in this stage is to arrive at a politically and economically viable concept for the lowest possible cost. Next, the developer will advance the design to the level required to seek and obtain formal approvals from the city.

Approvals Stage

At this early stage of the project, from the viewpoint of the public, the developer is often a solitary individual attending neighborhood meetings with a staffperson or an architect in tow. Behind the scenes, however, the developer's team is larger and will continue to grow. Developers are gener-alists and very knowledgeable but they lead as conductors and so, as Gerald Fogelson pointed out in Chapter 1, they must surround themselves with a wide array of specialists if they are to succeed. The design team will grow from that one architect to include landscape architects, land surveyors, geotechnical engineers, and structural, mechanical, electrical, and plumbing engineers. These different team members may be hired because they possess relevant expertise in the product type or because they have worked successfully with the developer in the past, or both.

As the design evolves, the developer will begin to consider which building systems—structural, heating and air conditioning, plumbing, and electrical—are most appropriate for the building and for the product type and how those systems will impact the economics of the project, including both costs and rents or sales prices. The marketing and sales team will help to improve elements of the design from the column bay spacing, window design, and ceiling heights for an office building to the unit plans, parking facilities, and common spaces for a residential building. Their combined efforts will be directed toward sharpening and differentiating the project's image or brand to ensure a competitive edge in the marketplace. In the background, the developer's real estate attorneys will assist with everything from executing real estate transactions—options, purchase agreements, and other contracts—to partnership agreements. Other attorneys will lobby local politicians and draft homeowners' association documents or other covenants, conditions, restrictions, and easements that will be applied to the completed property.

Throughout all of this, the developer will continue to meet informally and formally with city staff, politicians, community groups, neighbors, investors, lenders, and many others. The developer will receive feedback on anything from the height, density, and massing of the building to the mix and sizes of units, design style, colors, materials, site layout, and parking arrangements. She will strive to integrate as much of this feedback as is reasonably possible into the design, with the goal of maximizing the attractiveness of the product to potential buyers. At the same time, the developer will seek the support of these various stakeholders and will strive to increase their commitment to the project. If successful, the developer will gradually broaden ownership of the project by ensuring that the issues of key constituencies are reflected in the developing design as much as is technically and economically feasible. The developer will incorporate this information into the design and will complete drawings to the level of detail required by the city to submit for approvals and to present at formal public planning and zoning commission meetings. If successful, this stage ends with the city granting the formal approvals or "entitlements" to the developer for the submitted design that are required for the project to be built.

Design Stage

With entitlements in hand, key team members in place, and the developer's vision and project goals more clearly outlined, the team will begin to design the building in detail. More architects and engineers will join the team, along with a variety of other subconsultants specializing in everything from traffic engineering and parking structures to historic resources, lighting design, and interior design.

The contractor will use the approved concept design as the basis for a more detailed estimate of construction costs. These costs will include everything required to construct the building, from materials, labor, systems, and interior finishes to temporary heat, electricity, insurances, and fees to be paid to the city if a lane of the street must be closed or parking meters must be taken out of service. To this estimate the developer will add land costs, design fees, legal and other professional service fees, and all other "soft costs" to arrive at the "total project cost." Next, the developer will add an amount or percentage for profit to determine final pricing for the product. Once all of this information has been assembled, the developer will begin to fine-tune the project, working back and forth to reduce costs, increase value, and simplify the design from a construction standpoint while maintaining a certain level of quality. The contractor's input at this stage will influence everything from the architectural design and the selection of materials to the column grid, the locations of stairs, elevator and mechanical shafts, and the selection of structural, mechanical, electrical, and plumbing systems.

The developer will keep meeting with potential investors and lenders and will also commission a market study to help demonstrate the viability of the concept. This document will be based on national, regional, and local economic and demographic data as well as information about comparable products, or "comps," in the market. It will summarize existing inventory, how the project compares to similar projects in terms of location, features, and price, and how competitive the product is likely to be in the marketplace. If the developer is planning to use cheap appliances in a "luxury" condominium or providing one parking space per apartment unit when competitors are providing two, the lender either may be unwilling to make a loan without very good explanations for these decisions or may offer less favorable terms.

The marketing and sales team will begin to shape the image of the project from its name and logo to the design of its website and how it will be positioned, represented, and sold based on the target market—the buyers whom the developer hopes to attract. Developers differentiate their products to reflect the wants and needs of different types of buyers, and they vary their sales and marketing approaches for the same reason. Selling condominiums to first-time homebuyers on a budget, for example, is different from selling them to wealthy, retired, empty nesters. Similarly, leasing office space to small professional services firms is different from leasing to a call center filled with low-wage hourly workers in cubicles or to a prominent law firm that requires many large, private offices.

While the detailed design is being completed, the contractor will continue to fine-tune construction cost estimates, and the developer and sales team will determine final pricing. Marketing materials will be prepared, the sales center constructed, and the sales agents will be hired. The marketing team will grow to include public relations and media consultants; branding, graphic design, and creative firms; and an event planner. They will design brochures, signage, and collateral materials. Stories, opinion pieces, and ads will be placed in the local news media. And together they all begin to create excitement and "buzz" around the big and carefully planned grand opening of the sales center when the product will go on the market.

Construction Stage

Construction loans for real estate projects are secured by the future value of the completed property. Before a bank will make a loan, the developer must demonstrate this value by obtaining a specified number of purchase agreements or leases at or above projected prices to give the bank confidence that the project will sell out or lease up. The developer may turn to a bank with which she has a good relationship or she may shop around for the best loan terms.

As soon as the developer has settled on terms with a bank and closed on the loan, she will acquire or "take down" the land and break ground, with the goal of completing construction as quickly as possible. Throughout the construction stage, the developer will be involved in a million little decisions from materials selections to construction details to the review of monthly construction payment applications. Until the building is finished she will be constantly rebalancing the project's design, materials, systems, and costs.

Closing dates with tenants or buyers will drive the schedule. For large projects the developer may complete and sell or lease up a part of the project while the rest of the building is still under construction. High-rise residential and office towers are often completed and occupied from the top down, while horizontal developments like townhomes and office parks lend themselves more easily to phasing that matches market demand and absorption. Whether the first condo unit or an entire building, the completion of construction signals the beginning of sales.

Sales Stage

Once construction is complete and the building is ready for occupancy, the developer's objective is to sell or lease it up for the highest prices possible as quickly as possible. The developer must repay the construction loan with proceeds from sales. The longer it takes to sell out or lease up, the higher the interest costs on that borrowed money—the carrying costs—and the lower the developer's profit. During this stage the developer's attention will be focused on ensuring that buyers or tenants who have signed purchase agreements or leases remain satisfied and show up to close on those contracts.

The developer's involvement will not end until the building is completely sold out or, in the case of a rental property, leased up and then refinanced or sold. Some developers build to "hold" over a longer time frame and they will have ongoing responsibility for property ownership from maintenance to periodic capital improvements. When the developer does finally sell or "dispose of the asset," whether it is as soon as it has been leased up to a "stabilized" level of occupancy (for example 90 percent) or decades later, she will return all funds to lenders and make distributions of equity and profits to investors.

An Iterative and Fluid Process

The five stages outlined above offer an idea of the breadth of knowledge and experience required to be a successful developer. Each stage contains many tasks and many of those tasks span across some or all stages of a project. Many of those tasks are also different in character from one another, from negotiating a land purchase and directing an architect to drafting a pro forma and seeking the support of an elected official. So while they are sometimes portrayed as generalists who are "a mile wide but only an inch deep," developers must possess deep knowledge in a broad range of subjects—they must be a mile wide *and* a mile deep. They must also know when to bring in specialized expertise in those instances when they are less knowledgeable. And they must know how and when to approach these many different tasks. Pat Prendergast, a developer from Portland, Oregon, offers a different view of the real estate development process through his own detailed checklist:

REAL ESTATE DEVELOPMENT TASK LIST:
- Project Initiation
- Site Control: Option/Purchase/Venture
- Initial Development Entity
- Selection of Development Team
- Project Conception
- Alternative Development Concepts
- Development Program
- Market Evaluation
- Site Evaluation
- Economic Analysis (Pro Forma)
  - Gross Income
  - Operating Expenses
  - Net Operating Income (NOI)
    - Debt Coverage Ratio (DCR)
    - Debt Service Constant/Loan Constant
    - Mortgage Loan Amount
    - Total Development Cost (TDC)
    - Equity Investment
  - Debt Service
  - Net Cash Flow Before Taxes (CFBT)
  - Return Ratio
    - Economic: Return on Assets (ROA)/Return on Cost (ROC) (ROA/ROC = NOI/TDC)
    - Cash-on-Cash: Return on Equity (ROE)
    - Discounted: Net Present Value (NPV) or Internal Rate of Return (IRR)
- Socioeconomic Analysis
- Development Prospectus
- Development Proposals
- Development Planning

- Development Agreements/Deals
- Land Use Approval
- Private-Sector Commitments
- Public-Sector Commitments
- Equity Participation
- Permanent Loan Commitments
- Construction Loan Commitments
- Public Site Assembly
- Design Development
- Construction Drawings and Specifications
- Construction Bids and Awards
- Construction Management
- Preleasing Program
- Leasing Program
- Property Management
- Marketing Promotion
- Critiques and Evaluation
- Alternative Development

Other Tasks:
- Disposal/Sale of Asset
  (Include Presale OR Prelease)
      (Courtesy of Pat Prendergast.)

Prendergast's list reveals the scope and magnitude of the developer's job, but it is also important to recognize that while some tasks are shown on this list as one-time events in fact many of them are ongoing. These tasks span over some or all development stages and are messy and not easily confined to lists and frameworks. Indeed, the development process is an iterative and fluid one, as various ideas, constraints, different types of feedback, and new information are integrated into the process and the product comes into increasingly clearer focus.

For example, the original development budget will evolve from some numbers scribbled on the back of an envelope to a simple one-page spreadsheet to a spreadsheet with many tables. These tables will reflect increasingly finer assumptions and the accumulation of more information. Over a development timeline of five years or more, the pro forma will undergo

many iterations and revisions that incorporate new and changing information and assumptions from land price and construction costs to unit size,
mix, and price. Discussions with investors and lenders will also begin in the
first stage and continue throughout the process until the last unit is sold or
the last square foot is leased, the construction loan is repaid, and all investors have received their initial equity back, ideally with a return or profit.
Political work—meetings and negotiations with neighbors, politicians, city
staff, commissions, and other interests—will also be ongoing as will parallel
public relations and marketing and sales efforts. The design will evolve
continuously too, from a freehand sketch on a napkin or the back of an
envelope to a big stack of detailed drawings and specifications that the
contractor will use to determine the final costs of labor and materials and
to construct the building.

It sometimes helps to view development this way—as a series of stages
and as a list of tasks—but it can also be viewed as a process that is punctu-
ated by a small number of important milestones. These include property
acquisition, preliminary approvals, final approvals, achieving a predeter-
mined percentage of presales or signing a lease with an anchor tenant, closing on financing, completion of construction, stabilized occupancy, and
sale. Each of these is a required step on the way to a completed project and
each requires the careful management of myriad tasks through multiple
stages. While these lists of stages and tasks are easy enough to comprehend
in the abstract, they are more fluid and messier in practice. Because no two
development projects unfold in the same way, managing uncertainty and
the "unknown unknowns" is just one more part of the business. Real estate
development is a complex type of product development with high stakes.
Minor mistakes or omissions in any of the stages, tasks, or milestones can
derail or stop a project and cost the developer most if not all of his or her
financial resources. And just one bad project can wipe a developer out.

If real estate development is a form of product development, what
exactly is the finished product that developers make and how do they go
about doing it? In the next section we will explore these questions by considering the careers of two Portland developers—Pat Prendergast and John
Carroll. Each had a long and productive career spanning various product
types, and together they were the first to see the potential in an abandoned
railyard that has since become a neighborhood called the Pearl District. We
will hear how they each think about both the product and the process of

development, beginning with Prendergast, whose career story is a study in opportunism, adaptation, and product innovation over time.

Portland, Oregon: The Graveyard of the West

Pat Prendergast grew up in Dallas and attended Park City schools and the University of Maryland while he served in the U.S. Air Force. After he was discharged he returned home and took an entry-level position in a large bank. Three years later he moved to Houston to work in a smaller bank where he knew he could learn more about what the various departments did. The most profitable department in that bank was real estate construction lending, so Prendergast began to pay attention to the man who ran that department. "He was a darling of management and he brought in a lot of money so I gravitated away from the commercial lending side towards real estate construction lending."[6]

At the time, a big developer headquartered in Dallas named Trammell Crow pressured the Los Angeles–based commercial broker Coldwell Banker to come east and open its first location outside of California, in Texas. "Crow, who had become Coldwell's largest client in California, felt strongly that Texas was going to be the next Southern California and he ended up being right," says Prendergast. Five people came from Los Angeles to open Coldwell's Houston office and a year after meeting them Prendergast went to work for Coldwell Banker in commercial brokerage. "We were working with some of the largest national developers including Trammell Crow and Gerald Hines, who was based in Houston."

When Coldwell opened an office in Dallas, Prendergast moved back to his hometown. "CB was representing Neiman Marcus, which was based in Dallas, and Neiman was on an expansion program at the time. CB was also doing a lot of regional shopping mall leasing around the Midwest at the time so I did that for a couple of years." Then, in 1972, one of the original five CB people who had come from Los Angeles to Houston was asked to go up and open an office in Portland, Oregon. He recruited four other CB people from around the country to go with him and one of them was Prendergast. "My father-in-law had a lot of friends in Seattle and California, so when I told him I was planning on maybe moving to Portland he checked around. Back then, Oregon was known primarily for its poor,

lumber-based economy. 'Word I get,' said my father-in-law, 'is that Portland is the graveyard of the west.'"

Creating Capital to Do Other Things

Prendergast moved to Portland anyway. "Coldwell had a Seattle presence
at the time and they were all over California, so when we arrived in Portland that was the catalyst for Crow, Hines, Don Koll out of Newport Beach,
and some of the other larger players who wanted national brokerage representation if they were going to come into a relatively unknown market like
Portland." Soon, Prendergast wanted to get into the business on his own
but, at the time, Coldwell wouldn't allow its brokers to own real estate.
"They thought it was a conflict of interest and that as listings would come
in the brokers would cherry-pick the good ones." If he wanted to own real
estate, he would have to go out on his own, so a year after moving to
Portland, in 1973, Prendergast left Coldwell and formed his own development company.

"I started out doing build-to-suit commercial buildings on twenty-year,
triple-net leases for expanding companies like Denny's and 7-Eleven."
These large, national "credit tenants" could guarantee that the rent would
be paid, lowering Prendergast's risk and virtually ensuring a dependable
income for the duration of the leases, while leaving him with buildings that
could be sold as assets in the future. "Some of the banks were doing
branches and the savings and loans were still expanding so I did buildings
for them too. Until 1979–1980, we basically concentrated on those small,
low-risk, build-to-suits to create capital to do other things."

Late in the 1970s, Prendergast started doing some of the early speculative office-building developments in Portland, fairly close in to the core.
"Those went reasonably well considering there was nothing in the urban
center at that time, so in 1981 I did my first office building in the central
business district." This was a 200,000-square-foot building near Portland
State University that Prendergast did as a joint venture with New York–
based Merrill Lynch Hubbard. Between 1973 and the early 1980s Prendergast developed several million square feet of office space in Portland,
Seattle, and Denver. "Then, slowly but surely, the high-tech boom started
taking off in the early 1980s so we had a fairly sustained market for about
ten years. High interest rates in the early 1980s, however, followed by the
1986 tax act that closed a lot of loopholes and eliminated tax benefits as an
equity source, and then the savings and loan crisis in 1987 combined to

dampen the commercial office market throughout the United States for decades to come. The rest of the 1980s were a tough time nationally for office development," says Prendergast. "So, since the 1980s, we have concentrated largely in the urban center with the exception that I participated in some fairly significant land development and land sales in the 1980s, mostly on the west side, where high-tech was growing."

An Inkling of High Tech

As late as the 1980s, Oregon was still struggling to move beyond its historical, labor-based lumber economy, and real estate market cycles were short when compared to the rapidly growing Sun Belt. "A good market cycle in the commercial and industrial area would be eighteen months," says Prendergast, "but you have to have growth to have a decent economy, so the question then was 'How would Portland make the transition?'" The answer began to emerge when high-tech companies began to relocate to the region from California. "Growth started to occur in Portland metro with the advent of high-tech in the early 1980s."

At the time a new real estate product called "flex space"—a variation on the traditional one-story suburban industrial building—had come on the market and started to supply space for these companies. Flex space started with a basic high-bay warehouse or light industrial building. The innovation was that a strip of office space was tacked onto the front, creating an assembly building with offices. Flex space provides lots of flexibility by allowing office and manufacturing functions to be colocated in a single facility, but because it can house many more employees in its office space than a typical warehouse it requires much more parking. Most warehouses have few employees and just a handful of parking stalls but flex space is half office space, so it requires a much larger parking ratio to serve the same sized building, "on the order of a 4:1 ratio of parking to building area—four parking spaces for every 1,000 square feet of building area—as opposed to 1:1 for a typical warehouse."

New and growing tech companies in California needed lots of land, including room for expansion, and a good water supply. "But people had made a lot of mistakes in San Jose," says Prendergast. "As land costs skyrocketed in Silicon Valley, young tech companies tried to keep their costs down by buying smaller amounts of land that did not provide enough capacity for expansion, so when it came time to grow, they had nowhere to go. We had reasonable land costs in Portland, however, lots of water, and good planning, and so up they came."

Prendergast knew commercial office, which shared some similarities with flex space, so in the early 1980s Prendergast started doing flex space. "The land costs for flex space just took off because it is a suburban application that requires large land areas, so I went further west and bought undeveloped land that had just come into the growth boundary and just gotten utilities and urban services. Then, in 1984, the major users from Northern California started showing up—Epson, Fujitsu, NEC, Kyocera—it was a long list and we had a good run for the rest of the decade." By 2000, Intel's largest employment base was in Oregon, where it had between 16,000 and 18,000 employees—more than the headquarters in Santa Clara, California. "High-tech created a tremendous new economy that took the place of the timber-based economy of the early decades of the twentieth century so we capitalized on that and our major land development work on the west side led us to the Hoyt Street railyards."

A Big Transaction

"We had been partners with the Burlington Northern Railroad for some land they owned on the west side and in 1990 I sold that land to Nike for a significant profit but then I needed to find an exchange property to buy." Like many people who buy and sell real estate, Prendergast wanted to take advantage of section 1031 of the Internal Revenue Code, which allows sellers of property to avoid capital gains tax by using the proceeds of a sale to buy another property within 180 days. "So our company initiated the major acquisition of the Hoyt Street Yards, which was an obsolete railyard, from a former subsidiary of the Burlington Northern Railroad." Freight traffic had abandoned the city and moved north to a new intermodal yard, so the only rail service going into downtown Portland by that time was a single freight line and Amtrak passenger service. "The board of the railroad had decided to liquidate all nonrail properties and we had developed a piece of land nearby and that got us interested in the railroad's property."

Portland's Urban Growth Boundary (UGB) was created in the 1970s as a counter to sprawl and as a way to increase the use of transit and obtain the maximum value from other public infrastructure systems. "To a large extent it has served the city well," says Prendergast. "The city had a strong interest in putting jobs and housing close together and close to transit, and the UGB had the effect of making the urban core the center of activity and a more interesting place as a real estate market.

"So in 1992 we took our master plan for the Hoyt Street Yards to the city council and proposed a public-private partnership." The forty-plus acres that the railyards represented were made up of two big parcels and "it was a fairly risky deal at the time—there was a significant amount of environmental remediation required and the site needed planning and infrastructure." When the railyard was first developed in the early 1990s the old street grid terminated at its edges, so there was no power, water, sewer, or streets. The old Lovejoy Viaduct—a big automobile bridge that spanned over the yards—also had to go, "and it was going to be a $10 million problem just to take that down."

The railyard made up the northern end of a 100-block, 285-acre industrial area that was bounded by the Willamette River on the northeast and was filled with old factories, warehouses, and vacant lots. When the first urban pioneers began to move in, the buildings became home to numerous galleries and artists' lofts that—legend has it—one gallery owner characterized as the pearls inside the crusty shells of the warehouses. Local business and property owners were searching for a name for the area and, despite a handful of other suggestions, it soon came to be known as the Pearl District.

By 2010 the Pearl District was largely built out and had become a national model for high-density urban development. According to the 2010 U.S. Census, the Pearl was home to nearly 6,000 residents and 5,300 households living in warehouse conversions, new condominiums, and townhomes—all surrounded by countless bars, restaurants, stores, and theaters. But when Prendergast bought the old railyards in 1990 much of this growth was in the distant future. "At that time, before values were known, nobody, including us, knew if it was going to go, but we bought it right—at a good price—so we knew that at least we had an opportunity. We were also fortunate to be able to lease a significant amount of it back to the railroad for about eight years so that took care of a lot of the taxes that would have been due and provided some cash flow for planning purposes.[7]

"The point," says Prendergast, "is that from a development standpoint we knew what the goals were." The city leaders at that time wanted to capture as much of the region's growth within the city of Portland while obtaining the maximum value from publicly financed infrastructure, so the city had upzoned and encouraged higher-density development downtown. City leaders were also willing to try out creative new ways to invest in the infrastructure required to drive that density, such as the streetcar and the light rail line. Because the Portland Development Commission (PDC) had acquired a substantial amount of excess land around the railyards, the city was directly interested in development succeeding as well.

More important, says Prendergast, "because Portland had a history of successful planning to establish livable places stretching back to the 1970s, the city was used to working closely with the development community and developers were also used to working with the city." By the time Prendergast approached the city, "There had been many public-private developments and the city already knew how to do this stuff, so for each of those projects and for ours it was a simple case of 'if you do this, we will do that.'" The genuine attitude toward partnership from both parties and the level of financial commitment by the city were substantial. "Every time a block was developed it triggered four or five significant investments by the city," says Prendergast. "First, a local improvement district had been formed for the area within two blocks of the streetcar and any project within that jurisdiction paid a charge to the district and those funds were used to make public improvements—our development contributed three or four million to that district." Another typical arrangement was for a developer to donate a portion of his or her land for a park—for which the city would fund the improvements and operations—in exchange for the ability to build at a higher density. The city also made liberal use of tax increment financing (TIF)—the capitalization of future increased tax revenues for use at the beginning of a project—for the funding of public infrastructure. "And TIF is good," says Prendergast, "because the funds come not from the city's general fund but from future tax revenues, and in Portland TIF is structured so that the tax revenues come whether or not the project is actually successful, so someone is paying the tax bill.

"So we paid a lot for the basic infrastructure, but the city put in the infrastructure for light rail, which was the more expensive piece and also connected downtown to northwest Portland, which is the most densely populated part of the state." Later, the city extended the streetcar south, all the way down to Portland State University, and ultimately, during the 2000s, to the South Waterfront. In 2006 an aerial tram was built to connect Oregon Health and Science University—which was located up on a bluff and had run out of land for expansion—with the South Waterfront. There, large underutilized development parcels along the river's edge provided a new place for the institution to grow. "The city's strategy has worked well," says Prendergast. "Success in the Pearl District inspired confidence and that is the reason density has increased and more development has occurred."

Follow the Infrastructure

Because of Portland's focus on the downtown, Prendergast started doing development in the city and in the central business district in 1980. "After twenty years of developing we understood the growth trends and patterns, the planning efforts that had been completed and were known, and we knew the objectives of the city with respect to growth, transportation, and better air quality. So we followed the infrastructure that the city was putting in." This was a low-risk strategy that ensured smooth reviews by the city and kept development costs to a minimum. Prendergast did some condominiums and multifamily rental projects in the Pearl District, "because that was where the demand was—housing was needed to support the companies that were growing and relocating to Portland. Now lots of people live downtown and reverse commute back out to those companies in the suburbs—and that is where the demand came from."

As demand for downtown living increased, land became scarcer and more expensive. As land got more expensive, buildings grew taller, and as buildings grew taller, they became more costly to build. By 2010, Portland had been through three or four generations of product innovation and price increases. "The first condominium done in the Pearl District was a small, three-story, twenty-eight-unit project that sold retail for $110 per square foot," says Prendergast. "The next generation was four- to five-story buildings in concrete and steel priced at $150 per square foot. Midrise buildings followed at $200 per square foot and the last high-rise in the Pearl sold for $330 per square foot. The newest buildings in Portland, on the South Waterfront, reached the $400 to $500 per square foot range, which is still competitive when compared with Seattle or San Francisco."

Luck and Timing

"The public perception of developers—that they just make a lot of money, take no risk, and don't really know a whole lot—is just wrong." says Prendergast. "Development can be quite lucrative but things that are lucrative tend to be very high risk, and development is a very risky business. So to succeed in development you must have both an appetite for risk and the objective of making significant profits. To manage that risk, however, you have to be patient and factor in the public process and economic cycles."

Figure 12. The Pearl District before (top) and after (bottom). The Hoyt Street railyards are visible in the top photo (Google Earth, U.S. Geological Society, 1990) while the bottom photo shows all of the development that had occurred since (Google Earth, 2012).

More important, you have to be lucky—specifically in terms of timing. "Sometimes timing works for you and sometimes it works against you. For example, if you started a project in the spring of 2007 there is a good chance it was in serious trouble."

Indeed, many of the high-rise condominiums built on the South Waterfront in the mid-2000s were late to market, and numerous buildings were sold at a loss while others were converted into apartments. In 2009, Prendergast himself took advantage of the timing and the cheap rents being offered by distressed owners, leasing a luxurious penthouse apartment in a building called the Ardea as his personal residence. "Development is an exciting and rewarding process if your timing is right, and it can be incredibly satisfying because you create something that has a one-hundred- or two-hundred-year life and adds to the livability of your community if it is done well."

In his career, Pat Prendergast was able to move from commercial lending to real estate construction lending and then to commercial real estate brokerage before striking out on his own. As a developer he rode the commercial office wave and when that stalled he adapted by providing suburban flex space for the newly emerging high-tech industry. Next, by recognizing the progressive nature of planning in Portland, Prendergast was able to reduce his risk by moving downtown and following the infrastructure before migrating across product type again to develop housing for the workers in Portland's new economy. Prendergast himself had some luck, but he also succeeded in adapting constantly to serve the changing demands of the marketplace.

Prendergast concludes, "Design is where the developer really comes into play." Because development is market-driven, most developers will search nationally for best practices and the best examples of product types. "You want to know how it is put together and how it works and you want to understand the mix of units. That way, when you go to the architect you have a general sense of the number of units you want to build, and you will already know the zoning code and how high you can go. Then you set the tone for the exterior design and whether or not you want it to be traditional or contemporary. And finally, you have to balance all of that with the economics and what the market will pay per square foot when you finish it."

Another Portland developer's story expands on this discussion of the importance of design, as John Carroll explains how he thinks about the development process, illustrating just how much a developer's personal experiences can influence his vision and his projects.

Figure 13. The Hoyt Street railyards, before (top) and after (bottom), looking south toward downtown. Photos by Jeff Hamilton; courtesy of Ankrom Moisan Architects.

Never Be Afraid to Ask the Question

John Carroll's father was an ironworker, so when he was a child, he and his family were always in the back of a pickup truck, heading to the next job. "It was a particularly unsettling time in my life—I think I attended twelve different grade schools—and by the time I was in high school, the one thing I knew was that I didn't want to be an ironworker for the rest of my life."[8]

But Carroll didn't otherwise know what he wanted to do. "So I started out in the garment industry, pressing inseams on the production line, and I was smart enough to know to keep my mouth shut and to listen and observe." And after he had been through all of the positions on the assembly line, Carroll's supervisors asked him to get involved in engineering, which meant time-motion studies and the setup and improvement of production lines. "And through that work I learned something incredibly fundamental that has stuck with me and been the single greatest influence on my life.

Take that shirt you are wearing. You take that shirt, and you take it all apart, and you lay it all out on the table. You have to purchase materials so you have to lay it out in an efficient pattern because if you are 8 percent or 10 percent less efficient, then that cuts into your profits. Then once you have the material all cut up, you set up a production line for collars, cuffs, and so on. And when the finished shirt comes off the other end of the production line, you have time values associated with each one of the components. You also have costs associated with each of the components—the direct hard costs of the material and labor, the indirect hard costs for plant and utilities, and the soft costs, so in effect, you end up with a pro forma.

Real estate development is no different because you have to take whatever you are looking at and break it down to materials, design, production, packaging, and marketing. You have to look at the site and the land costs, the design and engineering component, what it is that is driving the design, and the costs associated with that particular design driver. Next you have to look at how fast the meter is running on debt and consider how fast it will run when the market is really good, when the market slows, and when the market craters. Once you have run those three scenarios, you may find that you have a project that is viable, but in all three cases you have to be able to reconcile it with that shirt that you took apart in the beginning.

For me, that has been the underlying principle and there hasn't been any business that I have looked at that I can't break down that way. In the end, you have to be able to reconcile whether or not you will be able to pay back your own equity, pay back your investor's equity, pay off your loan, and most importantly, whether or not you have just wasted five years of your life and not felt gratified

The House of Our Dreams

"What really kicked me off," says Carroll, "was not having had any money growing up." So Carroll bought a rental house and renovated it by using all of the money and practical experience he had. "I put in new linoleum floors in the kitchen, painted it, did up the yard, all that stuff, and then I turned around and sold it. And then I was looking at a check for my net gain—$1,785—and it was the biggest amount of cash I had ever had in my life. And do you know what I did with it? I had never been to Hawaii and had always wanted to go, so I took my whole family there for a vacation. That experience set me off on a different path for the rest of my life and since then I have never had another job or been on anyone else's payroll."

As a child, Carroll had never lived in the same place for very long or ever even had a house, and so he had always wanted one. "Years ago, I was over in Bend, Oregon, and the economy wasn't very good, and I was driving down the street and I saw a sign in front of a house that said 'for sale.' It was a beautiful cottage home just a block from Drake Park, which is the central park in Bend, so I knocked on the door and I said, 'I see your house is for sale; how much do you want for it?' And the guy who answered the door literally grabbed me and pulled me into the house and said, 'Do you want to buy it?'" Carroll told him, " 'I don't know, maybe, I don't have a lot of money, how much is it?' The man asked again, 'Do you want to buy it?' and I said, 'Yes, how much do you want for it—give me a price.' So he named a price and I said I don't have that, and then the man said, 'I'll sell it to you on a note and you don't have to put any money down.'" Carroll learned that the man and his wife were getting a divorce and that if he didn't have a deal by the end of the day she would have ended up with the house. "So we ended up in the house of our dreams for no money down and an excellent price.

"I share that story about buying my first home," says Carroll, "because I want to make a point about what it means to be entrepreneurial, and for me, it has always meant never being afraid to ask the question. You have to be willing to get off the main drag, drive through some neighborhoods, and poke around. I spend half of my day doing real estate, walking around, talking to people, doing windshield tours, and driving down streets I have never been down before. You also have to be willing to step up every now and then and get involved in the community." For example, in 1991, Carroll became involved in efforts to develop a streetcar system in Portland. "I was asked to give it three months and in 2011 it will have been twenty years and I have been the longest running member on the streetcar board." Carroll has since traveled all over the country to talk about streetcars and has had hundreds of people visit his office to find out how they might bring streetcars to their own communities. "Community involvement means being able to sit down with people, build deep relationships, create a long history, and develop and maintain a good reputation over many years." And, finally, when it comes to thinking about risk, Carroll says you always have to ask yourself the question, "What is my downside? The worst thing that can happen is that I would go to work in some nice restaurant and make people feel happy and get tips from them." Being entrepreneurial, concludes Carroll, "means that you take risks and are rewarded, but it does not mean that you take mindless risks—successful entrepreneurs do not take stupid risks."

From Flex Space to Urban Space

"It was just a strange collection of events that led up to the Pearl District," says Carroll. He started out doing flex office space in Beaverton and warehouses in northwest Portland. In the 1980s he went into partnership with Pat Prendergast and the two began working with Burlington Northern Railroad and its real estate company, Glacier Park Development. The two groups signed an agreement, entering into a joint venture for the development of a piece of land adjacent to a little startup company in Beaverton. But two days later, Glacier Park came back and told Carroll and Prendergast that they wanted to void the agreement because they had decided to completely liquidate all of their real estate holdings. "And we came to find that the agreement was in full force and effect, and now the railroad could not liquidate this billion-dollar company but for this one, little 123-acre site next to this little startup. So we acquired the land and, well, that little startup was called Nike. We ended up selling the site to Nike and that transaction was huge for us, so we used the proceeds to buy the old Burlington Northern railyards, in downtown Portland, in the area now known as the Pearl District." This was long before urban condominium living had started to take hold in Portland, and when Carroll and Prendergast first started doing master plans for the site they actually considered using a portion of it for a golf driving range. "The kick-off for us was getting involved in the railroads but then my interest shifted to urban development. At the time we were young and wanted to explore. Portland was not San Francisco or New York but I was really intrigued with urban development and with density and culture so we traveled to many cities looking for projects and communities that would fit into and challenge the Portland market." Carroll says he could have done well if he had kept building flex spaces and warehouses but that wasn't enough. He began to focus his attention on urban centers and on creating spaces that would attract people of all ages.

Where Would Andy Warhol Live?

First, before he started developing his own housing projects, Carroll wanted to get out of his own backyard in Portland and get some fresh ideas. "I had always wanted to go to San Francisco and look at the South of Market, or SOMA, and my question was 'Where would Andy Warhol live if he lived in San Francisco?'" Carroll imagined it would be a very simple place "with a sink and a toilet in the corner" but when he visited San Francisco, he found that they had a product that was very different—and more sophisticated—than what he had imagined or what he thought he would have liked. Carroll realized how much he had to learn when he almost immediately dismissed one condominium he was looking at because it was next to a freeway ramp. "I couldn't imagine that anyone would want to live that close to all of that constant traffic but then, after about fifteen minutes of staring out the window, the real estate agent asked, 'Are you ready to go?' and I realized I had been mesmerized by all of the cars going by."

Carroll's first project in the Pearl District was the 1995 conversion of the old Chown Pella Building, which had originally housed a window company, into sixty-eight loft condominiums and six commercial and retail spaces. Then he bought another half-block of land nearby and visited the two people who owned the properties that made up the other half of the block to ask if they thought they might ever want to sell. "They both said, 'No, no, we are never going to sell,' so I said, 'Well, if you ever do think

Figure 14. The Chown Pella Lofts, completed in 1995, is a classic warehouse-to-loft conversion. In the foreground is Carroll's next project, the Mckenzie Lofts, which was completed in 1997. Photo by Jeff Hamilton; courtesy of Ankrom Moisan Architects.

you want to sell, just give me a call.' About nine months later the first guy called me and said, 'Do you still want to buy our warehouse?' Then, a couple of days after that, the family that owned the other piece called and told me they were ready to sell. So I got it all under contract and then I had a full block. So, like I said, sometimes you just have to ask the question."

The Chown Pella Building was one of the first loft warehouse conversions in the Pearl District and two years later Carroll did another project. "Pretty soon we had one, then two, then three, then four projects, all within a stone's throw of one another—and you look back and you don't know how you got there, it all just happens." By 2010, Carroll had built seven buildings in the Pearl District—each different and increasingly larger than the last.

Times change, of course, and with the condo boom over, Carroll had to adapt, so he began to focus on urban senior housing. "You don't want to keep running into a concrete wall—so instead you go two or three degrees to the left or the right." Carroll's mother was eighty years old "and the people in her age group had an image of living in suburban senior housing, but the next generation of baby boomers are just now starting to think about senior housing and they are thinking about living downtown." So in 2010 Carroll began working on an agreement with the City of Portland to acquire a large public parking garage at the corner of Tenth and Yamhill Streets, in the heart of downtown Portland. The garage is an eyesore and the site of a lot of nuisance crime, yet it has an incredible location—"at the corner of main and main," as developers like to say. "It is a big, dumb, black hole in the middle of everything, and we are calling it 'Crossroads' because it is at the intersection of the light rail and streetcar lines. Brooks Brothers and Nordstrom's are both right across the street; it is a block from Pioneer Square; there are fourteen movie screens within three and a half blocks, ninety-two restaurants, ninety thousand people—it goes on and on." The plan was for a new garage with a tower on top and the uses would be focused on senior living and childcare and there would also be a clinic and a fitness center. "So we will have grandparents and kids together and when we are done the street will be much safer." By 2010 Carroll already had a tenant lined up for the top sixteen floors. "The architecture has not really started yet but we have done lots of sketches because the building looks down on a park and I want views from the terrace and the playground. And even though the base of the building is a parking structure I want to make it look good, so we are working on how to make it look better than just a glass curtain wall slamming into the ground." But the location was what really differentiated the project. "The only product we will be competing with is on the South Waterfront but our project is not on the South Waterfront and so we are not really competing with it."

A Big Life Story Making Its Way into a Building

Real estate development is a very personal process and often a developer's personal experience, ideas, and tastes actively shape his or her work. "You have got to have a focus when you see an opportunity," says Carroll. "Every effort must start out with some underlying, underpinning idea." Whether it is the renovation of an old historic building or new construction, Carroll believes that to be successful a developer must take the lead on design and all aspects of the project. "Design is so important—you don't want a building that looks like it was dropped in from thirty thousand feet—so the context and the evolving character of the neighborhood should be central to the effort. And it really takes a team that wants to work together, with the developer driving the vision."

Carroll's first new construction project in the Pearl District was the Mckenzie, a sixty-eight-unit condominium with nine commercial and retail spaces that was completed in 1997 that he named after his daughter. "When the building was finished the best compliments I received were when people told me, 'It was a great renovation of a historic building' or that 'it looked like an old building.'" Next came the Gregory, a 133-unit condominium tower with a four-story commercial space completed in 2001 that Carroll named after his son, followed in 2003 by the more contemporary Edge Lofts, a 125-unit condominium building that also houses one of the most successful REI stores in the country. And in 2005 Carroll completed the Elizabeth, a 182-unit condominium that was named after his mother. Each of Carroll's new buildings is based on a specific architectural style, so, for example, the Elizabeth was designed in the style of the Scottish architect Charles Rennie Mackintosh. A big fan of Mackintosh, Carroll had traveled to Glasgow, Scotland, and was walking around outside the architect's famous Glasgow School of Art building one Sunday. "The school was closed but then a student came along and we started talking and so I asked the question: 'Can you get me in?' He let me inside and gave me a complete tour."

Buildings are very personal for Carroll, and a more recent project called Eliot Tower, completed in 2006, was personal for him in a different way. The name Thomas Lamb Eliot is an important one in Portland. A Unitarian minister, Eliot had come to Oregon in 1856 and soon became the most influential religious figure in the city. He started Portland's library system and brought the firm of Frederick Law Olmsted—the landscape architect who designed New York City's Central Park and Prospect Park—to design the city's parks. But Eliot also started the Boys and Girls Aid Society and it was from this society that John Carroll and his wife adopted their daughter, Mckenzie.

Eliot Tower was also Carroll's first all-glass project. The architecture firm that designed Eliot Tower was Portland-based Zimmer Gunsul Frasca. Robert Frasca had worked for Pietro Belluschi, who had designed the Portland Art Museum, which is directly across the street from the Eliot Tower. For Carroll there is a reason or a connection behind every decision he makes and every opportunity he pursues, down to the names he gives his buildings. Says Carroll, "There is a reason for everything with each developer and each project is a big life story making its way into the building."

Figure 15. Exposed brick and timbers in a condominium within the Chown Pella Lofts. Photo by Jeff Hamilton; courtesy of Ankrom Moisan Architects.

Innovation—at the Margins

John Carroll's story offers a clear, linear illustration of product innovation in real estate development. The 1995 Chown Pella Building was a simple, sixty-eight-unit renovation of an existing underutilized warehouse building in an area that was still unproven as a residential market. The new product's identity and brand—as well as its economic model—relied on retaining the old building's original industrial character inside and out. The exterior was largely unchanged and the finishes in the lobby and the units were simple—sandblasted timber columns and beams and exposed brick. Basic drywall partitions and exposed spiral ductwork were used to subdivide the factory floor into units and adapt the old building to its new use.

Completed just eleven years later, the Eliot Tower was a very different product. An all-new, glassy tower designed specifically as a residential building, the Eliot's 223 units were more sophisticated in terms of design, materials, finishes, and appliances. Gone were the exposed ducts and sprinklers, and industrial sash windows were replaced by broad expanses of floor-to-ceiling glass.

Figure 16. The Mckenzie is a newer building designed to look like an old warehouse but with more refined finishes in the units. Photo by Jeff Krausse; courtesy of Ankrom Moisan Architects.

Over those brief eleven years, residential living in the Pearl District and Downtown Portland in general grew from a speculative idea into a mature market. The constantly increasing demand for housing in the area reduced market risk and allowed more developers to finance more and larger buildings. During the same period, construction costs rose, units became smaller, and overall unit prices increased. And demand grew from wealthier buyers who wanted to move into what had become a fashionable but established residential district rather than a largely vacant and undeveloped industrial area. Over these eleven years Carroll succeeded by being a cautious risk taker who innovated at the margins. He grew and learned from one building to the next, from the adaptive reuse of an old seven-story warehouse to a new, eighteen-story, glassy high-rise.

As more people moved into the Pearl, from the early adopters to wealthier people from the suburbs who came later, tastes and design styles changed too. Carroll's second building, the Mckenzie, was new but designed to look like an old industrial building because loft living was the

Figure 17. A contemporary kitchen design with high-quality finishes and appliances in a condominium unit in Eliot Tower. Photo by Kirsten Force; courtesy of Ankrom Moisan Architects.

image and brand of the Pearl District. With the Gregory and the Elizabeth, Carroll moved away from the warehouse aesthetic but continued to design in historical styles before shifting again to modern designs for the Edge and Eliot Tower. For each building, Carroll tried to design in a style that would fit into the rapidly evolving context of the Pearl District at a moment in time while providing a slightly forward-looking product and aesthetic.

Carroll's story emphasizes the importance of design to a successful development project. For community members who hope to engage in the development process, it is helpful to understand how architects think about and produce designs for real estate developers and how good developers drive the overall vision for the project, down to the details. In the next chapter we will look more closely at how developers think about architects and the design process—and how the architects who work for them think about working for developers.

Figure 18. The contemporary, all-glass, 223-unit Eliot Tower, completed in 2006. Ankrom Moisan with ZGF Partnership. Photo by Janis Miglavs; courtesy of Ankrom Moisan Architects.

Chapter 4

Developers and Their Architects

Every architect is an artist and if you let them go they will design
something artistic. In some cases they can become very anal about
issues of alignment and articulation but often in areas where only the
Almighty and the architect would ever know the difference. But we are
dealing in the real world and what is really important is that the
bedroom has to work. This is why the developer is the one who runs the
experience and the architect works for the developer and helps him to
shape that experience. Developers and architects typically butt heads
but no one's first idea is their best idea and in most cases the dynamic
created from this friction and push and pull will create a better product.
And lastly, while it is not the preferred way, sometimes you have to
remind the architect that it is your checkbook.
  —Buzz Ruttenberg, Chicago real estate developer[1]

Always design for your client's clients.
  —Morris Lapidus, Miami architect and designer of the famous
  Fontainebleau Hotel[2]

How Architects Think About Design

The sociologist Robert Gutman spent forty years studying, writing about,
and consulting to architects and he found that a powerful image survives
within the profession of the architect as "a free, independent practitioner,
operating on his own and cultivating personal relationships with an understanding client." The source of this image is "a romanticized view of an

architect-patron relationship that is supposed to have prevailed prior to the 19th century." What is most interesting is that this image survives, despite the fact that most architects do not practice that way and never have. The trend over the past half-century has been away from independence and toward more architects working in fewer, larger firms and public agencies. At the same time, architects have been commoditized as their work has become increasingly specialized. These trends have heightened the conflict between the romantic image of the architect-as-artist and the reality of the architect as a provider of professional services for fee-paying clients who require effective and economical technical and aesthetic solutions to their everyday problems. This internal conflict leads to friction between architects who hope to realize their own creative visions through the designs they do for their clients and clients who have pragmatic needs that must be addressed—program, function, budget, and schedule.[3]

Developers are different from traditional private, corporate, and institutional clients, and the risk-management and cash-flow-driven nature of the development business leads, in turn, to a very different type of design process. In the case of real estate development, a good design is a design that results in a product that can be built at a certain cost, will sell at a greater price, and for which there is a market of willing buyers. Architects who work for developers understand this and practice in a way that is very different from that of their colleagues who do not. They have a unique perspective on what it is developers are trying to accomplish—and what good developers do in order to succeed.

Design is an organic, fluid, and iterative process and even the most disciplined architects regularly find themselves making conceptual leaps and jumping forward and backward in the process. Most architects, however, try to overlay a linear structure on top of this process for practical reasons related to managing their client's decision-making process and budgeting staff time, resources, and fee dollars over the duration of a project. Indeed, the standard contract documents published by the American Institute of Architects that are used by most architects and contractors are based on a phased approach. Work begins with "schematic design," then moves to "design development," "construction documents," "bid and award of contracts," and "construction administration," and the fee and scope of work are allocated over these phases typically on a percentage basis. Each phase produces a more detailed and complete version of the design than the previous one as the design develops from the macro-level, big-picture idea into the micro level of detail required to actually build it. Doing architectural design for real estate developers, however, is a little bit different.

Designing from the Inside Out—and the Outside In

The Chicago architect Louis Sullivan, the father of the modern skyscraper, was the first to say, "form follows function," in his famous 1896 article, "The Tall Office Building Artistically Considered." But Herb Emmerman, a Chicago developer and marketing and sales consultant, demolishes any myth that development projects are designed from the inside out, with the end user's needs coming first. "The architecture does not start with the question 'Who is going to live here and what is the market?' Instead, it starts when the developer brings in a big-name architect who designs a conceptual model for the project that is all about 'How will this edifice fit into this environment and work with the municipality?'"[4]

The architect will design the exterior shell of the building, and then, to illustrate the basic idea, will produce a detailed rendering or model that will look real—from the existing skyline down to the little people and cars. The inside of the building, however—the column grid, plumbing risers, stairs and elevators, and unit layouts—will be designed only to the minimum level required to ensure structural integrity and determine the total interior area in square feet. "So the developer spends a lot of money designing this fancy picture or model," says Emmerman, "so that they can take it to the alderman, councilman, or mayor, and they either fall in love with it or they bastardize it first and then fall in love with it." Even then, elected politicians will not promote a project until the broader community has seen it and come out in support of it—or at least not come out in complete opposition to it—so the next step is to seek input from the neighbors. "So then you spend months dealing with the neighborhood and 'can you make it shorter, can you put the parking underground, can you put in flower boxes,' and still, we have not talked about how this building functions." By the time the developer commits to proceeding with the detailed design, after many months of promoting the architect's rendering or model, the image of the building's exterior shell has become fixed in the minds of the public.

"Then," says Emmerman, "when it comes time to really design the building, the name architect assigns the condo floor plans to their staff architect, who may or may not have significant experience designing unit layouts." A savvy developer will use market research, marketing and sales experts, and even trusted sales agents to figure out the unit mix first—how many studios, one-bedrooms, two-bedrooms, three-bedrooms, and so on. "If not, the unit mix will be the product of the staff architect too, and it will be based not on what the market may want but on what fits easily into the box that the name architect has created and the mayor, other politicians, and neighbors have come to accept as the exterior design of the project." At the same time, the structural engineer begins to figure out the elements of the structural system that will run the full height of the building—the locations of columns, elevators, stairs, other major vertical shafts for ducts and plumbing, and the vertical "shear walls" that contain structural bracing—to make sure they work for the units above and the parking spaces below.

"And, once you have figured out the typical floor plate based on all of these constraints," says Emmerman, "you try to fit the units into the space that is left over." One challenge particular to high-rises is that the structural engineering drives the overall building design and can place constraints on the interior layouts. The staff architect is often unwilling to challenge the structural engineer and probably doesn't have the authority to do so, trying instead to work within those constraints. "So sometimes, for example, shear walls end up in unfortunate places, like twenty feet from the edge of the building, which only allows for one-bedroom units in the corners." Corners offer panoramic views and more windows so they command a higher dollar-per-square-foot sales price and are better suited to larger and higher-priced units—two- and three-bedrooms. Cost-conscious buyers purchase one-bedroom units, and a developer cannot charge enough for them to make up for the lost value of locating them in corners. "So we argue back and forth with the staff architect and finally we turn to the developer and say, 'Hey, you are about to lose several million dollars.' Not until we convince them that making the change to the structural design will cost a lot less than the lost revenue from not being able to put larger, higher-priced units in the corners does the developer turn to the architect and say 'change it.'"

Emmerman believes that good design adds value but that there are limits based on economics. "For example, to make a building attractive, you will want to do a lot of articulation and stepping back of the façades. But given the reality of the city codes and regulations and the related land costs, you will also want to do everything to max out the allowable density on the site—the floor area ratio, or FAR—and use every buildable square foot you are entitled to. This means using a simple rectangular or square volume that may not be attractive but will be efficient and will maximize buildable area. Otherwise, the project will not be feasible and you will be leaving money on the table." This is because urban land is priced based on build-able area, so if you don't build the maximum, you must spread the same land cost over fewer units—which means charging more for the same unit as that of a competitor who does max out their site. "Most architects are just trying to build beautiful buildings, and we all agree with that, but saying it and doing it are two different things because everything you add to make it pretty costs money and makes the project more expensive and begins to affect the economics of the deal. There are some architects who really do understand the process, don't get their egos involved, are trying to build attractive buildings, and who understand the idea of compromise—with these kind of architects you can generally get a good-looking building."

Emmerman concludes, "When you say 'a building should be designed from the inside out,' no one really argues, but that's not how it really happens." And the reason has to do with money. It may cost $1 million to design the exterior of a high-rise condo building but it can cost $6 million to design all of the building systems, the floor plans, and the unit layouts. At the beginning of the project, design is a pursuit cost and the developer does not want to spend any more than necessary to obtain the support of local officials on the concept and determine that the building is marketable. The only way to do this economically is to develop the outside skin first and then wait until the project has obtained approvals or support before paying the much greater share of the fees required to design the rest of the building. "So what we really do as the marketing and sales team," says Emmerman, "is we re-design from the inside out and try not to change the skin very much since it has already been approved and accepted."

How Developers Think About Design—and Architects

Collin Barr of the Ryan Companies, a national development company based in Minneapolis, Minnesota, summarizes the developer's expectation of an architect. "First, architects must solve my economic model—it has to work fundamentally before we can spend any time or money developing the design. Next, good architects cut through the clutter of the marketplace to offer something that is distinctive, attractive, and marketable. And last but not least, good architects understand the value of self-management and discipline during the pursuit phase and they know that they cannot just spend a bunch of hours exploring angles but, rather, must be targeted and high-value added." This creates a paradox, says Mark Swenson, an architect who has collaborated successfully with Barr on numerous projects. "Developers have the least amount of money to spend on design at the beginning, and that is when my hours are worth the most. The highest value-added work we do is on the front end, often when the developer cannot pay us."[5]

David Haymes of the Chicago architecture firm Pappageorge Haymes agrees, concluding that the architect invariably has to work for free—"and that has been one of our gripes for many years. You have to give your best ideas and best works at the beginning of the project when you are not even going to get paid. It is always a frustration but you work yourself around that because of relationships." Unlike other clients who only build periodically, developers are sources of repeat business for the architects who work for them. As developers and their architects continue to work together, they get to know one another, and trust develops. And as Haymes points out, the various team members who work with a developer over and over again become that developer's "brain trust" because they understand what he expects and know how to work with him. That builds trust in both directions, and the repeat business that flows from it helps architects accept not being paid for the full value of their work during the pursuit phase. But lean fees during the pursuit phase and the unique nature of the architect-developer relationship results in a design approach that most traditional architects are unaccustomed to.[6]

Two Kinds of Architects: Developer Architects
and Traditional Architects

"We have been told in a positive way that we are a 'developer architect,'" says David Haymes. "Most of our work is for developers, and so we have not done as much work for corporate and institutional clients." Haymes has, however, partnered on development projects with several nationally known firms that typically do that kind of work, like SOM and Goettsch Partners. Working with those firms gave Haymes the opportunity to see the difference in working styles and methods between developer architects and more traditional firms that serve corporate and institutional clients. "Those firms wanted to try the development world and learn, but it was a struggle for them and you could tell there was some discomfort. Traditional architects are a little unaccustomed to their client having a strong viewpoint and they are more accustomed to being the one standing and talking in the front of the room while everyone else is listening. Their typical client is also better funded, so they can spend more time on design and charge higher fees."

To underscore the differences in design approach, Haymes describes one development project he undertook for a client whom his firm had worked with before but who had chosen to hire a large corporate firm. Haymes was brought in partway through to help get the project back on track. "It was tough because that firm's methodology was more corporate, they did not share the entrepreneurial spirit and urgency of the developer, and they did not realize that they had to move at a certain speed, so they couldn't turn the work fast enough for their client. They had so many people in the meetings that you never knew who was responsible and decision making was harder and took longer. And because they had a procedural approach that didn't make anyone truly responsible, no one was paying attention. So there were all kinds of errors related to code analysis and basic design criteria that were just intuitive to us."

Unlike corporate or institutional clients, private developers are often individuals or small groups who are able to speak with one voice and react very quickly. "Private developers are therefore very demanding and you have to be completely absorbed with their objective, be responsible and responsive to them, and recognize that speed matters." Haymes offers the example of a very large and successful development company that his firm worked with on many projects over many years that was owned by a father and his two sons. "That company was very tightly and intimately run and the three principals really functioned as a single individual and spoke with one voice. We spent ten years meeting every Wednesday morning and they came to every single meeting and they drove every single decision related to design." Many architects would find this level of involvement on the part of their client oppressive but architects who work for developers prefer it. "Other developers who are just in it for the money are not as good and bureaucratic corporate developers are even worse," says Haymes. "That is why we would rather work for an individual—or a group that can act like one."

How a Developer Architect Approaches a Project

Andrés Duany, a Miami-based architect and planner, is best known as the father of New Urbanism but his firm—Duany Plater-Zyberk—has also planned and designed scores of communities for developers, including the well-known Seaside, Florida, which played the role of the perfect town in the movie *The Truman Show.* Duany's father and grandfather were both developers and Duany himself has worked with many of them over the years. Yet while "they are all different," he has found a way of understanding them: "When I first meet and begin working with a developer, I try to figure out their 'six most important things.'" Duany maintains that every developer has half a dozen key ideas that are nonnegotiable, and he has to figure out what those are. "For example, a developer may have a favorite unit plan that has sold well in all of their previous projects, so don't argue about it. Or he may come in believing as an article of faith that developing a community around a clubhouse is the key, so don't argue about that." Time and again, Duany has seen architects "fly into the flames" by contradicting the developer over those very few things that are not up for negotiation. Instead, he sees his role as adding balance to the team and filling in the weak areas or gaps. "If there are fifty variables on a project and I can figure out the six that are most important to the developer, then I still have the flexibility to achieve New Urbanist principles with most of the remaining ones."[7]

Another Miami architect, Allan Shulman, offers a similar observation. His firm, Shulman + Associates, specializes in homes, condominiums, and hotels in Miami Beach and Miami, and as a result almost all of his work has been for developers. "Miami is a very competitive commercial environment and fashion is so important so most developers know that they must make a mark to compete and succeed and they see good design as one of the tools they can use to do this." As a result, Shulman says, "Most developers come in already thinking about design and know that it is worth paying a little more for something a little bit different." There are certain formulas that have always worked in Miami but these developers also understand the value of experimentation, aesthetic values, and trying something different. "We have had few experiences where we have had to educate our clients because they already get it—when you are working in a historic context and you are reusing existing structures you learn to think about more than just the pro forma and the number of rooms."[8]

Most developers whom Shulman has worked with also come with an idea. "The developer of one hotel came in saying, 'I really want this project to be all about a garden and that will be the centerpiece,' while another wanted to do an art hotel—a kind of hotel that was also a gallery. I love it when developers come with their own ideas and, in fact, I think I would feel a little lost in the undifferentiated world of suburbia, with empty land and a generic program." Shulman has moved well beyond the stereotype of architect-as-artist and embraced a more complex view of architecture. "I no longer think that architecture is born entirely out of my mind but rather that it is the product of so many ideas crashing together—urban context, history, neighbors, and the developer's vision—and that I could not have done it as well myself even if I tried." Shulman used to think that architects were the generalists in the development process but he has come to see that they are really specialists and that the developers are the generalists. "Developers must understand not only design, but finance, land, legal, and a host of other things. They are the synthetic glue, and when you work with developers you really begin to see where they make their money."

Shulman has never met two developers who think exactly the same way and so he has learned not to repeat the things learned from one project on another project. "One hotel developer might say, 'You can't make a small room work in this market, so we will have to do luxury suites,' while another might say, 'You can't make a large room work in this market, so we will have to do small rooms.'" Similarly, "One developer might maintain that 'hotels do not work based on selling rooms—they really make their money from the food and beverage side of the house,' while another might say, 'The rooms have to work first and foremost and the food and beverage operation is secondary.'"

Shulman has learned that all of these positions may be right even if they appear to contradict one another. "There are so many potential ideas and approaches, every developer has a different one, and I have never seen any of them match up." In several instances where a partially completed project was sold from one developer to another and then another, Shulman has had to adapt two or three ideas on the same project. "It is not as if some of their ideas did not make sense—they all did—they were just different. And because there is never just one answer, what makes a project a success—and the developer really effective—is when they come with a strong approach, a game plan, energy, knowledge, and passion."

Like Duany, Shulman concludes that his first job is finding out what is really critical to the developer. "The most important thing is the developer being able to articulate what he wants to do—and the one thing he can't live without—the sine qua non of the project. The developer was successful before he met me and he knows it—so he knows his market, knows what has worked for him in the past, and I know that I am not going to change his mind."

Riding Herd over the Details

Like Allan Shulman, the architect Jeff Hamilton's view of his own role in
design and city building has changed over time. "Architecture is not what
I thought I was getting into. We as architects think we create the world but
in the modern age I would say it is the developers who are deciding. We
are the pencil—we help them realize their visions and create the world we
live in."[9]

Hamilton is a partner at Ankrom Moisan, a large Portland, Oregon,
architecture firm that, like Pappageorge Haymes, Duany Plater-Zyberk, and
Shulman + Associates, works primarily for developers. "We try to avoid
fly-by-night developers who think we are a bank," says the firm's president,
Stewart Ankrom, "and instead, we focus on credible developers who want
to do good design in addition to earning good returns and who are really
tuned into sustainability, urban living, and quality buildings."[10]

Ankrom and Hamilton have been involved in scores of condominium
projects in Portland, Los Angeles, and elsewhere, including many of the
projects in the Pearl District and a number of projects for the developer
John Carroll, whom we met in the previous chapter. It all started in the
early 1990s when Hamilton did a study for one developer on how to turn
a small, six-story warehouse built in 1918 into an office building. "It didn't
work for parking so it just died but then one day I was sitting at my desk
when John Carroll called and said, 'I got your plans for a commercial office
building—what do you think about turning it into condos?' So we said
sure, and a year later we were building it." That was the Chown Pella Lofts,
a model New York–style warehouse-to-loft conversion. "That first time we
worked for John Carroll," says Ankrom, "he had just pulled away from Pat
Prendergast and I was thinking is John really a credible developer? So we
walked cautiously because we didn't know him and we hadn't done any
work for him but he turned out to be one of the greatest guys in the world,
indirectly teaching us a great amount about successful real estate development." The Mckenzie, Gregory, Eliot, and several more projects followed
the Chown Pella Lofts. Hamilton worked on fifteen of the sixteen projects
Ankrom Moisan did in the Pearl District, and he ran twelve of them.

"Economics and the market means that when you work with developers
you have to figure it out fast," says Hamilton. "Will it be a whole bunch of
little units or fewer big units? When you add more bedrooms it becomes
cheaper and when you make rooms bigger it also reduces dollar-per-
square-foot costs—but at the same time the total price goes up. We like to

have the contractor in the room at the beginning and figure out what will the excavation cost be, what will the concrete costs be, and then we compare his numbers with past jobs and get a very detailed budget very quickly." Design decisions can have a huge impact on success. "One Portland developer we worked with did a condo with no balconies, no fireplaces, tighter units, and shared parking, and then they hit the market at a bad time. They sold it off to another developer at a loss and now it is apartments."

But that story is not the norm. "It is funny how much some developers are tuned into the market," says Hamilton. "John Carroll is constantly asking, 'Who is my buyer, what are they interested in, and how can I market to them?'" Developers like Carroll know that they will only succeed if their project sells out or leases up, so they integrate the marketing and sales perspective into the design process from the very beginning. "They bring their salespeople along to the very first meeting and they are present from the beginning and the developer asks the sales team all the time, 'What do these people want?'" The answers range from unit size and mix to how many sinks to put in the bathrooms, how many cars to provide for, and which amenities will best support the lifestyles of the buyers that represent the target market. "They bring along their whole marketing group and they are constantly fine-tuning the mix and everyone is telling you exactly what is going to sell and why."

The other kind of developer couldn't be more different. "These are the hands-off, let-the-architect-do-it developers and they walk in and say, 'I want to put a building on the block, here is how big it is, tell me how many units you are going to get, and call me when you are done.' We ask, 'What's the mix, how many ones and twos,' and they say, 'I don't know, you tell me.'

"Both kinds of developers can be successful," says Ankrom, "but we like the first kind better. The hands-on developers are just more fun to work with—they really know their stuff. And developers like John Carroll are always on—daily, hourly, paying attention to the details of the unit down to the knobs on the kitchen cabinets." Hands-off developers are interested in returns first but career developers like Carroll take a more sophisticated view of the relationship between design, product quality, and profits. They do one project at a time, make sure that they get it right, and they try to do everything very well. "These developers have vision, are passionate, and they care about doing good urban buildings and making money doing it—but not the other way around. That is what makes the difference and as architects we like the kind of engagement that comes with working for them."

Ankrom Moisan has designed several buildings for another Portland developer named Ed McNamara, who specializes in for-profit affordable housing projects that integrate sustainable technologies as a way to optimize building systems and reduce operating and maintenance costs. Like John Carroll, McNamara creates the vision, promotes it throughout the team and the community, and remains very hands-on throughout the entire process. "We did the Sitka and Ramona Apartments for Ed," says Hamilton, "and he wanted to know everything about the building's mechanical systems. Since he is an owner of apartment buildings he is looking for sustainability and he wants to know every trick that will lower the operating cost, down to how often to change the filters. He cares about everything in the building and you have to know what you are talking about before you speak because he may know more about your business than you do—I have seen Ed turn engineers on their heads."

Hands-On Development

Ed McNamara grew up in a suburb of Philadelphia called Willow Grove. His father was a plumbing contractor, and McNamara worked for him during the summers when he was in high school. He moved out to Portland, Oregon, in 1970 to go to Reed College but after his freshman year he decided to take a year off. He moved back east and lived in Ventnor and Margate—at the Jersey Shore—where he learned carpentry. "Every weekend in the summer the place was wall to wall with high school friends but it was also cool to be there in the fall to experience the September storms and in the winter when the town emptied out." After six months, he moved back to Portland and soon became a framing contractor and then a general contractor.[11]

Finally, at the age of thirty, McNamara decided that he was really going to go back to college. "I loved carpentry, day to day, week to week, month to month, it was wonderful. I loved building things, I could see exactly what I had done, it was really nice, and I learned to appreciate that even more later. But year after year it was not that stimulating and I thought that my brain was going to atrophy even with complicated remodeling jobs, because even then the hardest thing was the execution and that's not that hard." So he applied to the University of Pennsylvania, in Philadelphia, and he was accepted and offered financial aid, "but I had a house that was torn up and in no condition to either rent or sell, so I deferred for a year."

During that year, 1983, a fledgling nonprofit in Portland called REACH Community Development contacted McNamara and asked him to come and talk to them. REACH was a small grass-roots community group that wanted to rehab some houses in southeast Portland and McNamara had previously estimated a project for them three or four times. REACH had finally found some funders, but they insisted on REACH hiring some more experienced staff. McNamara liked them and figured it would be fun to do for a year. Since he was planning to shut down his construction company the next year when he started school, it wasn't a difficult decision. "I was hired as construction manager but the only way I was ever going to build anything was by figuring out how to get loans so I learned how to do that." Two years later, with the organization deep in debt, the board laid off both the executive director and the business manager and asked McNamara to take over.

McNamara took a businesslike view of REACH's purpose and future, and within a few years of taking over, the organization's situation and reputation had improved. But as foundations and local government started to see it as successful they encouraged REACH to move beyond its successful program of rental housing rehabilitations and into homeownership programs. McNamara argued against that idea for four reasons. First, having a nonprofit build or rehab houses one at a time would be a very expensive way to get people into homeownership. "And besides, we were already starting to see some of our tenants save up enough money that they could go buy a fixer-upper without any subsidy." Second, the large amount of public subsidy that would be needed would be lost every time REACH sold a house but when that same subsidy was invested into rental housing, it could be used over and over again. Third, in the neighborhoods that REACH served, most of the housing stock was poorly managed and maintained multifamily apartment buildings that were dragging down the neighborhood, "and we needed to get those under control." Fourth, rental housing gave REACH an income stream and a balance sheet, so over time, the organization could pay off mortgages and have capital controlled by the community-based board. Then REACH would be able to reinvest as it wanted to rather than be dependent on the whims of public and philanthropic funders. "I had never thought that way before—that far into the future—but now it has been over twenty years since I left REACH and it has worked out great. They paid off some mortgages, refinanced some properties, and now they have cash flow, so they don't have to be entirely dependent on new development deals to generate fees to pay their nut." McNamara left REACH in 1990 to take a job working as the first executive director of the Neighborhood Partnership Fund for the Oregon Community Foundation. His job was to increase local community-based development capacity by getting training, technical assistance, grants, and loans to fledging and growing nonprofit groups. McNamara stayed for four years but while he believed in the organization's mission, "I didn't have the excitement for it that I had for development."

In 1994, McNamara was nominated for the prestigious Loeb Fellowship, a year of study at Harvard University's Graduate School of Design for mid-career professionals. He thought he would be going back into community development work when he finished so he wanted to spend some time working out how community development corporations could become self-sufficient, at least in terms of their business operations. "But that is not what I spent my time on at Harvard. I hung out at the business school as much as I could and gobbled up every class, including courses in real estate development, negotiations, and organizational management. I came in not thinking very much of MBA students but those classes were great, the kids were brilliant, and they were much more articulate than the kids at the Kennedy School of Government."

When he got back to Portland in 1995, he convinced the developer Pat Prendergast to hire him. Prendergast and John Carroll had purchased the old Burlington Northern railyards in 1990, the land that became the heart of Portland's Pearl District. In 1994 John Carroll had gone out on his own and Prendergast had brought Homer Williams in as an equity partner. By the time McNamara returned from Boston in the summer of 1995, the vision plan for the area had been presented to the public. "All of the activists had showed up at all of the meetings saying, 'You need affordable housing here,' and the city had made it clear that it wanted affordable housing as part of the deals. So I just kept on meeting people until someone made a call to Pat and Homer for me, and when I met Pat I said, 'You need to develop affordable housing, I know how to do it, you don't, and you should hire me.' I was sort of surprised that Pat hired me but I think Harvard looked good to him."

McNamara worked for Prendergast from 1995 until 2001 but in 1996 Prendergast and Williams split and Williams ended up with the land in the

Pearl District. "So we went over to the east side of Portland where I helped Pat with a project for apartments, condos, and a little subdivision on the site of an old car dealership, but then I became anxious to go out on my own." In December 2001 he took a job running a Hope VI project for the Housing Authority of Portland but after seven months he realized it just wasn't for him. "I took the summer off in 2002 and started working on my own, and that is how it all started."

A Nonprofit Approach to For-Profit Development

Since 2002, Ed McNamara has developed two apartment buildings: the Sitka, completed in 2005, and the Ramona, completed in 2011. When it comes to development, McNamara says he is a "one-at-a-time" guy. "I am involved in every aspect of it and I drive my architects crazy but they come to appreciate it and I think in the end they feel that they get a better product for it. They are not used to having a developer getting involved in all of the technical issues and details." McNamara does not build to sell; he holds onto his properties, so once the buildings are done, he remains closely involved as the owner-operator. "What I do is affordable housing, and this is not necessarily what I thought I would do but I am good at it and I like it. It is getting harder to get public subsidies as a for-profit developer of affordable housing even though I may be able to do so for less subsidy than most nonprofit developers." Unlike nonprofit affordable housing developers, McNamara must pay some property taxes and even then his rents are often lower and his buildings stay fuller. "So I do affordable housing, run well, not just as a commodity. For me it is about building a place that adds to the fabric of the neighborhood and is basically a good place to live so that maybe people are a little better off when they leave."

McNamara's latest project offers an example of how a hands-on developer works with his design team. The Ramona Apartments offers affordable family housing with 138 two- and three-bedroom units that are large enough for families with kids. The Ramona was financed with tax-exempt bonds, equity from 4 percent Low Income Housing Tax Credits (LIHTC), and a subordinate loan from the City of Portland. The building is in the Pearl District, and until this project, no other developers had attempted to provide family housing in the neighborhood—affordable or otherwise. "The Pearl District has not been seen as a place where kids live but the data tell a different story," says McNamara. "There have been amazingly high numbers of births in the Pearl in the past few years, so kids are being born here and they are staying here and families with kids are moving in too. I think family housing and larger units are still a little scary for condo developers so what I am hoping to do is to show that there is huge demand for family housing, even if it is in the affordable housing area."

Larger units are not the only feature McNamara provided at the Ramona. He spent about two years talking to the school district and was finally able to convince them to rent some space on the ground floor of the building. "Having a school in the building will help people decide to live there and having one in the neighborhood will help other families choose to stay." McNamara also rented some space on the ground floor to a community group that "does a lot of stuff with kids and families." The building's location is in the far north end of the Pearl, a mile away from the closest school and two miles from the south end of the Pearl, so people making decisions based on schools wouldn't move there otherwise. Where McNamara lived, in Northeast Portland, there were six schools within a mile and yet there were more births in the Pearl, which had no schools. Northeast Portland also had an older population of baby boomers and empty nesters who chose to stay after raising their kids. These shifting demographics and the related demand for urban schools were central to McNamara's plan.

"What I am trying to do," says McNamara, "is change the market in other ways and create a building where working families, lower-income families, and single parents will have a good place to live. I want to break down those barriers of isolation that come from living in the city and that is why we try to run the buildings in a way that people get to know each other." Part of it was recruiting those other things to the building to make it more than just a building. "That is what I do as a developer, I am a for-profit developer but I take a nonprofit approach to development."

Getting the Exterior Shell Right—and Tight

When he started to design the building, the first thing McNamara did was direct his architects to build eight to ten "massing models" of building configurations that they thought would work on the site, which was a full city block. He told them the number of units and the unit sizes, types, and mix so they knew how much square footage to design for. Once the models were done, McNamara had two calculations done for each: the ratio of rentable square feet to common area; and the ratio of exterior skin to building volume, "because skin is so expensive and such an energy leak."

Of the eight or ten models that the architects came up with, a scheme with a U-shaped plan was the best in terms of both of those calculations. "So then we went back to what worked best aesthetically and the U-shaped plan was also the best shape on the block and for the site." The closed end of the U faced 14th Street, which is a busy one-way street, and just across the street was the freeway. The open end of the U faced onto 13th Street, away from the freeway, so the noise would not reverberate inside the court-yard and the next planned city park was also in that direction. There was also some historical character to that side of the street and because it was an old industrial area the city encouraged property owners to build side-walks in the style of old loading docks, and those helped to resolve grade changes across the Ramona's site. "Everything about the block suited the U-shaped configuration and orientation, so it was a very efficient solution for the site," says McNamara, "and I do that kind of analysis and look at every detail the same way."

McNamara took the same approach toward the energy efficiency of the building and the design of the building's exterior, or "envelope." Individual building materials have different insulating properties that are measured in R-values, with a higher number providing more insulation. The total R-value of a wall assembly must take into account construction tolerances and can be increased or decreased by using different combinations of materials. "We modeled about twelve different ways to do the insulation, the air barriers, and the vapor barriers for an opaque wall with no windows and doors, and then the contractor priced them all and the engineer calculated the R-values for each model. We found that when we just looked at R-values on the opaque walls they performed very differently and that we could spend hundreds of thousands of dollars to get a significantly more efficient exterior wall and building envelope.

"The problem is," says McNamara, "that when you add in doors and windows it becomes something else." Windows transmit heat and cold much more than any other part of the building and even the best windows cannot achieve more than about an R-4. What really matters is the amount of overall window area on the building—the sizes and numbers of windows—and fewer, smaller windows is better. But window quality matters too, so McNamara looked at three different types of windows with U-values of 0.45, 0.35, and 0.29. U-values are the inverse of R-values, so the lower number the more efficient the window. The window with the U-value of 0.45 represented a very strong aluminum window but it wasn't

Figure 19. Exterior of the Ramona Apartments. Photo © Sally Painter Photo; courtesy of Turtle Island Development.

as energy efficient. The window with the U-value of 0.35 was the norm for LEED (Leadership in Energy and Environmental Design) buildings. The window with the U-value of 0.29 was something McNamara knew he could get but he was pretty sure the project couldn't afford.

"When we modeled the same twelve building envelope alternatives with the three different windows we found that the worst performing opaque wall with the best performing window had a better average total R-value than the best opaque wall with the worst performing window. So in other words, it was all about the window quality and we could spend an extra $300,000 on insulation and not get it right if we had a poor performing window." By working with his design team to carefully examine these variables McNamara arrived at his optimal alternative—the design that best balanced energy efficiency over the life of the building and initial construction cost without sacrificing livability

Next, and despite the recent trend of floor-to-ceiling glass everywhere in condominium units, McNamara decided to have the architects size the

Figure 21. A combined laundry room and children's play room.
Photo © Sally Painter Photo; courtesy of Turtle Island Development.

windows for function rather than form, letting interior use drive the exterior design of the building. This approach meant smaller windows in the bedrooms and larger windows in living rooms, but with sunshades to reduce heat gain. "Then we moved floor plans or flipped them over to make the best patterns on the building elevations so that, in the end, the sizing and design of the windows was driven by energy efficiency first and then we worked to make sure we got the aesthetics right second."

Designing for Performance and Durability

McNamara believes that sustainable design is the right thing to do, but that is not the only reason he does it. "I do it because I am going to own the building for a long time." Because he is going to own it for a long time, he doesn't care as much about green building ratings checklists. Rather, he cares about the actual performance of the building in terms of energy use over the long run of his ownership period—that is the vision that drives him when he hires and directs his architects and engineers. "That is why I measure all of this stuff."

McNamara's data-driven approach to design does not match up exactly with how the construction industry in general measures sustainability. Since 1998, the LEED rating system of the U.S. Green Building Council (USGBC) has served as the dominant framework for sustainable design in the United States. A building owner and design team work together to make decisions about building materials, systems, and assemblies that will earn them points on a checklist and if the design has earned enough points it may be eligible for a LEED rating of silver, gold, or platinum. "The problem," says McNamara, "is that you can game the system, and most people are doing that. You can earn a lot of points without getting great energy efficiency and the problem is that officials and the general public don't understand this—they think there is a correlation between LEED and energy savings and in many cases there is not a direct correlation."

McNamara did seek a LEED rating for the Ramona Apartments because of pressure from lenders, LIHTC investors, and local and state governments. "It was easier to get the LEED rating than to keep trying to explain why it didn't make sense. Our initial estimate was that we could qualify for LEED Silver and that was based on qualifying for a certain number of energy points in the LEED rating system." McNamara planned to maximize natural ventilation and leave out the air conditioning system all together, "but when we interviewed mechanical engineers, they told us, 'It is going to be tough to get that many energy points if we don't have air conditioning in the apartments,' so I said, 'Shouldn't the building be more efficient without air conditioning?'" The answer was that while it might be more efficient, it didn't necessarily get LEED points. LEED energy points—at least at that time—were based on the difference between the specific building being designed and the worst-case version of that same building that would be allowed by code. If that worst-case building had air conditioning and big windows then it would use a lot of energy. Using more efficient windows and a more efficient air conditioning system on that same building would produce gains in terms of LEED energy points even if the building still used a lot of energy. But for a building that had smaller windows and no air conditioning system at all, it was hard to show a big percentage improvement over the worst case. Even though McNamara's building—with an efficient exterior shell, small windows, and no air conditioning system—would clearly use less energy, because of the way the LEED rating system was structured he couldn't collect as many "points" for it.

Figure 22. Aerial view of the Ramona Apartments, with courtyard, green roof, and solar panels. Photo © SkyShots, Portland, Oregon; courtesy of Turtle Island Development.

The USGBC faced mounting pressure from owners and design professionals to increase the use of data from post-occupancy evaluations, or POEs, of buildings and to refine LEED criteria so that they reflected actual rather than prescribed outcomes. This direction is more in line with the approach that the Ramona's team took. Although they pursued LEED status, their primary focus was on the Architecture 2030 Challenge, which measured actual energy use compared to other buildings.

Good Design Is About Operating Costs

For Ed McNamara, real efficiency is all about operating costs and that's what he drives his architects and engineers to focus on. "My best education was doing asset management. Once I started overseeing the buildings that I had built and started watching the operating and maintenance budgets, I started asking questions like 'Why are we replacing that piece of vinyl trim so often?'" Using cheap vinyl trim may help to reduce initial construction costs but if it must be repaired or replaced regularly, then maintenance costs soon outstrip the value of the initial savings. "That is why, once we have completed a building, I review all of the work orders for the first year and I always ask our property managers 'What are we repairing?'"

Historically, building owners did not connect the dots between the first costs of constructing a building and the life-cycle costs of owning, operating, and maintaining it over many years. As a result, it was common during the design and construction phase of a project to cheapen the building systems, materials, and finishes as a way to meet a fixed capital budget. It was also common during this stage of the project to discount how those decisions would impact the cost of operating and maintaining the building in the future. So it was common for building owners to be "penny wise and pound foolish," by choosing to save a few dollars on initial construction while unwittingly increasing operating and maintenance costs for years to come in a way that well exceeded the value of the initial capital savings. Merchant builders—developers who are in the business of constructing and quickly selling buildings once they have leased up—have a difficult time justifying increased capital costs for a building they do not intend to own, but for people who do intend to own for a long time, these costs are more important. Increased understanding of these costs led to an increased emphasis in the real estate community on the total cost of ownership (TCO), which considers the total cost of financing, building, owning, operating, and maintaining a property over a long time frame. Real estate underwriters in the Pacific Northwest and elsewhere started accounting for this kind of holistic thinking, which increased the value of buildings that incorporated sustainable systems that were more costly to build on the front end but less costly to operate over the long run. Generally, however, this kind of thinking was not even on the radar screens of most developers except for a few like Ed McNamara, who had a bigger vision and knew how to use his architects to realize it.

Good Architects Help Developers Realize Their Visions

Architects who work for developers have to think differently about their work than do other architects. They must work quickly, maximize efficiency, and solve an economic model while finding room for good design. They must know how to identify the handful of design opportunities that will fit into the budget and derive a maximum effect—or return—for the dollars spent. As David Haymes says, "Sometimes you get only one move, and that could be a great landscaped entrance, a spectacular lobby, a unique amenity, or a formal shape on the roof, but it won't be all of those things, just one of them."[12]

Good developers have a vision and then ride herd over their design teams and all of the details. As Allan Shulman points out, it matters little if their visions are different or even in conflict—what is important is a strong vision, conviction, and drive—like that of Ed McNamara. Because he was interested in serving affordable housing users and owning his buildings for a long time, McNamara's definition of good design included not just aesthetics, but also maintenance costs, operating costs, and TCO. And because the Pacific Northwest was one of the most progressive regions in the country when it came to sustainability, the public's expectations of people like McNamara were higher to begin with. Indeed, many other developers in Portland genuinely embraced sustainable design while those in other regions paid it lip service while using only enough superficial "greenwashing" to serve marketing purposes. But how do developers in other parts of the country think about good design?

Figure 23. Entrance to the Ramona Apartments. Photo © Sally Painter Photo; courtesy of Turtle Island Development.

Chapter 5

Good Design

> The architects who benefit us most may be those generous enough to
> lay aside their claims to genius in order to devote themselves to
> assembling graceful but predominantly unoriginal boxes. Architecture
> should have the confidence and the kindness to be a little boring.
> —Alain de Botton, *The Architecture of Happiness*[1]

How Design Professionals See It

The previous chapter showed how successful developers and their architects
think about and collaborate on the design of real estate projects. The common thread is the developer's approach—a strong vision, leadership, and
attention to detail. Ed McNamara's story in that chapter exemplifies this
approach and also offers an example of one developer's idea of good design:
a building that not only offers a good affordable housing option but one
that will be cost-effective to own, operate, and maintain over the long run.
But how do other developers define good design? Do developers in different
parts of the country look at design the same way? How do their ideas about
good design compare with those of architects, planners, the public, and
those in the market for real estate—their potential buyers and tenants? To
answer these questions, we will hear the views of two other developers—
one from Chicago and the other from Miami—but first we will consider
how different people think about design.

One of the more typical criticisms of real estate developers is that they
just don't seem to care much about doing "good design." But not everyone

looks at design in the same way. Numerous studies in the field of environmental psychology stretching back to the 1960s have repeatedly shown that architects and nonarchitects experience buildings differently. In one study, by Kimberly Devlin and Jack Nasar, architects and nonarchitects were asked to look at photographs of two styles of residential architecture: "high" and "popular." Both groups favored "novelty and clarity or coherence," but nonarchitects favored "simplicity" and "popular" attributes and architects favored "complexity" and "high" attributes.[2]

A later study, by Robert Gifford, Donald Hine, Werner Muller-Clemm, and Kelly Shaw, focused more closely on the nature of this disagreement by evaluating not just the objective characteristics of a building but also the subjective meanings we associate with a building's properties. The objective characteristics or "physical cues" used in the study included arches, articulation, balconies, canopies, color variety, columns, ornament, glass, landscaping, metal, roof pitches, railings, roads, rounded shapes, sculpture, stone and brick, number of stories, triangles, stepped massing, and the size of the building. But it was the individual's subjective ideas about the properties of a building or place—whether it was clear, complex, friendly, meaningful, rugged, or original—that made the difference. Indeed, the researchers found that there was no correlation between objective physical cues and subjective meanings. While architects and nonarchitects agreed that "a meaningful building is an aesthetically good building," the two groups used none of the same physical cues as a basis for deciding what was "meaningful," and so there was "zero agreement" on what was a "meaningful building."[3]

Planners also have a different idea of what good design is. A study by Phil Hubbard that considered differences in architectural interpretation between planners and community groups in the review of urban real estate development projects found that, like architects, 70 percent of the planners focused on the objective, physical cues of the design—its materials, context, and design approach. Conversely, 50 percent of the community group members focused on "cognitive constructs"—what the authors of the previous study called "subjective meanings"—what the buildings reminded them of and their preferences for those kinds of characteristics. Hubbard attributed these differences in interpretation to the planner's professional training and socialization, which emphasize the technical and material qualities of the built environment and discourage a personal, subjective approach. He concluded with the suspicion that there are differences among the professions too and that planners see buildings differently than architects. The reason is that their professional training and socialization lead planners to put more importance than architects do on a building's functionality and its contribution to the public realm.[4]

The results of these and other studies about how experts—architects and planners—think about design reinforce a 1969 study by Robert Hershberger that found that "experts respond more to representational, physical meanings of architecture—objective physical characteristics or physical cues—while lay groups respond more to responsive, ethno-demographic meanings," or subjective ideas about buildings and place. Similarly, Linda Groat and, later, Kimberly Devlin found that architects are more likely to see buildings through stylistic and formal category systems while laypeople rely on functional categories. Robert Gifford and his colleagues speculated that architects might be more influenced by materials while nonarchitects are influenced by form.[5]

In other words, an architect is more able than a layperson to relate to a house designed in the modern style of the French architect Le Corbusier that is built of concrete and glass and has an asymmetrical façade, flat roof, and L-shaped plan with public and private wings. A layperson, on the other hand, identifies better than an architect does with a more traditional-looking house that is made of stone or brick, has double-hung windows and a pitched roof with dormers, and feels sturdy, warm, and welcoming.

Margaret Wilson and David Canter conclude that the primary reason why architects have different ideas about aesthetics is that they are socialized by their professional training in ways that "create or widen the aesthetic gap between themselves and the public." Hubbard adds that planners are similar to architects as their education "inculcates a distinctive knowledge structure" that laypeople lack. And Gifford laments that, while architects have been told for years that they must try to better understand the views of laypersons, users, and other nonprofessionals, this advice has fallen on deaf ears. As an antidote, he proposes that architects should be specifically trained to understand how nonarchitects think about buildings, concluding that "the greatest architects will be those with the creativity to design buildings that are delightful to design professionals and the public." As we will soon see, there is still a long way to go in achieving this goal because the general public—the actual buyers and users of buildings—has its own ideas about what makes buildings and places delightful.[6]

The Layperson's View: Style Versus Satisfaction

If architects and planners have different ways of evaluating buildings, then how do the nonexpert users of buildings—workers, residents, and members of the general public—think about good design? In a study of what constitutes good urban design in mixed-use and residential developments, Ann Forsyth and Katherine Crewe compared three planned communities that were developed at different times and designed in different styles—one based on early or high "modernist" principles, one based on more humanistic "late-modernist" principles that emphasized imageability and legibility of urban space, and one based on New Urbanism principles, which recall traditional, premodern communities. They then compared these communities on four dimensions—"objective aesthetics," "style," "place," and "satisfaction"—and determined that all three places conformed to some principles of "good design" but that these principles differed, resulting in criticism from architects and planners promoting different styles.[7]

Forsyth and Crewe define style as "the characteristic of a particular group or period or a manner of writing or building," but they emphasize that style "also connotes fashion." Further, "styles conform to rules and are intimately related to issues of 'taste,'" and as Herbert Gans has pointed out, taste ties to social position. As a result, one architect may judge a building according to the principles of one style while a different architect uses another style for his critique, leading to different judgments that reflect little more than the different "tastes" of the architects doing the judging.[8]

Nonarchitects, however, perceive their homes and communities in terms of "satisfaction" and "popularity." Satisfaction relates to how fit a place is for human activity and the fulfillment of needs, and it can be demonstrated through the use of a post-occupancy evaluation (POE). This survey measures and assesses the actual experience of a place after it has been occupied for some period of time, and because it is drawn from responses from many users it offers a much more informed and nuanced view based on a much larger amount of data. Conversely, an architectural critique is written by a single expert author, often not long after a new building or development has been occupied, and long before anyone has determined how successful it is from the users' viewpoint.

Forsyth and Crewe concluded that architectural criticism has tended to focus on style while planning criticism has tended to focus on resident preferences and overall functioning in terms of issues such as sustainability and affordable housing. Both viewpoints, unfortunately, neglect any discussion of "overall visual quality as such"—or how objective aesthetics, place, and satisfaction come together from a user's viewpoint. More generally, they conclude that debates about style are not the same as debates about aesthetic quality, because a project that is aesthetically good can, at the same time, be critically condemned by an expert who has different stylistic preferences. In other words, architects and planners do not talk about design quality from the viewpoint of objective aesthetics, place, and the satisfaction of the general population and lay users but rather from their own individual stylistic viewpoints. Thus, according to Forsyth and Crewe, any design that is deemed aesthetically good by nonprofessionals remains open to criticism and condemnation by architects and other experts.

Architects and planners, because of their education and socialization, have different ideas of what good design is than do the nonprofessionals who represent the majority of buyers and users of real estate. Where architects concern themselves with "subjective style" and planners consider social aspects, buyers care more about Forsyth and Crewe's "objective aesthetics" and "satisfaction." In other words, the user or buyer is concerned primarily with whether or not a place looks good to them and if it will be a good place to live. Developers must therefore concern themselves with both subjective style and the wants of their potential buyers. To succeed, a developer must not only balance these potentially conflicting views of good design but also resolve them within the context of a more important concern: who will buy their product and at what price.

Economics and the Tastes of the Market

Discussions of style, satisfaction, and objective aesthetics leave out one key ingredient that critics have little interest in but that developers cannot neglect if they hope to remain in business: price. A project must perform economically if the developer is to succeed, and this means that the final product must be something that can be sold for a price that is greater than the cost of developing it. Many of the "physical cues"—the stylistic design features such as details, material quality, massing, and façade articulation—that make a design look better both to experts and laypeople also cost more money. A developer must balance the costs of the various elements of a design with the price for which he hopes to sell the finished product because he is competing in a marketplace where he must be able to justify his price in the context of many comparable products. "And frankly," says Gail Lissner, a Chicago market research expert, "the market doesn't necessarily have great taste anyways."[9]

"Design quality definitely has an impact on the marketing and sales of condominiums," says Lissner. "In the early stages of the development boom of the 2000s in Chicago design was not as important but as soon as there was more competition it became increasingly so. Developers started using 'starchitects' and then everyone really started to get into the architecture." Design really does help differentiate a product from its competition and this becomes even more important when markets weaken. "A cookie-cutter building is simply not as valuable as a well-designed building," says Lissner. At the same time, architecture must have lasting power, and projects that are too trendy or cutting-edge do not translate well to the broader market. Projects that evoke a "love it or hate it" reaction are even more difficult to sell, particularly when the market softens. One project by a famous Chicago architect that had a very raw interior with a lot of exposed concrete sold very slowly and while Lissner thought, "as an architect I might find it interesting," she didn't like it personally. Indeed, being innovative and edgy is more likely to alienate certain segments of the market. "Another developer tried to do something that had moving walls but I just thought it was ugly." In the end, Lissner concludes, despite an architect's desire to focus his or her design on a "target market," the fact is that the market is diverse and the developer's first priority must be to create a product that will attract the largest possible pool of potential buyers.

As architecture has become more sophisticated, so too have buyers, but the bottom line remains price, which is critical, so a developer simply can't do something that is architecturally remarkable but costs 20 percent more. "Real estate is all about price and there is no amount of good architectural design that is going to cure pricing problems," says Lissner who, in her market research work, tries to look at a project the way the market—the buyer—would look at it rather than the way the architect does. So the questions become, "Do you have granite countertops? Do you have stainless steel appliances? What else are you offering?" Lissner also spends a lot of time looking at the sizes and mixes of units and critiquing the developer's unit layouts, focusing on details like kitchen designs, bedrooms, bathrooms, and closet space, "which unfortunately people have done away with." Her personal pet peeve is that with so many layouts you can see the toilet in the powder room when you are sitting on the couch in the living room. "Why," asks Lissner, "don't they teach that in architecture school?" Even among the people in Lissner's office there are differences in tastes. "My partner jokes that when we walk into a unit he walks up to the exterior wall because he wants to see the view and I always go look at the bathrooms first. It's not exactly true but there is something to it."

In combing over the unit layouts, one of Lissner's goals is to help keep the total sale price down and one way to do that is by trying to reduce the sizes of the units by making the design more efficient. "But we find that a perverse thing happens when you try too hard to reduce a unit's size—the living room layout suffers." The reason that happens is that the sizes and shapes of all the other rooms are dictated by a number of fixed dimensions. Bedrooms are based on the bed, furniture, and closet sizes and locations; bathrooms by the fixtures; and kitchens by the adaptability requirements of the Americans with Disabilities Act. "People made more and more use of breakfast bars as a way to reduce the dining area but then those started going away and the reduction in counter space in the kitchens really hurt the functionality of those units. Now developers are trying to go even smaller by basically putting the kitchen in the hall—kind of like a galley kitchen on a boat. In the end, the only room that can get reduced easily is the living room, which should be the most important room in the unit. And not only does it get shrunk but its shape becomes whatever is left over, including the notched-out corner of the semirecessed balcony."

And balconies are more important in people's minds than they are in reality. "We are big proponents of balconies and we talk about them a lot around here. Architects do not like them because they believe they have a negative impact on the exterior design but buyers want them—or at least they think they want them." In fact, people probably use their balconies a lot less than they think they will, so they are more important during "the buy moment." Still, says Lissner, "as someone who has lived in a high-rise without a balcony, I really wanted to be able to go out to check the temperature and see what to wear but in fact if I really had one it would likely just be a source of dirt at the balcony door." Even the details of a balcony design matter—should they be hanging, partially recessed, or fully recessed? Lissner prefers partially recessed. "Hanging balconies make me feel like I am too much on display, so I prefer partially recessed because they also give a feeling of security. Recessed balconies make the living room dark, take up too much space, and disrupt the unit layout. Even the design of the balcony rail matters because its material and height can obstruct your view when you are sitting down in the living room."

And while all of these things—layouts, closets, kitchens, and balconies —are constantly evolving, it can take a long time to notice a big change because as with most other products, innovation comes in baby steps. First, developers start by looking at their own location, what has worked, and what might work a little better. "But nobody gets too cutting edge," says Lissner. "It is very hard to deviate from the norm and so no one does. Besides, the two most important things to buyers are location and view. Then it comes down to a long list of features and amenities that people rate differently, so it depends upon the market and the person."

Despite opinions from architects, planners, critics, and everyone else, from the developer's perspective a good design is one that will attract a broad and deep market: it must sell—and sell out. More important, project economics are inseparable from design and are critical from the macro level of a multiphase, master-planned community to the details of individual unit layouts and finishes. The story of a high-rise tower in Chicago called Aqua offers one developer's idea of what good design is—at both scales.

Designing for the Resident

The Chicago architect and developer James Loewenberg admits to having "some heretical thoughts" when it comes to the value of good design. "The person who looks to buy or rent a unit in a high-rise," says Loewenberg, "only cares about three things: the location of the building, the layout of their unit, and the view from their unit. They don't care as much about the physical appearance of the building and it is my contention that they never really look above the third floor."[10]

Loewenberg maintains that the inside of the building, "where the person lives," is more important, so he focuses on the building floor plans, how people move around the building, and, most important, the unit layouts—down to the inch. He also pays attention to daylight, because large windows can make the walls transparent, creating the illusion of bringing the outdoors inside, which not only makes the unit feel bigger, but also makes it a more successful unit in terms of rent or sale price. "It is axiomatic," says Loewenberg, "that if you cannot see daylight out of a window within two steps of entering the unit, then you probably won't have as successful a building." Loewenberg concludes that his success as a developer is the result of his architectural approach to problem solving and knowing how to develop successful unit plans. "I make no bones about it," says Loewenberg. "After location, a unit's interior layout, finishes, and views matter most to buyers and this attitude has gotten me into all sorts of trouble with the architectural critics."

Blair Kamin, the architecture critic for the *Chicago Tribune*, has heaped scorn on Loewenberg's buildings, which he views as boxy and uninspired. In *Terror and Wonder: Architecture in a Tumultuous Age*, Kamin accuses Loewenberg of producing "designs of sterile symmetry and unarticulated surfaces that recall the old housing blocs of East Berlin." According to Kamin, "Former city planners lament the Loewenberg-ization of the Near North Side," where his "monuments to mediocrity" have led to the "uglification" of the city. Kamin blames the planners too, because their codes allow Loewenberg and all Chicago architects who design the typical high-rise scheme of a "tower-on-a-podium-of-parking-with-a-bad-base" to continue the proliferation of what he calls "plop architecture." Finally, Kamin is shocked and outraged that "Loewenberg is unapologetic about admitting that he designs to a budget and people don't look above the bottom of a high-rise—buyers want a decorated base and high-quality apartments."[11]

"Blair Kamin thinks everything should be beautiful and that it is good to do award-winning buildings, and he is right," says Loewenberg, "but economics matter." Loewenberg recalls being roundly criticized by another critic for a project with a parking garage finished in exposed concrete. "He asked me, 'Well, why are you putting marble thresholds in the apartments and why didn't you spend the money on better finishes for your concrete garage?' I guess it was heresy when I said, 'Because people don't care what a garage looks like and in fact they would rather see a marble or granite countertop than a magnificent exterior on a garage.' That critic," says Loewenberg, "was trained as an architect, so he looks at the outside of the building and thinks that no shortcuts should be taken and that you should only do beautiful architecture. I, on the other hand, would rather put my money where it counts, and I happen to know that it is the finishes that sell. Well, that critic, he didn't really quite get it, and what he and other critics can't really understand is this building, Aqua, which has great architecture, and how we were able to do what we did here." Loewenberg, of course, does get it. So while architects focus on design and style and developers focus on the economics and the tastes of the market, Loewenberg—as an architect and developer—is able to see development from both viewpoints. This unique perspective has helped him to develop an idea of what good design is that reflects an understanding of each, and that has fueled his continued success.

Developer as Master Architect

Loewenberg was born and raised in Chicago, where his father and uncle owned a successful architecture and engineering firm that dated back to 1919. The firm did a lot of residential development, and from an early age Loewenberg would go out with his father on Saturday mornings and afternoons to look at projects under construction. After high school he went to MIT, where he earned a Bachelor of Architecture degree and right afterward he went back to Chicago. "When I got out of school, in 1957, it was a golden time for architects developing high-rise residential buildings, although the definition of 'high-rise' in those days was a twelve- to twenty-story building. By comparison, I just topped out an eighty-seven-story building, and that's a high-rise building today.

"I came to development naturally, through an evolutionary process," says Loewenberg. "I got into a family business and took it over in the 1980s and have been a developer and architect ever since." But being both a developer and an architect has not always been easy. "When I got out of school, the American Institute of Architects [AIA] frowned on architects acting as developers and back then 'developer' was a dirty word." Loewenberg, on the other hand, thought that the AIA and the architectural profession had missed the boat. In fact, he argues that the first developer was the master architect of the Middle Ages, who was responsible for acquiring the land, preparing the site, designing the building, purchasing materials, managing accounts, and hiring and managing the whole workforce from masons and carpenters to artisans and laborers. "The guy who built Rennes Cathedral was an architect, but he ran the stone masons and all the other tradesmen, he lived in the building, and he lived, breathed, and died the church." But like some others in the profession, Loewenberg thinks architects lost their way in the late nineteenth century when, in an effort to minimize their own risk, they abandoned these broader responsibilities for a narrow focus on design, marginalizing themselves and their profession in the process. "That was the most tragic mistake ever made by the profession. I believe that by their training, demeanor, and import, the architect should be the master architect but he isn't and the reason—the problem—is that

Figure 24. Aqua Tower, Lakeshore East, Chicago. Photo by author.

the profession is so risk averse." But because he is not just an architect but also a developer, Loewenberg takes a very different view of risk.

"A lot of architects say to me, 'You are a developer—how do you do it and how can I become a developer?' and my answer is, 'If you have to ask then never mind, you will never become one.'" And the reason he says that is because the major thing required to become a developer is the willingness and ability to take significant risks. "Risk is a relative word and I don't mean stupid, idiotic risks," says Loewenberg. "I mean that you are going to have to leave the cushy position that the architecture profession has created for itself as not being responsible for anything, be able to evaluate something, and then be able to step into the frying pan and say, 'Yeah, I am going to do it.'" Loewenberg is a risk taker but he believes that if he hadn't been one he would still be sitting at a drafting board doing fee-for-service architectural work. Loewenberg's firm is still in business and still provides traditional architectural design services, but much of that work is in support of his own company's real estate development projects. "I am proud to say that I am a developer—I am not ashamed of it—but more important, my architectural training has been a wonderful asset to me in development. It has given me the tools to help me identify and solve problems, control processes, and get things done." Loewenberg contends that very few architects have the opportunity to take advantage of their educations and use these tools or to practice their profession as fully as he does and be the master architect. "The majority of architects are just too risk averse and it is hard to do something great if you are not willing to stick your neck out, get your head chopped off, and come back to fight the battle again the next day."

Loewenberg Architects is a full-service architecture firm, but Loewenberg is also one of two senior partners in a development company called Magellan. Loewenberg always had a sideline development business as a part of his architectural practice, and in the 1970s he had a partner who was using a lawyer named Joel Carlins for legal matters. "Carlins and I were talking one day in 1980, when Joel had access to a nice piece of property, and he asked, 'What should we do with it?' I said, 'Let's build a high-rise,' and so we did and it was a success." That building had a small office component in it and Loewenberg and Carlins soon moved their offices into that space. "We began to see more of each other and talk more to each other but there were no real development opportunities until around 1994 when markets started to open up again." Then Carlins and Loewenberg found a piece of land not far from their first building, obtained financing, and successfully developed an 809-unit apartment building. "We decided to do a couple of other things together, moved over to the new building and then we decided that as long as we were doing things together we may as well combine our two separate operations into one office that provides legal, architectural, and project management services." In 2002, Loewenberg and Carlins formally merged their organizations, creating the Magellan Development Group, and started to look for new opportunities.

Development ideas usually start with money, information, a user or tenant, or a property. For Loewenberg and Carlins, it was the last of these that caused them to embark on a huge development project called Lakeshore East. "We did a few more projects as developer and manager and some third-party stuff but then condominiums took off, Joel got bit by the condo bug, and along came this piece of property."

The Economics of Infrastructure

The property was a twenty-eight-acre parcel on Chicago's lakefront that was owned by a group of private investors that had backgrounds in office development. "In the 1970s they were doing office development but then the Sears Tower opened up, which shifted the office market from the East Loop to the West Loop. The site became a less desirable location, you couldn't get an office building financed anymore, and so their opportunity dried up. We offered to buy the property in a private transaction but they didn't like the price we offered and proposed something crazy and we said no. So they put it out for competitive bidding, the bids came back at 20 percent of our original offer, and we ended up getting it for a lot less than our original bid."

Loewenberg and Carlins closed on the property in 2002 and afterward they went to the city and had the land rezoned from office use to primarily residential use with some office and hotel. "At the time, the city was interested in downzoning, so instead of fourteen million square feet we were rezoned for nine million square feet. Since we only planned to build 8.2 million square feet, everyone was happy." The property was part of a larger planned unit development (PUD) of ninety acres that included a six-acre required park. The original plan included a long, linear park that would start at the west end of the development, at the elevated street called Upper Columbus Drive, and then slope and step down about sixty feet toward the lakefront. But rather than being built on grade, the plan was for the park to sit on top of a five- to seven-story parking garage. When Loewenberg and Carlins looked at the plan, they realized that, in addition to their land costs and other soft costs, they would have to invest $100 million in roadway and parking infrastructure just to build the required park.

The cost of a development project is usually split into three major categories—land, construction, and soft costs—and each must represent a certain percentage of the project's total costs. For example, a rule of thumb may be 15 percent land, 65 percent construction, and 20 percent soft costs. The costs of providing streets, parking, and utilities—the infrastructure—are included in the land cost. But if infrastructure costs are too high, then the land cost, total project cost, and the product price will be higher than the costs and prices of comparable products and the project won't be able to compete in the marketplace. Phased projects are even more complicated. For example, if a project is expected to be developed in three phases over ten or twenty years, it may seem logical—from a planning and design standpoint—to build the infrastructure for all three phases at the beginning. But it doesn't make any economic sense to do this because the cost of three buildings' worth of infrastructure cannot be borne by the sales proceeds or rental income from that first building alone.

Table 3 shows a phased development of three buildings, each with a development cost of $100 million and a market value of $115 million, yielding a 15 percent profit. If infrastructure represents 10 percent of the total project cost, when the infrastructure for all three buildings is built in the first phase, infrastructure costs drive up the total project costs so that they are greater than the market value of the first building. The second and third phases would each yield a whopping 28 percent profit and the three phases together would still yield an average profit of 15 percent but it would hardly matter: With its costs greater than its value, the first project would be "upside down," and if the developer did not have enough resources to span over to that second phase he would face serious financial difficulty. In the worst case, the developer would default on his construction loan, the bank would foreclose and sell the building, and that first developer would never realize the extraordinary profits from the second and third phases. The next developer, however, would stand to make a profit if she could buy it for a good price because much of the costly infrastructure would have been paid for. There is an old saying in real estate: "It is the third guy who owns the golf course who makes money." The point is that with a phased development, each individual project still must succeed on its own.

Table 3. The Impact of Infrastructure Costs on Profits

Building 1	Phased	Front-Loaded
Infrastructure	$10,000,000	$30,000,000
Other Project Costs	$90,000,000	$90,000,000
Total Project Cost	$100,000,000	$120,000,000
Market Value	$115,000,000	$115,000,000
Profit (Loss)	**$15,000,000**	**($5,000,000)**

Note: In this example, if the infrastructure for the whole three-building complex is financed and built with the first-phase building (front-loaded), that project loses $5 million. If the infrastructure is phased, however, those costs can be allocated across the three buildings to ensure that each building is profitable as a stand-alone project.

Equally as important, building all of the infrastructure in the first phase doesn't make any sense from the planning and design viewpoint either, because market cycles come and go, tastes for products evolve, and by the time the third phase is being built the master plan and the infrastructure needs may have changed dramatically. The shift from office to residential over four decades at Lakeshore East offers a perfect example. And because Loewenberg and Carlins planned on building not just three buildings but a dozen or more—over time—they wanted to find another way to comply with the PUD's requirement for a park without having to build costly underground parking garages that wouldn't be used for years to come, if ever. "It made no sense to build all of that infrastructure at the beginning, just to support a park, when the buildings using the infrastructure would be completed in phases over a number of years."

So Loewenberg had the idea of putting the park on the ground. He asked the international architecture firm of Skidmore, Owings & Merrill (SOM) to develop a master plan that reflected the new zoning for the land, a park on grade, and the phased development of infrastructure around the park that could be coordinated with the development of the individual buildings. SOM's AIA–award winning plan for Lakeshore East "moved the park back onto dirt, got rid of the costly infrastructure, and designed a road system that could be built incrementally, as part of the garages of the individual buildings."

By 2012, Magellan had completed ten major projects at Lakeshore East—seven condo and apartment towers, two townhome developments, and a retail center housing a food market and restaurants, all surrounding

Figure 25. A rendering of Skidmore, Owings & Merrill's award-winning Lakeshore East master plan, which shows the required park in the center of the development. Courtesy of SOM.

Lakeshore East Park. A handful of future tower sites still remain undeveloped. Loewenberg's own architectural firm designed some of the buildings but Magellan also hired several big-name architecture firms—SOM, DeStefano, and Solomon Cordwell Buenz—to design others. The buildings ring the park—the clad façades of their garages face into it—and the roads between the buildings sit on top of the garages for each building, at the elevated level of Upper Columbus Drive. More important, the plan allows Magellan to build the infrastructure needed for each building only when they are constructing that particular building. "So all we have to do is build the road that links to the next building and keep going around," says Loewenberg. "We got the infrastructure cost for the park down from $100 million to $17 million, and that is what made the project economically viable to do. And while the PUD required us to have the park complete by 2008, we finished it in 2005." But of all of the buildings that make up the development, the most striking is Aqua Tower. "There is a richness at Lakeshore East that you don't usually see," says Loewenberg, "and it is because of the variety of design styles—but Aqua is totally different from everything else here, and that is good."

The Simplest Box We Have Ever Built

In 2007, Loewenberg was at a dinner where he was seated next to a young architect named Jeanne Gang. Gang's award-winning firm, Studio Gang, had about twenty employees and their work was primarily small- to medium-scale community and adaptive reuse projects. She had never done anything close to the scale of a high-rise before. But Loewenberg and Gang hit it off, and soon Loewenberg had the idea of asking her to design his next high-rise project at Lakeshore East. Loewenberg hired Gang to do the concept design for the project, with his own firm serving as "architect of record" for the detailed design work. This would offer the best of both worlds, melding Gang's fresh, high-design sensibility with Loewenberg's great depth of experience designing high-rise, multifamily housing projects. "I had fun working with Jeanne. I am a demanding client because I am an architect, I can talk the talk if I want to, and you can't bullshit me too much, so a typical architect would have a harder time. But I had a problem, she had the solution, we both enjoyed it, and we got a great product." Gang also received national and international acclaim for the project and in 2012 she was the recipient of a MacArthur "genius grant."

Figure 26. The view from Aqua looking east across the park, which is surrounded on all four sides by townhomes and high-rises. Photo by author.

As inevitable as Aqua seems today, Loewenberg's ability to think about design from the viewpoint of both architect and developer emerges in the story of the scheme that did not get built. "Jeanne actually made two presentations to me of two completely different designs and I liked them both—but one scared me." In addition to the usual process of selecting a unit and various finishes and fixtures, Gang's proposed design would also allow the buyer to choose among five or six different exterior elevations for their unit. The idea was that this unusually personal and democratic approach would result in an exterior design that would be the product of all of the many buyers who would pick the elevations they liked, together producing an organic pattern—like a random quilt—on the four façades of the ninety-story building. "The idea intrigued me, I got to tell you," says Loewenberg. "I wasn't afraid of the architectural idea. What scared me, understanding the public as I do, was that I knew that 99 percent of the buyers would pick one design, and then we would have this whole building in one style but then someone would pick the one style that was different." Loewenberg was concerned that the interesting and diverse random pattern suggested by Gang's idea would not actually happen and that what would happen would not be good.

"You have to think of it like a suburban single-family subdivision," says Loewenberg. "As a homebuilder you might offer four types of homes, each with three types of elevations and six color schemes. But then you have to establish ground rules that prohibit you from putting two houses with the same design next door to one another." And the reason you need those rules is because it is the only way to enforce any kind of diversity of style in a development. Otherwise, says Loewenberg, "everyone will want Tudor." Loewenberg wondered how to go about creating a set of rules for a high-rise with both vertical and horizontal adjacencies. "It was a really interesting idea, and if I had the guts I would have tried it but I just didn't think we could pull it off. I just knew that everyone would want design 'C' and one guy would want 'A' and it would be in a bad place compositionally."

Aqua is a good name for the scheme that Loewenberg did select, because its elevations undulate and the windows appear to be pools of water within the concrete balcony edges that extend out and then recede back to the building face in a pattern of freeform waves that form the high ground. Computer software helped to generate the random patterns on the façades, but, according to Loewenberg, "it is the simplest box we have ever built, and in fact, the hardest part of the job was convincing the contractors that other than the cost of the materials to extend the balcony slabs this would be no different from building the basic box." Ultimately, Loewenberg was successful: "I finally browbeat the contractors enough to talk them into it." There were just a couple of little problems that had to be solved first.

The building would be a poured-in-place, post-tensioned concrete frame—a typical "table job"—where the concrete contractor uses molds or "forms" that look like giant tables standing on the floor to pour the next floor up. Once that floor has been poured and the concrete has set—just a matter of hours—the tables are lifted or "flown" by crane up to the next level to pour the next floor. A good concrete contractor working with a simple building plan can pour a full floor in just three days. The only wrinkle with Aqua was that the balcony slab edges extended as much as twelve feet out beyond the building frame. Loewenberg's solution was to have the structural engineer use upturned beams on the top of the balcony slabs, between units, to provide the necessary structural support required for the balconies once they were built, but one question remained: how to pour them in the first place. The structural engineers would not allow the bearing of the formwork—the tables—on the cantilevered balconies below because they could not carry the loads, so instead they designed a system where the tables for the slabs would be attached to the much stronger vertical columns and cantilever out from the edge of the building. "The problem was actually a godsend," says Loewenberg, "because the solution also created a larger work area around the perimeter of the building, more room to store materials, and a much safer place to work."

The next problem was finding a reusable edge form that would allow the concrete contractor to pour slightly different curving edges at each level without having to buy new formwork for each one. "So we had the miscellaneous metals guy give us some samples that could be bent and would spring back and when we found one that worked the process became very simple: Two guys would walk around with a copy of the plan and an 'idiot stick' and nail a series of tacks into the plywood surface on the top of the table form. Then they would take the metal edge and wrap it around the tacks and then they would pour the whole floor. And the beauty is that there was no premium required for accuracy—who cares if the edge is off an inch or more?"

In the end, the only additional costs incurred to realize such a unique exterior design were the material costs of the extra concrete at the extended balconies and the labor costs of the two workers installing the edge form on each floor. And what were these costs? Loewenberg does some quick math: "Each floor took three days and was done in two pours, and it took an hour and a half to install the edge form for each half, so three hours per floor times two guys is six extra labor hours per floor, on top of the three days. If you assume each guy costs $100 per hour including benefits—it is less than that but let's just say—two guys is $600 per floor. The building is eighty floors, so that's $48,000 in additional labor costs. The balcony extensions ranged from zero to twelve feet, so if the average is six feet, then there

Figure 27. This construction photo from below shows the cantilevered table forms that support the curving concrete balconies while they are being poured. Courtesy of Tudor Van Hampton/ENR.

Figure 28. The flexible, reusable metal form that created the curving balcony edges. Steel reinforcing bars ("rebar") are put in place, and concrete is poured on the right-hand side of the form. The area to the left of the form is used as a lay-down space for materials but is open air once the table is removed. Courtesy of Tudor Van Hampton/ENR.

is six more feet of concrete around the perimeter. The total cost for all of it was probably a couple of hundred thousand dollars, which is nothing on a building of this size." Aqua is eighty-two stories and contains nearly two million square feet of hotel space, apartments, and condominiums, and its total cost was about $500 million, so a couple of hundred thousand dollars to get that magnificent effect truly was peanuts. "The great magic of this building is that we were able to accomplish what we wanted to do because we were able to convince the contractor that he could build it at virtually no additional cost. That is the fun part of architecture, getting all of these guys to think in these terms. And that is what architects should be doing as master builders."

"Waves of Creativity"

So who is right about good design—Blair Kamin or Jim Loewenberg? Gail Lissner comes down on the side of Loewenberg. "Jim Loewenberg has received criticism over the years for generic design, but the whole thing is, his buildings make money. He does good interior design, good layouts, makes good use of interior space, and there is never extra space. He gets it—he is practical, there is never any fluff, and that is why he has been very successful as an architect and as a developer. He also has his ego under control—at Lakeshore East, Magellan was careful to disassociate his name from the architecture of the project." Magellan's decision to use SOM for the master plan and to use Skidmore and other well-regarded architecture firms, including Jeanne Gang, DeStefano and Partners, and Solomon Cordwell Buenz, for the buildings ensured diversity of design at Lakeshore East and virtually eliminated Loewenberg as a target for architectural critics. Says Lissner, "Loewenberg knows what he is doing."

With Aqua, Loewenberg, Carlins, and Magellan Development succeeded on all fronts. The building was a critical success with the architectural press—appearing on the cover of *Architectural Record* in the summer of 2010—and has won dozens of awards. It was also a hit with the market—an economical and competitively priced project enhanced by the innovative use of computer-aided design and concrete that yielded a huge bang for the buck in terms of design, image, and brand. Even Blair Kamin was uncharacteristically effusive. "Aqua, the spectacular new Chicago skyscraper with the sensuous, undulating balconies, is the pearl of the long-running, now-ending Chicago building boom, a design that is as fresh conceptually as it is visually."[12]

Figure 29. Completed balconies looking down on Lakeshore East Park. Steve Hall © Hedrich Blessing; courtesy of Studio Gang Architects.

Yet the design of Aqua and the larger strategy for phasing the infrastructure at Lakeshore East both illustrate how economics and design are inextricably entwined and are simply two sides of the same coin. Those who do not understand this simple truth of development economics are doomed to misunderstand both how our cities are built—and the motivations of the builders. They are also unlikely to influence private developers like Jim Loewenberg and Joel Carlins.

What is most important about the Aqua Tower is that, in the end, it is a simple, conservative, well-designed stock product wrapped in an exterior that is so fresh and new that it leaves its competitors in the dust. And as another developer in Miami named Jorge Pérez says, "Using design to differentiate your product is one of the most important things a developer can do if he hopes to succeed in a crowded marketplace."[13]

Designing to Stand Out in the Marketplace

Since founding his Miami-based Related Group in 1979, Jorge Pérez has built or managed more than fifty thousand residential units in Miami. He has built affordable and market-rate apartments, condominiums, and hotels, and he has owned more than fifty condo towers in various stages of completion in South Florida and Las Vegas. During the height of the condo boom, his staff numbered over 450. In 2007, Related entered *Builder* magazine's "Builder 100"—a list of the largest homebuilders in the country—in thirty-third place and by 2012 it was ranked twentieth with $1.4 billion in revenue. In 2004, *Hispanic Business* ranked the Related Group as the "largest Hispanic-owned business in the USA." *Time* named Pérez one of the twenty-five most influential Hispanics in America in 2005, and in 2008 *Forbes* ranked him at 377 on its list of the 400 richest Americans with an estimated net worth of $1.3 billion (Pérez has graced the magazine's cover twice). In 2009, the Related Group completed the Trump Hollywood condominiums, in Hollywood Beach, Florida, using the Trump name under license. Pérez remains friendly with Donald Trump, who wrote the foreword to his book, *Powerhouse Principles: The Ultimate Blueprint for Real Estate Success in an Ever-Changing Market*, and Pérez himself has even been called "the Trump of the Tropics."[14]

Even after the housing bubble burst and Pérez watched his business come to a complete halt and his net worth plunge, he remained one of the country's largest developers, and a philosophical one too. Pérez told the *Miami Herald*, "If I die and am worth $50 million as opposed to $3 billion, it is really not important." He then started up his own vulture fund to buy distressed real estate—the very type of product he and his company as well as his competitors had been mass-producing in recent years.[15]

Pérez is an avid art collector and arts and design philanthropist. His own collection of Latin American art, an interest that started in childhood, fills several homes as well as his headquarters building and includes work by Fernando Botero, Diego Rivera, and many others. In 2011 Pérez spearheaded the capital campaign for the Miami Art Museum with a $35 million gift—$20 million worth of art and $15 million for design and construction of a new building. The Pritzker Prize–winning architecture firm of Herzog and de Meuron designed the building, which opened in 2013 as the Pérez Art Museum Miami. Pérez is also intensely interested in architecture and design. When he saw the drawings for a new architecture school building at the University of Miami, designed by the founding New Urbanist architect Leon Krier, he "fell in love with the building" and made a major gift to ensure its completion. The building was completed in 2005 and named the Jorge M. Pérez Architecture Center.[16]

Pérez started out with a city planner's background and sensibility, and he remains committed to revitalizing downtown Miami as demonstrated by both his project choices and his decision to build Related's headquarters on Biscayne Boulevard. But he also developed and honed his personal interests in architecture, design, and art, and he continuously integrated those interests into his professional work. And Pérez has shown remarkable resilience and an ability to adapt to changing conditions. Over three decades he and his Related Group have developed multiple residential product types from affordable apartments to luxury condominiums. Finally, the sheer volume of housing produced by Pérez and the Related Group has been virtually unmatched by almost any other urban real estate developer in the United States. So, having developed so much residential real estate over the past thirty years, how does Jorge Pérez think about good design? Like Loewenberg, he focuses on the resident's experience—and on using design to ensure that his products stand out in the marketplace.

Making Design a High Priority

The son of Cuban parents, Pérez was born in Buenos Aires, Argentina, and raised in Bogotá, Colombia. After immigrating to Miami in 1968, he attended Long Island University and then the University of Michigan, where he earned a master's degree in planning before coming back to Florida and going to work as a planner for the City of Miami. He moved up quickly and soon became an economic development director but after a couple of years, when he was in his late twenties, Pérez left the city to join a large market analysis firm called Landauer Real Estate Counselors. "Landauer was the Rolls Royce of the business at the time," says Pérez, "and through that job I met some developers." Pérez soon went out on his own with one developer but then, in 1979, after a chance meeting with Steven M. Ross of the Related Companies, a big developer in New York City, the two agreed to join forces and together they formed the Related Group of Florida.[17]

"I started out in affordable housing," says Pérez, "because I did not have a lot of money and at the time it was possible to finance almost 100 percent of affordable housing projects." Over the next decade, the Related Group became one of the largest developers of affordable housing in the country. Pérez attributes part of this achievement to an emphasis on good design. "We have always differentiated ourselves through design," says Pérez. "We use design, landscaping, and art to separate ourselves from our competition." Because it was affordable housing, however, Pérez did not actually have a lot of money to spend, so he focused his design efforts on landscaping and community amenities and he remains proud of the projects he built in lower-income areas that have withstood the test of time. "Our projects never felt like affordable rentals—they felt like a country club when you walked into them. The pool areas are still nice and the landscaping has grown in—they are jungles now—and they are all very livable places. I have always said there is no prettier building than a tree.

"That was a great ten years," says Pérez, "so then we started getting involved in market-rate and mixed-use rental apartments and commercial projects and we became the largest rental developer in Florida." After Pérez started doing market-rate rentals he became the industry leader in Florida again. "And then we got involved in condominiums and we became the largest condominium developer in the United States." Pérez has always tried to make sure that everything Related did within a class was the best in that class. "I can't make a $100,000 rental unit look like a $2 million condo—I don't have that kind of magic—but I can give the person who is going to rent that $100,000 unit from me a place that they are going to be very proud of for that price level."

And the way he does that is by making design a high priority. "We don't cut corners on architecture and design—we use the best architects to design our products." Like other developers, Pérez has worked with many of the same architects over and over again. "We have worked with these architects for thirty years and they know the program. So if I say, 'Hey, I am going here, I can get these kinds of rents, now design toward a product I can build,' they know what to do. They understand what sizes the rooms need to be and how the balconies should work—all of that." Although good architects may be more likely to push the envelope on the budget when it comes to design, in the end, says Pérez, "I would rather work with a good design architect and then whittle them down and pull them back on the budget rather than work with a dumb architect and have to say, 'That's ugly.'"

Like Jim Loewenberg, Pérez also has a very particular idea of what "good design" means. And while Loewenberg's story illustrates the importance of staying focused on the product and, more specifically, the unit layout—"where people live"—Pérez offers insights into how building design, interior design, art, landscaping, and "amenities" combine with the unit design to create a complete package with a strong, coherent brand that people identify with, buy into, and then experience as residents. In the past decade Pérez has taken this approach further than many developers, partnering with big brand names from Donald Trump to the industrial designers Philippe Starck and Karim Rashid to create one-of-a-kind, co-branded projects and transform mere buildings into unique and highly marketable designer products. Pérez also uses art and amenities to help differentiate those products beyond basic building design and landscaping.

Great Artists and Museum-Quality Art

Pérez is a passionate collector of art and he brings that passion to each project, integrating art into a building's design and its public spaces. "Whenever I have done a building, particularly in the past ten years, art has been an integral part of the process." And as with interior design, Pérez uses different types of art for different types of buyers. The art in the high-end Apogee condominiums on South Beach is more classical in style, but when Pérez was developing lofts that were designed to appeal to a younger market, he chose to use photography. "We have a fantastic piece that we lent to one building—it is a series of thirty-two 32- by 48-inch color photographs that, when put together, make one big picture of a market in Latin

America and it is filled with the reds of the candles and the yellows of the bananas. It makes the lobby."

Art has become an integral part of Related's marketing program too, and sales agents use it as a selling point in the same way that they use the names of the architects and designers. In recent years Pérez has even had catalogs made for each project that include photos of all of the art pieces and information about each of the artists. A copy of the catalog is given to all homebuyers when they move in. "I put great art in and sometimes it is not easy on the eye or easy to understand but I tell them, 'This guy is in MoMA or some other gallery, he's a rising star,' and the residents become educated. People want to have pride in the place they live and art is a part of it so they buy into the idea that they want good art." Other developers have introduced art into their projects—notably Craig Robins in the Design District—and art has become an increasingly integral part of real estate products in fashion and design-conscious Miami. "Art is important in real estate," says Pérez, "and when you walk around the Design District art is everywhere—the place revolves around the art—and that is good. You also see more art now in Midtown—in the new restaurants—and in Winwood. But I think we have become known as the developers who brought art into buildings in a large-scale way and that was very important to us."

Lastly, although Pérez uses great interior designers, he doesn't let them select the art that goes into his projects—he does that himself. "I pick great artists and I put in museum-quality art by younger, up-and-coming artists and in the end it costs almost the same as those damned framed lithograph prints that the interior designers wanted to put in."

Amenities That Make Living Easier

Finally, Pérez differentiates his projects through the design of the amenities. "Amenities in urban living are extremely important," says Pérez, "because most units being built today in New York City, Chicago, Miami, and elsewhere are smaller than your typical single-family home, so the amenities provide you with what the yard in the single-family home typically offers. When you live in a small unit like that it is very important to be able to get out of your apartment and enjoy open spaces. So we love big pool decks with infinity pools looking at the water or a park or some other feature and great exercise rooms that become a place not only where people exercise but also where they can congregate. We also like movie theaters where people can watch Monday night football or a tennis match—social gathering places."

Related has also focused increasingly on technological amenities that increase convenience like electronic tablets that residents can take with them and use remotely to turn on the air conditioning or the television in their units or just to watch a movie by the pool. "And if you can have a hamburger or a drink served at the pool instead of having to go back into your unit to cook it that is a great amenity. Things that make living easier are extremely important in a busy urban environment." More important, "even if people don't use the amenities as much as they think they will, it is important when they are making the decision to buy, because they visualize themselves with their girlfriend in this great hot tub even if they never really use it."

Knowing Your Buyer

Pérez also knows that good design means different things to different people. "It is very important for me to understand my client and, as with art, in real estate you cannot be so selfish or egocentric to think that everyone is going to like what you like." Pérez took a conservative approach to the design of the Apogee condominiums, in South Beach, which were some of the most expensive condominiums built in Florida when they went on the market, with penthouses starting at $3–4 million and going as high as $20 million. "I knew who the buyers were going to be so we didn't use Philippe Starck. Instead we used a great interior design firm out of Toronto called Yabu Pushelberg and we did a design that was contemporary, classical, very tasteful, and very expensive. The art, the rooms, the community areas, the amenities, and the wine room are all fantastic."

Finally, when Pérez talks about design, he usually means interior design. While he hires award-winning architects to create his building's exteriors, like Jim Loewenberg he also knows that it is where people live that matters, and that is why he focuses on the interior design of the public areas and the amenities.

Putting It All Together with the Icon Brickell

Pérez took this strategy to the limit with the design of his magnum opus, the Icon Brickell, a one-thousand-unit condominium and hotel complex on Brickell Boulevard facing Biscayne Bay. It is a beautiful building and Pérez is rightfully proud of it. "We went all the way doing that—with Arquitectonica, Kelly Wearstler on interiors, and Philippe Starck." Despite the sheer scale of the complex, the elegant designs for the building exteriors combined with rich interiors bring a high level of sophistication to the project, inside and out. But it was international design phenomenon Philippe Starck's contribution that really branded the Icon. His Easter Island–inspired sculptural columns at the entry to the Viceroy, the complex's boutique hotel and spa, have become well-known symbols of the sophistication of the project's exterior design but it was Starck's design for the spa that exemplified Pérez's willingness to push design to the limit.

"We didn't want the spa to be the usual whirlpool and sauna. Instead, we wanted it to be something that you went into and experienced—something really different and interesting. Philippe is great at creating interesting spaces—that's what we wanted and that's what we got." What Pérez got with the 28,000-square-foot Viceroy Spa was a spa like no other. Whirlpools, cold-plunge pools, a sauna, and his and her private treatment rooms are all arranged around a huge, two-story central space that is half modern luxury spa and half stylized period library. Floor to ceiling glass runs along one long wall while the ends of the room each have a fireplace with a large mirror above the mantel and shelves on either side filled with white painted faux books. A living area with period furniture and an oriental rug faces one fireplace, and in the center of the room an enormous chandelier made of yellow glass hangs over a winding "serenity pool." The floor and columns are covered in Carrera marble and the room feels stylish, expensive, and very sophisticated. "Some people may like these designs and some may not," concludes Pérez, "but the level of detail and the standards were very high and Philippe says it was his best work ever."

Adapting to What the Market Gives You

By 2006 Pérez was concerned enough about the condo market to shut down another major project in Las Vegas called Las Ramblas but he chose to move ahead on the Icon Brickell. Unfortunately, the building did not open until late 2009—after the housing bubble had burst—and it remained largely empty in 2010 when Pérez handed the keys back to the lender in a "friendly foreclosure." A 30 percent cut in prices in 2010 led to increased sales, and by 2012, there were only twenty units remaining to be sold, proving that despite unfortunate market timing, Pérez's Icon remained a desirable product.

Like most developers, by 2010 Pérez was frustrated and bored. "Now we are not doing anything. We are acquiring as opposed to developing, unfortunately, because that is not what turns me on." But, as Pérez says in

Figure 30. The Icon Brickell. © Robin Hill; courtesy Arquitectonica.

Figure 31. The rooftop amenity deck at the Icon Brickell and Viceroy Miami.
© Robin Hill; courtesy Arquitectonica.

Figure 32. The Philippe Starck–designed columns at the entry to the Viceroy Hotel and Spa. © Julio Espana; courtesy of Arquitectonica.

his own book, "the way you survive is by adapting to what the market gives you, and what the market is giving us now is a different type of business." Pérez went into acquisition mode because there was a glut of housing stock that was a product of the recession, overfinancing, overdevelopment, and the collapse in real estate prices. When real estate prices fall, investors with cash on hand can buy existing property for less than the cost of building new, which is why Pérez created a vulture fund to buy up distressed condominiums and put new development efforts on hold. "Whenever you are able to buy below replacement costs it makes no sense to build."[18]

In 2010 Pérez saw that the only development possibilities in the near term would be rental apartments. Apartment development virtually stopped during the condo boom but not only was very little new product built during the 2000s, but many older apartment buildings were converted to condominiums, further reducing supply and leading to rising occupancy rates and rents in those apartments that remained. "We are seeing occupancy rates continue to creep up and we are seeing rents that are going to make it worthwhile to build new. And that is what we are going to be doing in the next three years,

Figure 33. The Philippe Stark–designed spa at the Viceroy with a yellow glass chandelier. © Robin Hill; courtesy Arquitectonica.

so we are brushing up with developers who have done that kind of thing and we are actively looking for apartment sites." But Pérez clearly longed to design and build big things again. "These apartments are going to be great projects but they are not going to be the Icon Brickell."

A Value Deal with Great Design

Over the course of a decade, Pérez had licensed the Trump name for two projects and used Starck on the Icon as well as the canceled Las Ramblas project in Las Vegas. He had also come to increasingly value collaboration with big brand names that could help differentiate and promote his products. And by 2010, in the trough of the recession, he was already laying the groundwork for his next co-branding deal—and for getting back into the condominium business.

"There are a lot of pretty standard condominium towers on Brickell and elsewhere in Miami that are modern 'but traditional in their modernism,'" says Pérez, "and even many of mine, while great, are not particularly showy." But the Icon Brickell set a new standard. "The Icon is mindblowing—people said, 'Holy cow, where did you get that chandelier?'" So for his next project Pérez sought to work with what the market had given him while at the same time taking product design to an even higher level. "This next project will be an even wilder design—I wanted something different and this is a brand-new product."

Pérez's newest idea was to use great architecture and design to build high-rise condos that were very low in cost. Since the housing bust, the costs of land and construction had dropped, so rather than the highs of $400 to $600 per square foot during the boom, Pérez thought, "If I can produce a brand-new product for $250 per square foot, I can sell it to South Americans and they want it." Despite a glut of empty condos on the market in Miami—many of which had been dramatically reduced in price and value—Pérez thought that new product would still have appeal. "I am going to tell them, 'For the same $250 per square foot you are going to spend on that old product, if you wait for three years I'll give you a new unit.'"

And once again Pérez lined up a world-class team to design and create the market buzz for his new product. Arquitectonica—the Miami-based designers of the Icon Brickell and many of Pérez's other projects—did the architectural design for the building, and the award-winning, Miami-based Raymond Jungles provided landscape design. Most important, Pérez recruited the world-renowned industrial designer Karim Rashid to design the interiors. "His designs are really cool and really funky, with bright colors like hot pinks and lime greens," said Pérez. "With Karim I am bringing a new designer into the real estate world—he is the new Starck and he is a world-class guy."

But despite the hype, like Jim Loewenberg's Aqua, Pérez's new product is actually pretty straightforward. "The architects will play with the building's exterior envelope to create a very interesting pattern," says Pérez, "but otherwise it is a basic box and there will not be any structured parking, which will help keep the cost down." The units would be small too—for example, a one-thousand-square-foot two-bedroom unit for $250,000 and a seven-hundred-square-foot one-bedroom unit for $150,000—which would also help keep the cost down. They would be marketed to local buyers who were really interested in design and to the younger, middle-class South Americans who wanted apartments or condos in Miami. And Pérez expected to get a lot of bang for the buck from the interior design. "Karim is designing the units, including our own furniture, and there is lots of pink. I told him about art and he is so excited to work with me to find modern pieces that go with what he does. We will open up the market again and our buyers will get amazing design for that price—so it is a value deal with great design. And like we were the first with Starck in Miami, we are doing the same with Karim."

It is a value deal in part because Pérez was able to reduce costs and prices by taking a unique approach to the problem of parking. Related's previous plan for the site included a ten-story structured parking garage but true to Pérez's vision of providing a "value deal with great design," he was able to avoid the cost of building a new parking structure. Instead, he effectively "bought" existing parking at lower than replacement cost by striking a deal with a Related-developed condo next door that had a surplus of parking spaces. Residents would park in the neighboring building under what Related called a "friendly agreement," and that is how Pérez was able to price the units as low as $159,000. Related launched preconstruction sales for the project, mybrickell, a 28-story, 192-unit condominium development, in 2011.

New Financing Structures

Pérez took his first step back into the water by offering a lower-priced condo product with mybrickell, but his confidence grew, and he soon announced a higher-end condominium project targeted at a different type of design aficionado. Rather than using renowned product and graphic designers, the project would feature interior designs by Pininfarina, the famous Italian automobile design house that had given shape to Ferraris, Maseratis, Rolls-Royces, and other luxury supercars since the 1930s. The building design would be by Carlos Ott, an internationally known Uruguayan architect based in Canada who designed two of Miami's largest and most luxurious condominium projects, Jade Beach and Jade Ocean. Millecento is a 42-story, 382-unit condominium with prices starting at $226,000 for studios and going as high as $550,000 for two-bedroom, two-bath units.

Perhaps the most interesting thing about Pérez's two most recent projects is how they will be financed. While the lending community remained uninterested in writing mortgages for new condos even in 2014, Miami is a global city with an economy—and real estate market—that is different from that of the rest of the United States. A gateway to Latin America, Miami is a place where immigrants with cash form a whole separate buying market—which means that absorption can be much quicker than in other

Figure 34. Jorge Pérez (left) and Karim Rashid at the opening of the
mybrickell condominium sales center in 2011. Photo by Andrew Goldstein;
courtesy of the Related Group.

areas of the country. Indeed while Miami was known as the epicenter of
condo overbuilding and rumored to be awash with forty thousand empty
condos in 2007, by 2011 the *Wall Street Journal* had recognized that in
Miami "the condo glut is coming to an end."[19]

Still, obtaining a mortgage for a new condominium remained difficult,
so for both mybrickell and Millecento, Pérez adapted to what the market
gave him and simply required that buyers pay cash in installments at key
milestone dates. For mybrickell, a buyer was required to pay 20 percent at
contract signing, 20 percent at groundbreaking, 20 percent when the tower
reached the halfway point at the twelfth floor, 20 percent at the topping
out of the tower, and 20 percent at closing. Millecento's structure is similar
but with a larger balance—50 percent—due at closing. These financing
structures only work for buyers with the cash to make these significant
payments but apparently there are enough of them for Pérez. By June 2012,
92 percent of the units at Millecento had been reserved while deposits had
been received for 180 of 192 units at mybrickell. Related broke ground on
Millecento in the fall of 2012 and completed construction in the fall of

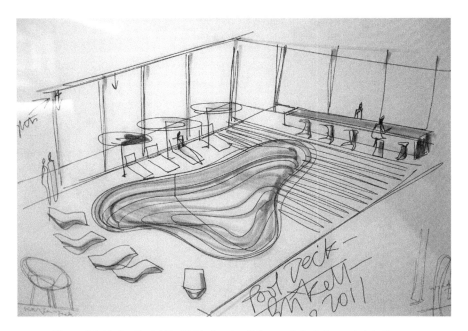

Figure 35. Karim Rashid's 2011 sketch of the pool deck for mybrickell.
Photo by World Red Eye Productions; courtesy of the Related Group.

2014. Mybrickell broke ground in early 2012 and was completed and
opened in January 2014.[20]

Good Design in Different Places

Ed McNamara, Jim Loewenberg, and Jorge Pérez each offer slightly different ideas about what good design is, but at the core, there is more agreement than difference of opinion. All three take an active interest in shaping
their projects, from concept through design and down to the details. They
are all three different, in background and emphasis, and those differences
reflect their professional and personal sensibilities—builder-owner, architect, and planner–art collector. They also develop in three different parts of
the country, which sheds some light on how cultural differences between
regions influence design.

The Pacific Northwest is a hotbed of sustainable design and so it has
become a more integral part of development in Portland than elsewhere in

Figure 36. The grand opening party on the pool deck at mybrickell in 2014. Photo by World Red Eye Productions; courtesy of the Related Group.

the country. Chicago is a large city in a northern climate with long suburban commutes so high-rise living has been an accepted lifestyle for decades, and architects design units there to be lived in. Design in Miami is influenced by fashion, high design, and sex appeal, in part because speculators played such a large role in the condo boom there. Because so few of them actually intended to live in their units, the layouts were less important than the creation of a brand that integrated amenities, lifestyle, and image.

Still, all three developers strive to create products that integrate design and development economics. They are also keenly aware of who their buyers are because, in the end, their products must sell, and to sell they must be marketable. "Marketing is the most important thing," concludes Pérez, "and marketing is creating the perception that you are moving into the greatest thing in the world and you've just got to have it." In the next chapter we will look at how developers create desire for their products and how another Miami developer was able to build a brand around the image of lifestyle as nightlife and, more recently, around the idea of the trophy condominium.

Chapter 6

Selling Real Estate

> People don't really buy the physical real estate. They buy the
> enhancement of their self-image and the benefits they'll derive after they
> take possession.
>
> —Herb Emmerman, Chicago real estate developer and marketing
> consultant[1]

Why We Buy

In the past several chapters we have considered how developers work with
their design teams to give form and shape to real estate development projects. We have looked at how architects, planners, and the general public—
the buyers—each experience buildings differently and how, for the developer, a good design is one that accounts for both project economics and
the tastes and demands of the marketplace. We have also seen how a good
design, from the developer's perspective, is one that is attractive to a lot of
people. This is because the developer knows that to succeed he must make
his project appeal to the broadest cross-section of people possible to maximize the pool of potential tenants or buyers. We have seen that while good
design improves use and function, it also plays an important role in the
sales process. In this chapter we will look more closely at how products are
marketed and sold generally and then we will see how real estate developers
position their products to create interest and excitement and attract potential buyers.

In his book *Where Stuff Comes From: How Toasters, Toilets, Cars, Computers, and Many Other Things Come to Be as They Are*, Harvey Molotch

observes that when it comes to goods, while we think most about their design, production, and consumption, the way they are distributed and sold is also an important and integral part of the experience of enjoying a product. Different types of products lend themselves to different sales media, and products and sales media shape one another to create a total consumer experience. For example, the purpose and use of the kinds of products sold through print media like those Sky Mall catalogs in the seat compartments on commercial airplanes must be made clear to the reader with a short text explanation and one or two illustrations. On the other hand, television, says Molotch, is the best place to sell goods that require a physical demonstration so that the potential buyer can understand how they work, particularly products that use different technologies to get the same results as more traditional products. The most famous examples of these types of products include the famous Veg-O-Matic, Ginsu Knife, and Popiel Pocket Fisherman, of the 1970s and 1980s, and, more recently, the ShamWow. TV can help connect a product with an audience, says Molotch, and some products are even made for TV, where the medium shapes the product. More recently, the web has had a similar influence in shaping goods through online consumer ratings that give producers rapid feedback. And evolving technologies also shape goods as in Apple's iPad, Amazon's Kindle, and Barnes and Noble's Nook, which initiated a massive transformation in the way that books were produced, marketed, licensed, distributed, sold, and read. But while print media, television, and the web have played an increasingly important role in the selling of goods, for some products the best medium remains the experience of shopping in a physical retail environment.[2]

For the successful sale of goods in a retail store or showroom, Molotch says that two things must happen: the first is physical and the second social. First, buyers must have the ability to "get up close" and touch, use, and experience the goods being sold. They must be able to see what it is and what it does. More important, an enjoyable and entertaining sales environment and a well-designed product together must "stimulate the buyer's desire for the product. . . . You must create a physical allure of the product and you must make the environment enjoyable."[3]

The second thing that must be provided is a social context—the enthusiasm of others who make up a common shopping audience. Shoppers and bystanders "can create a specific buzz for one another over the goods." The combination of the physical and the social has always been part of the distribution apparatus. "The commercial spot is the happening place because people seem to rally around goods and enjoy watching others make their choices," reflecting a process that Herbert Blumer, a sociologist interested in fashion and shopping, called "collective selection." Examples of commercial environments that successfully integrate these two crucial aspects of physical and social contact include the coffee shops, general stores, and hair salons that make up our communities—those places between home and work that Ray Oldenburg called "third places." Other third-place shopping environments include high-end boutiques, clothing stores, sporting goods stores, and automobile showrooms.[4]

At a popular level, department stores bring in stunts and attractions to drive retail traffic while elegant showrooms become attractions themselves for the up-market crowd. These attractions, together with collective selection, create what Molotch calls "retail theater." One example is the Apple Store, which provides a complete experience from the ability to easily play with the products and buy them—by letting the salesperson just swipe your credit card on a handheld device—to the nonthreatening "Genius Bar" service, and free herbal tea or hot cocoa, all wrapped in a sophisticated and sleek architectural package.[5]

Like an Apple computer, real estate is a form of "stuff" too, and it is sold in much the same way—through a variety of media from print ads and radio spots to websites, brochures, and a physical sales center. But how do the "middlemen" of real estate sales think about creating a similarly integrated experience and heightening the allure of their own products? There is nothing more personal or emotional than buying a home—a major purchase that many people can relate to—so let us look more closely at how developers think about selling that product type.

The Emotional Stepladder

"Most real estate is a discretionary buy," says Herb Emmerman of EMS/Garrison LLC. "You don't need it—you want it." Emmerman, whom we met in Chapter 4, and his company have been in the business of marketing and selling condominiums in Chicago and throughout the United States for over twenty years. Emmerman and his partner, Garry Benson, have developed real estate themselves—primarily conversions of apartments to condominiums in Chicago—but the mainstay of their business has been providing consulting and sales and marketing services to developers of multifamily, for-sale housing. Their company helps developers conceive of, brand, design, market, and sell a project. And Emmerman has a very personal interest in making sure that the match between product and market is the best that it can be, because the lion's share of his firm's compensation comes from sales commissions, so the product must sell.[6]

"Real estate is a point of purchase sale," says Emmerman, "so buying real estate is very similar to buying a luxury automobile at a showroom." Real estate is also like a luxury automobile because "where you live tells people who you are and if you doubt that," says Emmerman, "ask yourself what you would think if you met someone who lived at Trump Tower. You would make an immediate set of assumptions about that person, their wealth, etc. For this reason, home purchases are all about self-image and self-fulfillment, so when you sell real estate it is a matter of creating heightened desire and enthusiasm: Nobody buys unless they are excited."

When Emmerman trains a new salesperson he first tells him or her that most people have an "emotional stepladder" that they must ascend, that they won't buy until they get to the top, and that the salesperson's job is to help potential buyers make the climb. "Most people start at the bottom rung or even lower because they are fearful of getting a heavy sales treatment. They may have been following the project for three months and are very interested but they don't want pressure, which is why we never ask 'can I help you?' Instead, we start to walk them up that emotional stepladder and we use the views, the amenities, and the model unit to help people imagine themselves living there." Every sales center also has floor plans for each unit type, even though few people can read floor plans. So why have them? "The reason you have plans is that they are another way to keep someone talking and keep them in the sales center so that you can get to know them, because you cannot sell to someone you do not know." Even under the best conditions, people rarely get to the top of the emotional stepladder on the first visit to the sales center, "although," says Emmerman, "younger people can sometimes get there more quickly."

If you don't close in that first meeting, the next step is to obtain some other kind of commitment from the prospect. "For example," says Emmerman, "you might say, 'We only have three of this model left, so would you like to put one under contract?' If the answer is no, you can then say, 'Well, then you can reserve this one for $2,000 while you keep looking around and it is fully refundable.' No? 'Well, then, can you give me an idea of where you are in the process and how long it may take you to decide if you are interested?' No? 'Well, in that case, would you like to make an appointment to come back again in two weeks?' No? 'Can I call you three weeks from Tuesday?' If the answer is still 'no,'" says Emmerman, "then this is probably not a really good prospect."

Emmerman's firm rates all of its prospects from A to D. "An A is a ready, willing, and able buyer and you should be ringing their doorbell every day. A B is able, but either not ready or not willing, at least not yet. A C is able but neither ready nor willing. And, finally, a D is not able, so they are dead and not a real prospect." By the strength of their level of commitment, you can then determine how to pursue various types of prospects, what kinds of materials to give or send to them, how to contact them, and how often.

The first step in this process is when the prospect puts his foot on the bottom rung of that stepladder by walking in the front door of a sales center. The sales center is a carefully constructed environment where skilled salespeople use a variety of props, tools, and media to create and reinforce a brand image while giving people an opportunity to physically experience a product that has not yet been built. The well-designed sales center stimulates Blumer's "collective selection," which, for the right combination of price, product, and location, will help people climb up that stepladder and lead to sales for the developer. But what exactly is the developer selling and to whom?

What Is Our DNA?

"In a perfect world we are introduced to the design process early on," says Jim Losik, a former senior vice president at Herb Emmerman's firm. "That way we can have an influence on unit mix, unit sizes, unit locations, unit design, and the design of common areas and amenities." But the first question, according to Losik, is, "who are we, what are we designing, and what is our DNA? Are we designing a slick, urban loft infill project with small units and concrete countertops that will appeal to first-time homebuyers, or are we creating a more luxury-oriented product for empty nesters?" Once he understands the positioning and the target market, then Losik gets involved with the advertising agency and begins to shape the image of the product. "What is the name of the project going to be? From the name, logo, and colors flows everything else—stationery, business cards, brochures, and other collateral materials, the website design, the overall image of the project, and most important, the sales center."[7]

By the time a potential buyer actually visits a sales center, he has probably already seen color advertisements in newspapers and magazines. He has probably not, however, seen all of the advertisements placed in the many magazines targeted at different markets. So an advertisement in a suburban lifestyle magazine popular with the "empty nester" crowd may show a smiling, good-looking, silver-haired, "active senior" man with his arms wrapped around an attractive younger woman Photoshopped onto a balcony on the thirtieth floor with the premium view of the skyline, the ocean, or whatever view is being sold, in the background. The ad in the alternative lifestyle magazine, of course, will have the same balcony and view except the Photoshopped couple will be two very fit younger men, one with his arm around the shoulder of the other. The buyer may have also heard advertising on the radio, read stories about the project in the newspaper, or even seen stories on television news. Even the music and the voice of the person describing the project on the radio will have been carefully selected. The marketing and sales and public relations team will shape all of these ads and media events so that the message is coherent and that everything that the public experiences—from the key words and phrases to the graphics and colors—consistently represents the product and its brand.

The potential buyer will have also visited the project website that has a variety of information from renderings and view photography to unit plans and square footages, information about amenities, and pricing. But the project website will also have a unique "feel," from graphic effects to custom music and even the voice of the announcer. Creativity increases with competition, and at the peak of the condo boom some projects posted short films and serialized fictional stories on their websites to create buzz. All of these efforts are designed to introduce and reinforce to potential buyers the coherent, integrated, and distinct brand of the project.

Elevating Your Emotions

The sales center is the most important part of the sales process, however, "and of all the sales tools," says Losik, "if I could have only one, I would have a great model unit." This is a life-sized copy of an actual unit that will be in the building. Sales centers have come a long way in the past few years, from a trailer in the middle of a cornfield with a few plans mounted on foam core and some tile and countertop samples. While they vary in cost and quality, the best sales centers can be very expensive—several million dollars and upward—and they are very deliberately designed to help guide you up Emmerman's emotional stepladder.

With a sales center, you are creating a "Disneyland for real estate," says Losik, "where there is a method to the madness, the flow is carefully designed, and nothing is left to chance." First you enter and are greeted in the reception area by a sales agent, but over her shoulder you can see the scale model of the project. The model is in its own special area or room with windows so that it can also be seen from the street. It rests on a beautiful wooden base and is surrounded by a thick glass case held together at the corners with fancy stainless steel fasteners. The model is populated with little people, cars, and trees, and it lights up on the inside. It looks very realistic—and expensive. The scale of the model is chosen to ensure that it will be taller than the average person—it should feel big. The room is wallpapered with stunning view photography and spotlights shine on the model so that it looks unique and valuable, like a piece of art.

While architects often prefer monochromatic models in white, gray, or simple woods that highlight the abstract ideas and the massing and proportions of their designs, these rarely resonate with nonprofessionals. Developers know that potential buyers need something more realistic and representative that clearly illustrates the arrangement of the site and buildings, as well as scale, colors, and materials. "I am a lawyer by trade," says Cathy Tinker, a model builder in Chicago, "and I don't know what a model is supposed to be so I just make a good marketing tool. I make the development look like something that is going to appeal to people, so people will want to live there." Which is exactly what Tinker's developer clients want her to do. Tinker's models are very realistic considering that they are small-scale representations of much larger buildings. She uses sophisticated machines, processes, materials, and painting techniques to give the impression of brick, concrete, glass, metal, grass, and trees. "And we make them light up. . . . Architects, particularly if they are really well regarded, say that our models are 'cute' and they don't want a 'cute' model, of course, because 'cute' is derogatory. They would rather see a model painted all white that focuses on the form of their building and they usually don't want their models to light up. But the developers we work for have a much better idea of what is going to sell so we try to make sales tools that are absolutely beautiful three-dimensional representations, more like dollhouses, like a Disney World thing." Finally, Tinker points out that her models serve another important function in the sales center—that of Blumer's collective

Figure 37. A sales center with a light-up scale model of a high-rise condominium tower surrounded by lifestyle photos. Photo by author.

selection. "They help to engage people, so you can talk about the model and then work into talking about buying the property. And if you have a mobbed sales center people can spend some time looking at and enjoying the model until a sales person can get to them. Our models just create a wow factor when you walk into the sales center."[8]

As the sales agent walks around the scale model with you, she will describe the product, using a laser pointer to show you where the entrance lobby is, where the amenities are, where the parking is, and where the various unit types are. She will also ask how you learned about the project, where you live now, when you are thinking of moving, what type of home you are looking for, what is important to you in a home, whether you think you are interested in a two-bedroom or a one-bedroom plus den, and how much you can afford. "The point," says Losik, "is that they are not just chatting with you, they are also carefully prequalifying you." So when the agent takes you over to the unit floor plans, she does not show all twelve of them to you; she just shows you the two or three that she has prequalified you for. Then she talks to you about the unique features of your unit, the layout of the rooms, the finishes, and the prices. You begin to look around and take in displays on the walls that illustrate the building's amenities and offer lifestyle photographs of liveried doormen, good-looking couples shopping at the local farmer's market or laughing on a balcony, and fit men and women working out in a fitness center. You may also visit a touch-screen kiosk that allows you to call up actual panoramic aerial photographic views from the different unit floor plans and from different floor levels. By now you may have noticed that the whole sales center and everything in it is designed to reflect "the DNA" of the project, so that the style of the furnishings and the colors and finishes all correspond with the brochures and letterhead, the website, the colors of the building materials, and even the design of the building itself. Like an Apple Store, the purpose of the sales center is to immerse the buyer in a potential lifestyle experience and help him to imagine how much better his life will be after he purchases the product.

If you have come for the "grand opening," the sales center will be crowded and you may have to take a number and wait your turn to meet with a sales agent. The sales agent may be wearing a headset so that she can receive instructions from the sales manager in the back office or she may be carrying an electronic tablet from which she can place your order in real time so that you do not miss out on the unit you want. "The headset and the tablet really do work," says Emmerman, "but they aren't all that important to the efficiency of the sales transactions. Rather, they are props that help to enhance the project's image, create an atmosphere of sophisticated commerce, and heighten the buyer's perception of urgency. They get the buyer thinking, 'If they are wearing headsets and carrying the electronic tablets, then this is serious and I better buy unit #504 before that guy over there does.'"

While you are milling around, you may notice that there are a lot of people trying to buy units and you may get concerned that if you don't place your order fast enough then your unit will be sold to someone else or its price will increase while you are waiting. You may then notice an illuminated diagram of the building that shows all of the units with little pegs in little holes under the unit numbers—and you may notice that a lot of the units have already been reserved or sold. You will begin to feel a sense of "urgency" and you will fear that if you do not buy you will be missing out on something that everyone else around you has figured out—and nobody wants to be a sucker. If the developer's marketing and sales team has done a good job of designing this experience then your emotions should be very elevated by now—you are ascending Emmerman's stepladder.

Then, the agent walks you around the corner and into the model unit. This is an exact copy of one of the larger typical units in the building, so that while it may not be affordable by all buyers, it is just one or two steps up from what a typical unit—your unit—will be like. It is also a corner unit so there are lots of windows and just behind the windows are backlit, full-height, full-length transparent prints of aerial photography taken from the roof of the building next door or from a helicopter or a small remote-control blimp. The views in the living room are daytime, with a clear blue sky and bright green grass or fall foliage far below, and the bedroom views are taken at dusk or at night and show a magnificent cityscape of lights. The interior design work in the model unit is perfect, from the sleek kitchen appliances, cabinets, and lighting to the exotic lavatory basins and faucets in the bathrooms. The furnishing of the unit is complete, from the high-quality original art to the books on the shelves in the den, the place settings on the dining room table, the wine in the glass-front wine cooler, the fake flowers in vases, the bric-a-brac and expensive art books that grace the coffee table, and even the photos of the grandkids of the fictitious empty nesters who live there that line the walls of the study.

"When the sales agent walks you into the drop-dead gorgeous model unit with backlit nighttime views from the thirty-fifth floor," says Losik, "your emotions get elevated, and you start to think: 'Man, oh, man, this is cool. I could live here. Maybe not in this exact unit—it is kind of expensive—but some of the floor plans will work for me. I can move out of my crummy apartment and into this cool place. I can see it now. I can see the kitchen, I can see the finishes, I can see the views, and I can see my life getting a lot better.' Then," says Losik, "you walk them out of the model unit and into your sales office and say, 'Sign here, please.'"

A buyer usually will not sign the first time he visits a sales center but Emmerman and Losik help explain how a carefully created brand experience can create urgency, elevate a person's emotions, and cause someone to make a significant purchase that is purely discretionary. And if sales agents do their jobs really well, they elevate a lot of people's emotions at

Figure 38. The author standing in the living room of a model condominium unit with backlit photographic transparencies showing views from the thirtieth floor. This model unit was located in a temporary, one-story sales center building in the parking lot on the building site. Photo by Silas Crews.

the same time to create Blumer's collective selection, leading to what real estate developers call "sales velocity."

Not all developers and sales teams take an approach that is as conscious, deliberate, or sophisticated as the one that Emmerman and Losik describe but they do all share the same objective, which is to heighten a person's emotions and cause him or her to make a major discretionary purchase. The market for commercial office space is different from multifamily housing but the sales process is not. Sales centers for new high-rise office towers use the same methods and technologies as those for condominiums—scale models, aerial views, lifestyle photography, model interior spaces, and video monitors with testimonials. The purpose is also the same—to create a sense of brand and to elevate the emotions of the prospective buyer or tenant. A developer of commercial office space is usually seeking a major anchor tenant or two and then, once those leases have been signed and publicly announced, to create excitement and sales velocity around those tenants and then backfill the rest of the building with smaller tenants. As with condos, the developer hopes to appeal to the egos and aspirations of corporate CEOs who want the best new address—and image—for their headquarters. The marketing and sales programs for retail spaces and industrial warehouses are more routine than for a class A office, but for all product types, the goal is to get the potential buyer or tenant excited about your property. Still, purchasing a home is much more emotional than renting an apartment or leasing office, retail, or industrial space. In the next section we will consider an extraordinary story of how one creative developer in Miami identified a market niche, designed a new product, and then elevated the emotions of his potential buyers to the point of causing a real estate feeding frenzy.

Selling Real Assets to Real Buyers with Real Wealth

In 2003 real estate values in Miami were about to explode. Miami Beach was where all the action was but downtown Miami, on the mainland, was still unpopular, and Biscayne Boulevard, which runs along the edge of Biscayne Bay in downtown Miami, was nothing but parking lots and the Freedom Tower. Hank Sopher, the owner of Kwik-Park, owned most of the parking lots and he also owned an old, boarded-up Howard Johnson's on Biscayne Boulevard, just south of I-395, one of the causeways that spans Biscayne Bay, connecting the mainland and Miami Beach to the east. A thirty-three-year-old developer named Gregg Covin who had three or four successful projects under his belt got Sopher to let him up onto the roof. A young architect named Chad Oppenheim accompanied Covin. He had designed Covin's latest project, an eighty-unit, five-story condominium in Miami Beach that had been a big success. A rising star on Miami's architectural scene, Oppenheim was champing at the bit to add a high-rise to his design portfolio. "When we saw the view we said, 'Wow, this is the best view in the whole city,'" remembers Covin. "You could see straight out through government cut—the main shipping channel—and you could see the cruise ships, the port, and the lights of South Beach. It was incredible. So we went back downstairs and said, 'Hank, we want to buy the hotel.'"[9]

Maybe I Am a Developer

During World War II, before being deployed overseas, both of Gregg Covin's grandfathers, Sol Brown and Michael Covin, were posted in Miami

Beach, where the military had taken over all of the Art Deco–style South Beach hotels to billet troops. Michael Covin was an army cook and Brown served with the Seabees—the militarized construction force of the U.S. Navy that built advance bases, often under withering fire. They did not know each other at the time, but both were from New York City and after the war they each returned home, took a quick look around, and then, like many other GIs who had been posted in Miami Beach, moved back permanently.

Michael Covin took advantage of the 1 percent mortgage program offered as a part of the GI Bill and bought a house in North Miami Beach. He lived on the Isle of Normandy, where the street names included Marseilles Drive, Calais Drive, Biarritz Drive, and Rue Vendome, all in honor of D-Day. He began a construction business and started building duplexes and multiplexes in North Miami Beach and then he built five or six two- and three-story hotels around South Beach. This was after World War II so these hotels were not in the Art Deco style of the 1930s and 1940s but rather the midcentury Miami Modern, or "Mi-Mo," style. Gregg Covin was born in 1970 and when he was growing up he spent a lot of time working with his grandfather on construction sites, building single-family homes in places like Pinecrest, in South Dade County.

In 1985, when Gregg Covin was fourteen, his father passed away and he began to assume more responsibility at home, helping to take care of his father's estate and his mother and little brother. After high school, in 1988, Covin enrolled at Tulane University in New Orleans but he came home after a year. "I partied too much—a lot of people only attend Tulane for a year." He spent his first summer back in Miami, in 1989, working as a stockbroker for Drexel Burnham Lambert, cold-calling people and trying to sell them stocks. "Being a stockbroker sounded like a good idea at the time," recalls Covin, "but it was the worst." At the end of the summer he enrolled at the University of Miami. "I had no idea what I was going to do and after switching around between business and English I ended up majoring in fiction and nonfiction writing, and now I am a developer, of course." But not long after starting at the University of Miami in 1989, Covin's grandfather Michael began to show early signs of Alzheimer's disease and had to stop working. Covin had to step in again and learn finance to sort out his grandparent's personal affairs. His grandfather was forgetting things, paying bills twice, and "it was just a mess." His grandfather passed away a couple of years later and Covin found himself responsible for his whole family—his mom, little brother, and now his grandmother. He never did finish college.

But one day, before he left college for good, Covin was sitting around his fraternity house at the University of Miami, talking to a guy whose father had hosted a radio show about real estate. "I was talking about how I wanted to buy some real estate and the guy said, 'It is crazy for you to buy anything retail—there is this new thing called the RTC [the Resolution Trust Corporation, created after the savings and loan crisis in 1987], which is selling off all of these foreclosed properties for pennies on the dollar.'" He helped connect Covin with a realtor, and Covin started buying apartments around the University of Miami. He rented each of them out for $900 a month to students, made some money, and then sold all of them and thought "this is great!"

Covin also wanted to buy his own home in Coconut Grove, the Miami suburb where he had grown up. He was a young, single college student and he wanted a cool, modern place but there was nothing to be found. It took months of digging and working with a realtor before he finally found a townhome development designed by the architect Robert Altman called Apogee. "It was way ahead of its time and unlike anything else," remembers Covin, "and my friends would come over and just be amazed at how cool it was."

After leaving college, Covin started working for a friend's father who was a contractor building custom homes in Coconut Grove. He started taking construction courses at the same time and soon earned his contractor's license. "Then my friend's father built a house on spec and sold it," says Covin, "and then he built another on spec and sold it, and I thought 'I want to do that—maybe I am a developer.'"

Were They Shooting at You?

In just a few years Gregg Covin had learned three things that would shape his career. First, he learned from his apartment experience that a well-timed purchase would increase his wealth and that, as some developers like to say, you make your money when you buy. Second, he realized that he could use his increased wealth to develop and build his own projects. And, third, he was confident that he could succeed by serving a market that he knew, and he knew from his own search that there were very few cool, modern homes in Coconut Grove.

So in 1991 he bought two dilapidated houses in Coconut Grove, knocked them down, and built a complex of six detached townhouses. He hired an architect named Greg Neville to design the "Richard Meier knock-off" styled homes and they called the complex Atrium in the Grove. "I did everything and my little brother helped," said Covin. "I did all the permitting, all the drywall, laid all of the tile, and built the whole thing myself. It seemed like it took forever," said Covin, "and it didn't really make a lot of money but they were a big hit—nobody else was doing anything like it." Covin remembers that "other builders were asking me why I was doing what I was doing—they told me I was crazy and was giving too much away and leaving money on the table by doing expensive, double-height living room spaces, but I didn't care. I wanted the project to be so nice that I wouldn't have any problem selling it, and I didn't—I sold four to South Americans, one to a European, and one to a guy from New York City."

While he was building Atrium in the Grove, Covin remembers coming home and complaining to his other grandfather, Sol Brown, the former Seabee, about construction problems only to have him say, "Were they shooting at you?" Covin would say, "My plumber didn't show up today," and his grandfather would say, "Did somebody shoot him? No? Then what are you complaining about?" Covin points out that the Seabee logo is a grimacing, six-armed bumblebee in a Navy uniform swooping down with hammer, wrench, and blazing Thompson submachine gun. Covin's view of real estate development was becoming that of a builder rather than an investor, and both of his grandfathers had taught him how to keep the uncertainties of construction and other challenges in perspective.

South Beach Was Starting to Become Cool

Until the 1990s, recalls Covin, "Miami Beach was gross, dangerous, and filled with crack heads—you could get killed on Ocean Drive. Back then everyone went to Coconut Grove to party, but then nightclubs started springing up here and there and soon everyone started to come to South Beach. The social scene started to play up the celebrities and people like Sylvester Stallone and O. J. Simpson used to hang out there. This woman started throwing all of these parties and then suddenly there were all of these famous people in South Beach. Around the same time, developers Chris Blackwell, Tony Goldman, and Craig Robins started buying up and renovating old Art Deco hotels on Ocean Drive and South Beach was starting to become cool."

In the same way that his own search for a home had helped him spot an opportunity to develop a new style of housing in Coconut Grove, the young and single Covin saw how nightlife—and the people who followed it—was shifting away from Coconut Grove toward South Beach. Sensing opportunity, in 1996 he bought a vacant piece of land at 360 Collins Avenue, at the southwest corner of 4th Street in South Beach, and hired Greg Neville again to design a small condominium project. The first plan was for a U-shaped building with parking in the courtyard in the middle. Covin and Neville took their plans to the city of Miami Beach for review, where they met with Tom Mooney, the head of design review, and William Cary, the director of historic preservation. "They gave us a big lecture," recalls Covin, "about how we were in a historic district where all buildings have a lobby in front, a center corridor, no exposed parking, and that since this was a corner lot at the gateway to South Beach, we would have to emphasize that corner. They basically kicked us out and my head was spinning—in the other places like Coconut Grove I had just brought in the plans and received my approval so this was new." Covin and Neville went back and redesigned the building with the parking off the alley and concealed beneath the building and a four-story, curved, galvanized metal façade at the corner of Collins and 4th. When they went back, Mooney and Cary liked the new design, and Covin and Neville got their approval.

They called the project Neville Lofts and the twelve two-bedroom condos sold for about $200,000 each. Covin hired a real estate broker named Jeff Morr to sell it and it was one of Morr's first contracts for a new construction project. Morr and his company, Majestic Properties, sold that project and went on to become big and very successful, selling many large new condo projects on South Beach and in Miami. Completed in 2000, Neville Lofts sold out fast and made money. At the time, the Related Group's huge Portofino Tower was also starting to come out of the ground just a few blocks away and the area was starting to turn around. But in addition to his good timing, Covin was proud that Neville Lofts was one of the first high-quality new buildings on South Beach. "The better contractors all worked on Brickell in Miami or in Coconut Grove so finish quality was terrible and until my project there were no smooth walls anywhere on South Beach."

Hotels Are In and This Should Be a Hotel

In 1997, a year after buying the land at 360 Collins Avenue for Neville Lofts, Covin decided to buy the old Hotel St. Augustine, just behind the Neville, at 317 Washington Avenue. He had only done new construction before and had never renovated a building, "so this was a whole new experience." When Covin first went to see the St. Augustine, "it was a gutted crack house with homeless people living in it." At the time, all hotels were still "flag" hotels—Marriott, Radisson, Sheraton, Hyatt, Hilton, and so on—but Ian Schrager of Studio 54 fame had just opened the newly renovated, Philippe Starck–designed Delano Hotel on Washington Avenue in South Beach. This kicked off the boutique hotel movement and soon another boutique hotel, the Hotel Astor, opened up nearby. Covin talked to his sister-in-law, who worked in the hotel business, and decided, "Cool—hotels are in and this should be a hotel." He hired two high-end interior designers: Peter Paige and Patrick Kennedy, who had just finished another hotel called the Saga-more. "This was the first time I ever worked with high-end designers," says Covin, "and I learned more than ever before."

Covin financed the St. Augustine with a construction loan from a bank and used the money he had made from the Neville as equity, but unforeseen conditions increased his costs and he ran out of funds before construction was complete. "One day, I was talking to Jeff Morr," said Covin, "and I said, 'I'm out of money, workers are walking off the job, what do I do?'" Morr gave Covin the names of two "private lenders." Covin had never heard the term before but Morr told him they are like banks except they were basically very wealthy individuals. Covin called the first one, Brian Gaines, who liked the project, so he came in and paid off the bank's first mortgage and loaned Covin the rest of the money he needed to finish the project at 15 percent. He has been a partner in every project Covin has done since. "One important thing I learned doing the St. Augustine," says Covin, "is that I would always prefer to have an extremely wealthy investor partner. That way, if I go over budget or run out of money, I can go back to my partner and get more. The worst thing that can happen is that he will squeeze me down on my share of ownership but the project still gets completed and I don't have to go through foreclosure with the bank. You will never hear about me going through foreclosure proceedings."

Covin paid $650,000 for the St. Augustine in 1997, put $1 million more into it, sold it in February 2000 for $3.5 million, and made $1.5 million for his efforts. "That was my big deal. Prior to the St. Augustine I was living like a college student but now I had finished three successful projects, including Atrium in the Grove and the Neville, and when I sold the St. Augustine, I was, like, 'now I am retired.'" But Covin wasn't really ready to retire—he was just getting started.

I Want to Do a High-Rise

When Gregg Covin was younger, his mother used to talk about how as a little girl she had to wear fancy gloves to go shopping on Lincoln Road, the old east-west commercial street in Miami Beach that was built by Miami's first big developer, Carl Fisher, in the 1920s. By the time Covin was a teenager, however, Lincoln Road was in steep decline and it was "horrible, abandoned, and ruled by skateboarders—it was all you could do to try not to get in a fight with gangs." Lincoln Road has come back since the 1980s and by the 2000s it was home to some of the most valuable commercial real estate in the world and all of the most expensive stores, which paid some of the highest rents in the country. Covin had done the two projects south of 5th Street and had seen how shopping had become popular there, so in 2001, after he sold the St. Augustine, he decided that he wanted to do something near Lincoln Road. He found a vacant parcel just a block away, at 17th and Meridian that was owned by a big real estate investment trust (REIT). Covin had a realtor friend call to find out about it, only to learn that the REIT also owned a big building across the street and wanted to sell the two properties as a package. But two years later, in 2003, the city had bought the building and the vacant lot was still available so Covin had his realtor friend call again and this time the REIT agreed to sell. "So I quickly got it under contract." The property was actually three adjacent parcels, with the old, Art Deco–style Montclair Hotel in the center, sandwiched in between two empty lots.

Covin started telling people that he had the site under control, "and a little buzz started because it was such a great site, 'at the corner of Main and Main.'" Soon, Alan Lieberman, the other private lender whom Covin had called when he was looking for cash to finish the St. Augustine, contacted him. Lieberman had not financed any of Covin's previous projects but he had watched him successfully complete the Neville Lofts and the Hotel St. Augustine and had become interested in working with him. Covin had modest plans for converting the old Montclair Hotel into condos and building something similar with low-scale additions next door on the two adjacent parcels. But Lieberman met him in his Bentley and said, "Let's do something big—I'll sign for it." When Covin reviewed Lieberman's financials he realized just how wealthy he really was. "So when I went to Mellon Bank with Lieberman's personal guarantee and said 'I want to borrow $12 million,' the bank said 'done' and I was instantly approved."

One of the people who worked with Lieberman suggested to Covin that he hire Chad Oppenheim to do the design work because he was "the hot new guy." Covin met with him and said, "Chad had a bunch of renderings out there, like all the other architects, but Chad's were the coolest so I picked him even though he had never delivered anything this big before." In addition to nightlife, South Beach was increasingly becoming a place known for style, arts, culture, fashion, and design, and although Oppenheim was relatively untested, Covin and Lieberman both knew that Oppenheim's reputation as an emerging talent would raise the profile of the project and increase its value. Having successfully completed his three previous projects, Covin was also confident that he could augment Oppenheim's experience with his own.

Covin and Oppenheim worked together with the city and came up with a design that allowed them to keep the old hotel's façade and tear down the rest of the building and build three new five-story additions of eighty thousand square feet wrapping around the old façade. This created 80 lofts, each averaging 1,100 square feet, all with ten-foot ceilings. The project was completed in 2005 and sold out fast.

By 2003, Covin had built a niche doing successful low-rise and midrise projects on Miami Beach and he was thinking, "I'm not going to do anything too big, I'll just stay in my niche, but then Chad started in with 'I want to do a high-rise.'" Covin and Oppenheim enjoyed working together on the Montclair and had become friends, and Oppenheim's father-in-law, Armin Mattli, was the wealthy owner of a Swiss cosmetics company called La Prairie. "So Chad said, 'My father-in-law is going to back us on a project and we want to use you because you are the only guy in the town who seems to get it and to get things done.'"

Everyone Thought We Were Nuts

When Covin and Oppenheim came down from the roof of the Howard Johnson's and told Hank Sopher that they wanted to buy it, Sopher said the price was $10 million. Covin offered $8 million but then Sopher said, "Look, don't buy the Howard Johnson's, I'll sell you the parking lot next door instead for $6 million." Covin wrote him a check for $20,000 on the spot. It was 2003 and the condo boom was just taking off, but with a difficult regulatory environment and few large sites left, development opportunities on South Beach were limited. Downtown Miami, however, was

Figure 39. Gregg Covin and Chad Oppenheim's high-rise, Ten Museum Park. Photo by Totus Photography; courtesy Oppenheim Architecture + Design.

virtually unregulated, had lots of underutilized land along Biscayne Boulevard, and was the only place left to develop condominium projects on the waterfront. Covin was certain that his site would be perfect for a high-design, high-rise condominium tower that offered views and amenities like no other.

Next, Covin and Oppenheim assembled a team of investors. Covin got his own investors together and they came up with half the equity while Oppenheim's father-in-law put up the other half. "Everyone thought we were nuts," recalls Covin. "There was nothing but crack heads on Biscayne Boulevard but we went ahead and designed the building and then built an awesome million-dollar sales center—you couldn't even tell it was a trailer. Next," says Covin, "I sent a woman who worked for me up in one of those little helicopters and had her hang outside and take pictures, and we printed an amazing fifteen-foot-high picture, made a wrap, and put it on the exterior wall of the sales center." Even Jorge Pérez from the Related Group came and said, "Wow, what an amazing sales center!" Covin settled on a lifestyle theme for the project and since a cosmetics company was investing, the team decided to incorporate a Clinique La Prairie spa into the building as a major amenity. The second only in the world—the other is in Montreux, Switzerland—this luxury spa would fill two floors of the building and offer a variety of services and facilities including a wellness center, cabins for VIPs, massages, beauty care, thalasso facilities, a "hammam" room or Turkish bath, six swimming pools, a "sky garden," and even a room where snowflakes fell from the ceiling. Then Covin decided to do something no one else had ever done before and redefine lifestyle as "nightlife"—and access to celebrities.

A Big Party

Covin remembers his grandmother telling him about a time on Miami Beach in the 1940s and 1950s when every weekend there was an opening party for a new hotel. This time around, the only difference was that the product was condos, competition was increasing, and each party was glitzier than the last. And in Miami, where nightlife, glamour, and spectacle are everything, Covin knew he had to do something extraordinary if he was going to successfully promote and sell the development he was calling Ten Museum Park.

So he called on an old friend, Michael Capponi, to help. "Michael is famous in Miami now," says Covin, "but I knew him when he was a young

surfer." In blighted and vacant South Beach in the 1980s, Capponi promoted a series of roving parties that were held in a different place every
weekend—a vacant hotel, theater, or retail space. The reason was to avoid
police and regulatory authorities and the only way to find out where the
next party was going to be was to call an unlisted phone number. But these
subversive "Avenue A parties" attracted huge crowds, including rich locals
and celebrities, and began to cement Miami Beach's reputation as the place
to go to party. Capponi became a fixture in the Miami Beach nightlife and
club scene and as celebrity partying became the trademark of Miami Beach
nightlife, he also became the go-to guy whom all of the celebrities from
Madonna to Lil Jon would contact before coming into town. No one had
ever promoted real estate with nightlife as an amenity before, but Covin
knew that all the real estate agents and brokers went to Capponi's parties,
so Covin made him a codeveloper and "ambassador of residential services."
Capponi's first job would be to plan a grand opening party like nothing
anyone had ever seen before.

"The first thing I asked Michael," says Covin, "was 'How are we going
to get all of your A-list celebrity people from South Beach to come to
Miami for our launch party?' At first he said, 'No way—nobody goes to
Miami,' but I pushed and finally Michael had an idea. 'Listen,' he said, 'Joe
Francis—the guy who owns *Girls Gone Wild*—is coming to Miami to party
for his birthday and all of these celebrities follow him around because he's
got real money and a jet. If you pay for his birthday party on Saturday
night, I'll get him to come in on Friday night and bring all of his celebrities
to your party.'" Covin immediately agreed to pay $20,000 to $30,000 for a
birthday party, including all of the food, alcohol, and decorations, for Francis at Opium, a nightclub in South Beach.

Then Covin and his team began to plan their own event, the grand
opening for Ten Museum Park, which they billed as a giant party to cele-
brate the rebirth of downtown Miami on the night before Francis's birthday
party. Covin got permission from the City of Miami to hold the party in a
park across the street from the site of the project and he spent $200,000 to
rent a huge, clear tent and to hire caterers. "I even hired an acrobatic troupe
from Cirque de Soleil," said Covin, "and they were all swinging from
ropes." Michael Capponi invited so many people that three or four thousand showed up at the party, "and then Joe Francis arrived in a stretch
Hummer limo and he's got with him Ashton Kutcher, Tara Reid, Andy
Dick, Mario Lopez, just a whole slew of A-listers." Local celebrities came

too, and even Donatella Versace was there. "Miami's mayor, Manny Diaz, was there," recalls Covin, "and at one point he was saying to me, 'Is that Ashton Kutcher over there?'" It was just a huge hit of a party, recalls Covin, "and everyone was wondering, 'How can all of these people be in downtown Miami, which is so dilapidated, and what are all these celebrities doing here?'

"Next," says Covin, "I hired three supermodels and one good-looking gay guy and said, 'Now you are all real estate sales agents,' and a month later, on January 6, 2004, we opened the sales center. We sold out the whole building in nine days—200 units, $150 million of inventory, and $28 million in deposits," recalls Covin. "People were camping out in front of the sales center, fighting to get in, and fighting over units—it was crazy." Ten Museum Park actually sold out in eight days. Covin and his sales team had to close the sales center for one day in the middle because they had been overwhelmed with cash deposits. Miami is the gateway to the south, and Latin Americans drive much of the city's economy by buying homes and stashing cash as a hedge against coups and political instability. "The joke around here," said one high-end Miami condo salesman named Philip Spiegelman, "is that every time Venezuelan president Hugo Chavez opens his mouth, we sell more condos. He should be our salesman of the year."[10] Covin's problem was that he was accepting 5 percent to 10 percent deposits for his condos but so many people paid in cash that he had to lock the doors and call in his comptroller from the Hotel St. Augustine and some other friends to help count all of the money. "People were banging on the door and screaming while we were in the back room running cash through counting machines all day long," said Covin. "It was like a scene out of the movie *Scarface*."

Covin says that he was the one who started the downtown Miami condo boom and that within thirty days of his grand opening virtually all of the other vacant parcels on Biscayne Boulevard in downtown Miami changed hands as "Hank Sopher sold all of his parking lots." At thirty-three, Covin was a lot younger than most of his competitors in Miami, many of whom were fifty or older and had more experience, so while other developers began to plan large, high-density projects with as many as five hundred units, Covin kept his ego in check and stuck to two hundred. His reasoning was simple: in the City of Miami, for two hundred or fewer units a developer must obtain a Class 2 Permit, which takes only about sixty days. "My four-year-old daughter can walk in and get a Class 2 Permit," says Covin.

Figure 40. The thin, elegant, two-hundred-unit Ten Museum Park, with larger buildings that required MUSPs on either side. Photo by Robin Hill; courtesy Oppenheim Architecture + Design.

But for a project with more than two hundred units a developer is required to obtain a Major Use Special Permit (MUSP), which can take a year or more. "I didn't want to do a high-rise in the first place and now I was getting sucked into this," recalls Covin. "So while everyone else got a MUSP for five hundred units on Biscayne Boulevard, I said, 'Give me my two hundred units and I am out of here.' We were already ahead of our competition when we opened, but that decision really helped us to beat everyone to the market and close most of our units before the bubble burst."

It took two years to build Ten Museum Park and it was completed in early 2007. By then Covin was becoming concerned about the condo market. "I could really see the writing on the wall and I had to really, really massage it to get it closed." From the beginning, Covin had a resale program and his agents were constantly flipping units for a 6 percent commission each time. The original buyers—those who bought units in those first nine days after the sales center opened—were allowed to sell their units before they were even completed. Many units were resold four or five times to new buyers before construction was finished but the prices were getting bid way up and Covin had to tell his sales staff, "Slow down, there is no way that guy will ever be able to close for a million dollars." As construction was nearing completion, Covin's team was finally able to get rid of most of the investor flippers but then the market began to turn and people started coming in and saying that they couldn't close, "so we worked with as many as we could, moving them into cheaper units." By the time the financial crisis hit in the fall of 2008, 196 of the 200 units had closed. In 2010 the developers handed over the condo association to the residents and were finishing up the warranty work. The association sued over a number of small things but the developers had kept a reserve and were able to settle with the association. In the end, the project made $30 million and Covin earned 8 percent, or $2.4 million. But since the bubble had burst there were no more condos to be built.

Everything Is Different This Time

Throughout 2009 Covin sat around thinking about what to do next, and finally he decided to get into the senior housing business. He had a passion for Alzheimer's and dementia care because of the experience he had with his grandfather. "Nursing homes are crummy," says Covin, "but the worst part is the dementia wing—you go through that door and it is the worst part of the facility."

In 2010, Covin bought a building from Broward County that had been a drug-rehab facility, gutted it, and renovated it into a one-hundred-bed assisted living facility that specialized in Alzheimer's care. "As a developer," says Covin, "I have to follow the money, and there was money out there for health care. I was able to use Obama dollars to fund the construction by using an SBA [federal Small Business Administration] guarantee to get a small bank in Dade to give me a construction loan and Medicaid basically pays all of the costs. So federal money paid for the construction, and Medicaid pays the revenues. On average, Medicaid is $1,800 a month plus $600 in social security so $2,400 a month gets a resident three square meals and two snacks."

But the building type was also a perfect fit for Covin's background because in many ways assisted living facilities are very similar to the hotels he had done on South Beach. "They both have little rooms with little counters," says Covin, "except instead of a bartender there is a nurse and instead of a liquor license I had to apply for a Medicare license." Covin hired the interior designer who did Hyatt Classic Residences—Hyatt's senior living product—to design his facility like a little boutique hotel and then he hired a management company to run it. "My product is so different and so attractive because no one had done it this way before and it has been full since it opened. So that's what I'm doing now," said Covin in 2010, "and while it is not as exciting as condos, it is more stable."

But then the market began to return and by 2013 Covin had made a bigger plan than he had ever made before—for a much bigger condo tower on Biscayne Boulevard. The area had changed a lot in ten years. "Downtown Miami was dilapidated when we started Ten Museum Park, but now it is the financial and cultural capital of Latin America," says Covin. And he had learned a lot from Ten Museum Park so he brought a whole new attitude and a very different approach to this new project. "When we did Ten Museum Park it was all about parties, creating a frenzy, and flipping units. We were selling for 5 percent down and the buyers were not real—they never intended to live there. We barely completed and closed before the market really turned and while it was a success that was not a good model and in retrospect I would never do it that way again."

Even if he wanted to, he could not do it that way in 2013 because there was no construction financing available for condominiums in Miami. So like Jorge Pérez, in the previous chapter, Covin's latest project would be sold to buyers who had the wealth to pay cash for their units. Not only was the financing different, but so too were the buyers, the units, and the architect. Covin took the trend of hiring famous "starchitects" to a new level by hiring Pritzker Prize–winning architect Zaha Hadid. Then he had Hadid design the project—1000 Museum—for very wealthy buyers who could afford large, expensive units. The building would be sixty-two stories when it was completed. Most of the eighty-three units were full floors and there were some half-floor units. The smallest unit in the building was huge at 4,600 square feet, and the lowest-priced unit cost $5 million. Buyers would pay cash in installments at key milestones, including contract, groundbreaking, topping off, and closing. And despite the high prices, by February 2014, nearly half the building was sold and Covin was making plans to break ground.

"Everything is different this time," says Covin. "These are condos for real buyers with real wealth who can afford to pay for larger, more expensive, higher-quality units. They are investing in a trophy condo designed by

Figure 41. Event for the opening of the 1000 Museum sales center with the building's architect, Zaha Hadid, on the screen in the background.
Photo by World Red Eye Productions; courtesy of 1000 Biscayne Tower LLC.

a famous architect that will become a valuable asset." And because the buyers and product are different, so is the sales process. These buyers are not flippers, so rather than an open launch party with A-list celebrities and four thousand people, sales for 1000 Museum started with a very small, invitation-only party for serious potential buyers.

With Ten Museum Park, Covin proved once again the idea introduced in Chapter 2, that successful developers are skillful at identifying and minimizing their risk. Although his grand opening event was as splashy as any Miami had ever seen, his underlying real estate strategy was far more conservative. Rather than simply trying to maximize profits, he focused on mitigating his risk by seeking a tolerable balance of profits, sales velocity, and speed to market. The developers who chose to do larger projects and seek greater profits had to wait longer to receive their MUSPs and then watch helplessly as the window closed before they could sell out, leaving them with hundreds and in some cases thousands of vacant units.

Figure 42. Attendees at the opening engage in "collective selection," looking at unit floor plans on an interactive touch-screen display. Photo by World Red Eye Productions; courtesy of 1000 Biscayne Tower LLC.

But later Covin came to realize that the dominant marketing and sales model at that time—a model based on small deposits that allowed speculators to create a frenzy and boost prices—was both risky and unsustainable. So with 1000 Museum, he adapted to the lack of construction financing while shifting to a new and more robust model that relied on more stable financing—cash. While 1000 Museum is much larger, more costly, and more valuable than Ten Museum Park, it is also arguably more conservative and safer because it is based on those real buyers with real wealth.

More generally, Covin's story illustrates how developers must adapt to changing times and markets while at the same time they grow and evolve through their work. His story also illustrates how successful developers must always be thinking in terms of what people will want, what developers can provide to meet that demand, and how they will sell that product to those buyers. And Covin's story also illustrates the importance of timing, for while he barely completed Ten Museum Park in time, many other developers who were late to market got crushed, which brings us to our next chapter, and the impact of leverage and timing on risks and rewards.

Figure 43. The future view from the balcony of a condominium unit at 1000 Museum Park, looking southeast through Government Cut toward South Beach. Rendering by Zaha Hadid Architects; courtesy of 1000 Biscayne Tower LLC.

Figure 44. The future view looking east over Biscayne Bay, South Beach, and the Atlantic Ocean. Ten Museum Park is the second building from the left and 1000 Museum is to its right. Rendering by Zaha Hadid Architects; courtesy of 1000 Biscayne Tower LLC.

Chapter 7

Market Cycles, Leverage, and Timing

> Thus, while we have heard of blundering swiftness in war, we have not
> yet seen a clever operation that was prolonged.
> —Sun Tzu, *The Art of War*[1]

Market Cycles

Real estate development is a game of large numbers, and timing plays a
huge role in profitability. It takes years to develop a project and get it to
market but market cycles are relatively short, tastes change over time, products evolve, and competitors are constantly increasing supply, so everything
is fluid. For these reasons, development is less a business of marginal gains
and losses and more one of bold plans and potentially huge swings between
profit and loss. Development uses other people's money to create leverage
and enhance returns to investors so it is also a game of cash-flow management and risk management over long time frames. Success is directly
influenced by market cycles, leverage, and timing and being late to market
can have devastating consequences, as the following three experienced
developers can attest:[2]

> It was all timing. We sold the first one out in a weekend. We sold
> the second one out in a weekend—I think we made $20 million on
> that one. The swing was as much as $60 million on the third one,
> so we could have made $40 million but we lost $20 million. We
> sold it out but nobody closed. We lost everything. We got crushed.

Everything we were doing that was not finished by 2007 we lost everything on.

We will spend about half of all the profits we earned from the ten buildings we have done in the past fifteen years getting out of that last building.

We opened the sales center and sold out the whole building—250 units—in three weeks, so we started construction and then started sales on the second building. We sold out 175 out of 275 units in a couple of weeks and started construction on that one too. Then everything stopped. All of the buyers on the second building fell off and we could only close about half of the buyers on the first one. We were left with 400 empty units. We are not a development company anymore.

In his book *Real Estate and the Financial Crisis*, the economist Anthony Downs cites National Bureau of Economic Research data showing that there were thirty-two market cycles in the United States between 1854 and 2001, with an average duration of 4.5 years from peak to peak. Between 1945 and 2001 there were eleven cycles averaging 5.6 years, although the recent troughs of 1991 and 2001 were milder than previous ones.[3]

Downs believes that market cycles are caused by two human traits. First is the inherent tendency of self-interest to generate financial exploitation, leading to excessive self-interest or "greed." Second, self-interest, in combination with a little success, can lead people to overestimate their own skills, knowledge, and powers. As their reputation for success grows, they will become overconfident and begin mistaking luck for skill and their arrogance will make them increasingly vulnerable to bad decision making as they start "believing the hype that surrounds them in society." But how do these two traits lead to booms and busts?[4]

Traditional economic theory holds that supply and demand should seek equilibrium and that boom-and-bust cycles should not occur, but since they do, then they must be the result of bad private economic decisions and misguided government policies. But this explanation seems inadequate, so Downs turned to the theories of the economist Hyman P. Minsky, who concluded that money and financial markets play a leading role in creating and aggravating the instability that is inherent to capitalism. According to Minsky, most private firms need to borrow money to operate and produce, and firms tend to engage in three different types of borrowing: "hedge," "speculative," and "Ponzi." Firms that hedge borrow against near-term future profits that are relatively well assured and then repay their debt on a quarterly basis with after-tax profits. Firms that borrow speculatively cannot fully repay their debt in the short run and must continue borrowing until profits realized in the future can be used to repay debt. Firms that use Ponzi borrowing can never generate enough profit to repay their debt, so they must continue borrowing until their product reaches the end of its life cycle. At that point these firms must be able to sell their assets at higher-than-market prices to cover their debt or, more commonly, they will default, leading to big losses for their investors and lenders.[5]

Minsky theorized that when the economy is coming out of a recession, at the beginning of a market cycle, firms are conservative at first, using hedge borrowing to operate and produce. As the market strengthens, confidence turns into overconfidence and firms take greater risks, increasing their borrowing and using more leverage to increase returns to equity. The same overconfidence causes lenders to relax their underwriting standards and increase their lending so that they too can generate greater profits. Over long periods of economic growth, says Minsky, firms move from hedge to speculative and, ultimately, Ponzi borrowing, and this is how financial markets and money help create booms. Overconfidence and hunger for excess profit drive borrowers to overestimate their own skill and borrow more while increasing leverage. At the same time, lenders continue to relax their underwriting standards and lend more money in search of excess profits. When the market turns, there is an oversupply of product, prices are too high, buyers are scarce, and there is not enough income to cover debt so producers default and lending freezes up as the banks come to grips with the extent of their own bad loan portfolios. This is exactly what happened in the housing boom and bust of the 2000s.[6]

Recent research, says Downs, has validated Minsky's theory and has also shown that, by increasing leverage during growth periods and constricting leverage during downturns, lenders are "pro-cyclical." This means that banks actually contribute to the problem and make things worse by fueling speculation just when they ought to be tightening up on leverage and then, after the peak, shutting off leverage just when lending would help to smooth the transition into the trough.[7]

Minsky attributes this well-worn pattern to excessive risk taking and a lack of prudence over long periods of prosperity during which success breeds more confidence until firms get too leveraged and cannot defend

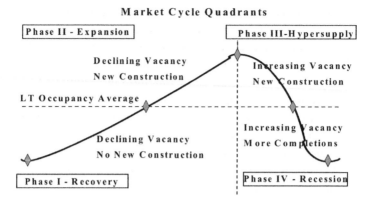

Figure 45. The four quadrants of a real estate market cycle. Note that the market takes longer to rise through Phase I and II but that it turns down quickly in Phase III. The top of the curve represents the point of lowest opportunity and highest risk, when the market is booming and oversupplying product, while the recession at the bottom of the curve represents the point of highest opportunity and lowest risk for developers who still have capital to spend on undervalued assets. Used by permission of Glenn R. Mueller.

against price drops in a downturn. Downs also finds Nicholas Taleb's theories of randomness to be helpful in explaining boom-and-bust cycles. Taleb explains, for example, that success is often a product of luck but if someone is lucky two or three times in a row, she and others might begin to think that she knows what she is doing—and she may begin taking bigger risks. Taleb's bigger point is that financial markets, economists, and people in general are incapable of developing robust models that predict and accommodate major unforeseen events—"black swans"—that invariably occur and affect markets.[8]

Real estate developers fit nicely into Minsky's theoretical framework. They start with a small project first and then, as success breeds confidence, lenders continue to increase leverage. Increasing leverage means the confident developer can initiate more and bigger projects with the same amount of capital. To perform on these projects, the developer must increase his organization's size and capacity, which also increases operating costs and risk. There is only a brief window, however, during which a developer knows that opportunity is at its greatest so he tries to make hay while the sun shines and before the market invariably turns down, which happens suddenly and sooner than was hoped for. The crisis comes when the developer is at his apex, with a bunch of big, highly leveraged projects in the pipeline and a large organization with a substantial payroll and the many contracts required to execute on those projects. As we saw in Chapter 2, entrepreneurs are optimistic and often overoptimistic, so it takes time for the reality to sink in and for the developer to come to grips with the fact that he will never realize the profits or recover all of his costs from the latest, largest, and riskiest projects. Low on cash and with no income, the developer drastically reduces costs by letting go of staff and stopping payments to consultants, vendors, contractors, and lastly, lenders, even to the point of risking default. At this point, everything that is nonessential goes over the side of the boat and the developer hunkers down and waits until the market begins to turn and lending loosens up.

For those few developers with cash on their hands, the recession will provide huge opportunities to buy undervalued or "distressed" real estate for substantially less than "replacement cost" or the cost of building new. Buying distressed real estate is not as sexy as developing new projects but as developers like to say, "You make your money when you buy," and those with the cash to do it when the market is in the trough can increase their holdings and their wealth at that point of maximum opportunity. After that it will be a few years before any new projects get started. But how do market cycles influence how developers are compensated and where they add value to a project?

How Developers Are Compensated: Time, Fees, Rental Income, and Proceeds from Sales

As discussed in Chapter 2, entrepreneurial real estate developers make their money by creating value. They do this by buying resources—land, construction, and professional services—and combining them together to make a new product that they can sell for a price greater than the cost of those resources. The difference between costs and sales proceeds—the profit—is a developer's compensation. But what exactly does she get compensated for and when does she actually get paid?

Developers earn their money for different reasons and at various times throughout a project; these payments can be grouped into four basic categories: monthly expenses for time and overhead, development fees and other fees, income from rents, and one-time profits due to appreciation realized at the time of sale. Over the duration of a project a developer typically charges for overhead—the costs of her own time, staff time, office rental, and other basic overhead expenses—and these costs are allocated to the project. The developer may personally fund overhead until a project is proven up and investors and lenders begin to contribute, at which point those dollars can be used to cover operations going forward. The developer will earn a percentage-based development fee on top of the overhead. She may also collect a fee or earn an entrepreneurial profit when she closes on the land if she has increased its value, and again at the closing on the construction loan or at other construction benchmarks. When the project is complete she will earn one-time profits from the sale of the product. In the case of a rental property, she will earn profits in the form of net income every month as long as she owns the property. The developer may earn other fees, for example, if she manages the rental property. And when she does sell the property she will earn a profit if the property has appreciated in value as measured by its annual cash flows. These four types of income correlate roughly to four basic types of value that developers bring to a deal.

Where Developers Add Value: Time, Expertise, Pursuit Costs, and Exposure to Ongoing Liabilities

First, developers spend time pursuing and implementing development projects and they reasonably expect to be compensated for their time, including time spent on projects that do not go ahead. Over the course of their careers, developers also gain relevant experience and expertise, and they expect to be compensated for this as well, in the same way that any other professional expects to be paid for knowing their business and providing quality products and services for sale to willing buyers.

Developers also expect to be compensated for the costs of determining if an opportunity is worth pursuing further or the "upfront risk." A developer can invest a substantial amount of money only to determine that a deal does not make economic sense or is too risky, in which case the money is lost. In real estate, these "pursuit costs" can be very large sums and they are concentrated into one or just a handful of win-or-lose opportunities. Developers must achieve a successful "hit ratio," for example, 1:3 or 1:4, and they must be willing to part with the money spent on the two or three deals that do not go ahead. Thus a developer's return on a successful project must not only cover the costs and compensate for the risks associated with that project but must also cover the lost pursuit costs from the other projects that never went ahead.

Developers expect to be compensated for the risks associated with the ongoing liabilities they assume when they develop real estate, whether they sell the building in the short run or hold on and operate it as the owner for the long run. In the case of for-sale housing, when a developer completes and sells a single-family home or a condominium unit, state laws typically protect homebuyers by requiring the developer to guarantee or warrant certain building systems for some period of time, such as ten years for major structural and mechanical systems and two years for interior finishes. If a part of the building's structure—the roof, windows, or exterior wall— begins to leak or requires a major repair during that warranty period, the developer is required to correct the problem. If the cause was faulty design by the architect or shoddy construction by the contractor, then the developer may seek assistance and monetary damages through those vendors and their insurance companies. But often he must use his own funds to begin correcting the problem because he is liable first and cannot wait to settle those claims.

The long-term ownership of rental property presents another form of ongoing liability because the building owner must pay the mortgage every month—regardless of whether or not the building is leased up and earning enough rent to cover its debt. As a developer named Tanya Bell says, "If you put a dollar into the stock market, the worst thing that can happen is that you lose that dollar, but if you put a dollar into commercial real estate, you can not only lose that dollar, but you can then still have ongoing liabilities." Developers expect to be compensated for the risks associated with these ongoing liabilities.[9]

Being compensated for their time, expertise, lost pursuit costs, and ongoing liabilities helps to explain how developers think about risk and reward. But a developer does not just receive a steady paycheck every other Friday, because compensation is also related to cash flows and the size and timing of returns. And because the developer is not the only contributor of capital to a project, his returns are influenced by the amounts contributed by others and by when those contributions are made. Indeed, the developer's invested capital is often just a fraction of the total project cost, as development deals rely on many different sources of funds.

Sources and Uses of Funds

One of the basic components of any development pro forma is a simple table called "sources and uses of funds." "Sources of funds" means the total sum of money that will be used to finance the project and includes investor equity and debt—sometimes known as "other people's money" (OPM). On a complex project there can be many sources of funds, including the developer's equity, the equity of any number of wealthy individual investors, the equity of an institutional investor such as a pension fund or life insurance company, debt in the form of a construction loan or first mortgage and sometimes a second mortgage, and various forms of public subsidy. The sum of all of these sources is sometimes called "the capital stack."

"Uses of funds" means the total sum of the project costs—what the funds will be spent on—and these include land, construction, and "soft costs" such as design fees, legal fees, marketing and sales costs, overhead, and profit. Sources must equal uses and if sources are inadequate, then the developer must find a way to reduce costs—without reducing value—or must secure "gap financing" in the form of public subsidies such as tax increment financing, grants of money or land, grants for pollution cleanup, low-interest loans, and so on.

But a sources and uses table is a static projection of project economics —a snapshot from a moment in time—and therefore an abstraction of a complex picture that changes constantly as a project is developed. For example, the developer does not commit to spend all funds at the beginning of a project but rather spends a few dollars in architectural fees to get a concept sketch and test an idea. As the idea becomes more concrete, they commit more funds to developing the design further. At the same time, the developer does not have all of the required funds in hand at the beginning—usually he has just his own cash. Throughout all of this, the project—and the sources and uses table—is constantly changing to reflect new information. For example, the developer may adjust or change anything from product type, building height, and gross square footage to parking requirements, structural systems, and finish material quality. Over the duration of the project the developer will constantly adjust the sources and uses table to reflect these types of changes.

When the developer determines that an idea makes sense and chooses to move forward, he must spend more money—and at some point he will seek investors as a source for this additional cash. These investors will have

Table 4. Sources and Uses of Funds ($10 Million Project)

Sources of Funds	Amount	% of Total
Equity	$2,500,000	25%
Debt	$7,500,000	75%
Total Sources	**$10,000,000**	100%
Uses of Funds		
Land	$1,000,000	10%
Construction	$7,000,000	70%
Fees and Soft Costs	$2,000,000	20%
Total Uses	**$10,000,000**	100%
Gap: Sources Less Uses	**$0**	**0%**

Note: In this simple sources and uses table for a $10 million project, sources include equity (the cash of the developer and the investors) and debt in the form of a construction loan or permanent loan or mortgage from a bank. Uses of funds include the costs of acquiring the land or property; construction costs, including labor and materials; and design fees, legal fees, sales and marketing costs, commissions, and other soft costs. If uses exceed sources, then the difference must be made up with other funds, such as a government subsidy.

Table 5. The Capital Stack ($10 Million Project)

Sources of Funds	Amount	% of Total
First Mortgage	$5,500,000	55%
Second Mortgage	$1,500,000	15%
Institutional Investor	$1,500,000	15%
Investor #3	$500,000	5%
Investor #2	$500,000	5%
Investor #1	$300,000	3%
Developer	$200,000	2%
Total Sources	**$10,000,000**	100%

Note: The capital stack is a more detailed breakdown of all sources of funds. These can include the equity of the developer and any number of participating investors, an institutional investor such as a life insurance company or pension fund, and one or more bank loans. In the case of a shortfall or gap, the developer may seek a government subsidy such as tax increment financing (TIF) that would be added to the list of sources.

different expectations for returns based on how much money they contribute, when they make their contribution, and their perceived assessment of risk at that time. So how do these other capital contributions influence the developer's return on his initial invested equity?

Equity and Debt: OPM

Whether it starts with a property, an idea about the next desirable location, or a hunch about demand for a product, at the beginning of a project a developer will spend some of her own cash to investigate or "prove up" whether or not her basic concept makes sense. Costs might include the purchase of an option to buy land or property, fees for architectural and engineering design work to determine how a certain type of building might fit on the property, the costs of a market study to determine demand for the product, and legal fees. Together, these costs may represent a very small share of the total estimated project cost, perhaps 5 percent or less, but at this point the uncertainty of whether or not a project will be completed, let alone be successful, is at its very greatest. The project is so speculative that these dollars are 100 percent at risk.

As the project develops, uncertainty and risk are continually reduced. In the beginning, a developer may not know whether she can fit a big-enough project of the right type on the site to justify the land cost, but after spending some cash on architectural design, she will have a better idea. At this stage, however, she may not know whether the local community and city will be receptive to these plans, so she will be required to spend time meeting with elected officials and city staff and attending neighborhood meetings. She may also pay her designers to revise the drawings several times to reflect the input received from these various stakeholders. Once she has developed a conceptual design that is generally acceptable to most of these stakeholders, the likelihood of receiving needed approvals has been increased and the risk of the project going forward has been reduced, so at this point the developer will begin to line up investors and start talking to banks about the terms for a construction loan.

Next, the developer will spend more money to complete the drawings required to submit the design to the city for review to determine if the plan is in compliance with the city's planning, zoning, and development regulations. When the project receives formal city approvals, the "entitlement risk" will have been largely eliminated and if the market study confirmed that there will be demand for the project, then the "market risk" will have been reduced as well. At this point the developer will need to commit yet more resources to develop the design to a level required to firm up building systems, costs, and sellable or rentable square footages. She will also need to spend money to launch the marketing and sales program, including brochures, collateral materials, website design and maintenance, advertising, the leasing or construction of a sales center, and payroll for sales agents. This work will require a substantial amount of money and at this point the developer will ask potential investors to contribute to help cover these costs.

Next, the developer will bring the project to market. Whether it is for-sale homes, apartments, or office space, the developer will seek commitments that she can take to the bank and use as security to obtain a construction loan. These commitments include signed contracts from buyers or signed leases from tenants. As the developer markets the project the design team will work to complete the drawings and specifications—the "construction documents"—to a level of detail required by a contractor to price and build the project. This is the most costly phase of the design process, so the developer will commit yet more cash to design fees. And when the developer has demonstrated that there is demand for the project through presales or preleasing, the "market risk" has been further reduced and the developer can close on the bank loan, close on the property, and begin construction.

By the time the project is complete the developer will have recruited a handful if not dozens of private investors, perhaps an institutional investor, and a lender or two. And because each of these investors and lenders contributes their capital to the project at a different point in time, they expect to earn a different rate of return based upon their individual assessment of the risk at that time. So the developer who invests the first dollars required to initiate the project may expect to earn a 30 percent to 50 percent return on her invested equity and if the project really succeeds she may double or triple her money or even better. Other private investors—wealthy individuals—who contribute during the concept or pursuit phase may expect to earn 20 percent or more. Large institutional equity investors—such as pension funds or life insurance companies—that invest their dollars at the same time that the developer is closing on the construction loan may expect to earn 15 percent. Finally, the bank making the construction loan may expect to earn 8 percent interest.

At every step the developer hopes to eliminate uncertainty and reduce risk. But somebody must invest the first, highest-risk dollars at the beginning and that is usually the developer, who invests her own cash and time—sweat equity and footwork—which she hopes to see repaid when the deal goes ahead. But while the developer may have contributed enough cash to get the project started, she will soon come to rely on the capital of private investors, institutional investors, and lenders to complete the project. All of the investors and lenders have different expectations related to the order in which they expect capital and profits to be returned, beginning with the bank.

Banks and Loans

A developer rarely funds the entire cost of a project. Instead, he borrows from a bank—either a construction loan or a permanent loan—to cover the majority of project costs. The bank lends at a loan-to-cost ratio, so, for example, if a bank agrees to loan at a 70 percent loan-to-cost ratio, then the developer will be required to secure the remaining balance of 30 percent in equity—his own cash and that of his investors.

There are two main reasons why a bank will not typically loan the full amount of the total project cost. First, by loaning a lesser percentage and being in "first position," the bank's risk is reduced because in the case of default it has the first right to take possession of the asset and sell it for whatever price it can obtain. So while the bank may only be earning 8 percent interest, if it can sell the project for 70 percent of its cost, it can still recoup its principal—its depositors' funds. The developer and equity investors, however, lose everything.

This leads to the second reason why a bank is only willing to loan a part of the total project cost. The bank would rather see the project succeed, and one way to increase the odds of success is to ensure that the developer is committed to success and that the developer's interests are aligned with those of the bank. A developer who has more to lose is a developer who will work harder to ensure a successful project. And if he has much to gain if the project exceeds its profit expectations, then it is all the better for everyone. In other words, as the billionaire investor Warren Buffett would say, the bank wants the developer to "have some skin in the game."[10]

Banks base loan-to-cost ratios on their assessment of risk and the amount of capital flowing into real estate, which typically increases over the duration of a market cycle, as Minsky predicts. At the beginning of a market cycle, when credit begins to loosen, loan-to-cost ratios are low—60 percent, for example—which means that only very well-capitalized individuals and companies are in a position to develop because so much equity is required. On the other hand, a 90 percent loan-to-cost ratio opens the door to anyone who can scrape up the last 10 percent of equity required to close a loan. Ten percent of a $10 million project is still $1 million and a lot of money to raise but 40 percent is $4 million and a whole lot more.

Uncertainty, Risk, and the Timing of Returns

The cash-flow timeline in Table 6 illustrates the relationship between decreasing rates of return and levels of risk as a project moves from inception through completion. Assuming a $10 million project and a five-year schedule, the developer's relatively small amount of equity—the first cash into the project—is at the greatest risk during the pursuit phase because it may cost $200,000 just to learn that the project is not viable, in which case the money is lost. On the other hand, if the project is successful and earns a profit of 16 percent, then the developer can expect to triple his money. At the end of the pursuit phase, the developer may have an idea that he has a viable project, and he may have secured some informal approvals as well as a market study that supports the proposed pricing, so the risk has been reduced somewhat, although the risk for investor #1 is still significantly greater than other investments such as the stock market. During the development phase the developer will continue to reduce risk and uncertainty by securing final approvals and fine-tuning the design, cost, and pricing information. When development is complete and the developer has secured enough purchase agreements or leases, he can borrow the balance of the money required to finance the project from a bank at a much lower rate. The bank is willing to offer a construction loan at that rate because the market risk has been reduced and the completed asset will serve as security for the loan.

Once the project is finished and sold or refinanced, the bank must be completely repaid. Only then does the institutional investor, if there is one, receive equity and profit. Last come the early investors and the developer. Although the developer does not receive his returns until everyone else has been repaid, he does stand to receive a significant share of any excess profits, so if the project is successful, his rate of return could be enormous. And why shouldn't it be? The developer has taken the greatest risk over the longest period of time.

Table 6. The Cash-Flow Timeline ($10 Million Project)

Phase/Risk Level	Pursuit 4 (Highest)	Concept 3	Design 2	Construction 1 (Lowest)	Total/Average
Duration (Months)	4	8	12	16	40
Source of Funds	Developer	Investors	Inst. Investor	Bank/Lender	
% of Total	2%	3%	25%	70%	100%
Amount of Funds	$200,000	$300,000	$2,500,000	$7,000,000	$10,000,000
Amount of Return	$400,000	$150,000	$500,000	$550,000	$1,600,000
Total Return	$600,000	$450,000	$3,000,000	$7,550,000	$11,600,000
% Return	**200%**	**50%**	**20%**	**8%**	**16%**

Note: This table illustrates how anticipated rates of return decline with levels of risk. The first dollars in, the developer's own cash, are at the greatest risk of being lost so the developer expects to earn a much greater return of 200 percent. The bank requires only an 8 percent return on its much larger construction loan that will be funded later, when most of the uncertainty and risk have been eliminated from the project.

But developers don't just use other people's money to complete the capital stack. They use it to reduce their own exposure on an individual project, and if they have enough capital this allows them to invest in multiple projects and diversify their risk rather than investing it all into a single deal. Most important, developers use other people's money to enhance their own returns to equity through what is called "leverage."

Leverage—Positive and Negative

The developer's rate of return is influenced by the loan-to-cost ratio, so while the overall rate of return on a project does not change when the loan-to-cost ratio increases, the rate of return for the developer grows as his equity becomes an increasingly smaller share of the total sources. This is called leverage. A construction loan or mortgage is typically the largest part of the capital stack, and while interest rates may increase to reflect the added risk of a higher loan-to-cost ratio, they are still relatively low as compared to the overall rate of return. For example, if the project is expected to earn 15 percent and the interest rate is 7 percent, the more the developer borrows at 7 percent, the higher the rate of return on their increasingly smaller share of equity.

Consider a project with a total cost of $10 million that is expected to increase in value by 20 percent by the time it is completed and sold out or

Table 7. Positive Leverage ($10 Million Project)

Leverage Debt/Equity	Low 40/60	Medium 60/40	High 95/5
Loan-to-Cost Ratio	40%	60%	95%
Total Project Cost	$10,000,000	$10,000,000	$10,000,000
Debt	$4,000,000	$6,000,000	$9,500,000
Equity	$6,000,000	$4,000,000	$500,000
Appreciation	20%	20%	20%
Sales Value	$12,000,000	$12,000,000	$12,000,000
Debt Repayment	($4,000,000)	($6,000,000)	($9,500,000)
Equity Value (Liability)	**$8,000,000**	**$6,000,000**	**$2,500,000**
Return on Equity	**33%**	**50%**	**400%**

Note: With positive leverage, high leverage yields very high rates of return if the project meets or exceeds its profit expectations. With 95 percent leverage, someone who can find $500,000 can develop a $10 million project, make a huge return, and then have five times his or her original capital ($2.5 million) to invest in the next, larger project. On the other hand, the developer who used only 40 percent leverage made a very good return of 33 percent but still left a lot of money on the table when compared to the first developer. All developers use leverage to increase the amount of capital under their control, which allows them to do more and larger deals in the future.

leased up. With a 40 percent loan-to-cost ratio the developer has to contribute $6 million in equity for which he will earn $2 million in profit—a 33 percent return. For the same project with a 60 percent loan-to-cost ratio, the developer must invest a smaller share, $4 million, and he will earn the same $2 million in profit for a 50 percent rate of return. But if the loan-to-cost ratio goes up to 95 percent, then the developer only has to contribute $500,000 but he earns the same $2 million in profit for an astonishing rate of return of 400 percent—four dollars earned for every dollar invested. So, with high leverage a developer has to put up less equity, thus lowering barriers to entry along with exposure and risk, and for this he earns a much higher rate of return. When it works, this is called "positive leverage."

What could possibly go wrong? Well, if the developer overestimated the demand for his product, if he overestimated what people would be willing to pay for it, if construction costs went up, or if he could not sell out as fast as he had hoped and had to pay additional interest charges and other "carrying costs" over a longer time frame, then he probably won't be able to sell it out or lease it up for the prices or rents required to repay the debt and the equity and still earn his expected profit.

Table 8. Negative Leverage ($10 Million Project)

Leverage Debt/Equity	Low 40/60	Medium 60/40	High 95/5
Loan-to-Cost Ratio	40%	60%	95%
Total Project Cost	$10,000,000	$10,000,000	$10,000,000
Debt	$4,000,000	$6,000,000	$9,500,000
Equity	$6,000,000	$4,000,000	$500,000
Appreciation	− 20%	− 20%	− 20%
Sales Value	$8,000,000	$8,000,000	$8,000,000
Debt Repayment	($4,000,000)	($6,000,000)	($9,500,000)
Equity Value (Liability)	**$4,000,000**	**$2,000,000**	**($1,500,000)**
Return on Equity	**− 33%**	**− 50%**	**− 400%**

Note: When profits are lower than expected, high leverage quickly becomes negative leverage and a liability. For the developer using 95 percent leverage, a 20 percent loss in value means all equity is lost and, worse, there are not enough funds to cover the debt and he or she may be at risk of default. The low-leverage developer is in a better position. He or she may not be happy about losing a third of $6 million in equity but he or she still owns the building. And although it may take years, if that developer can make it through the recession and wait for prices to rise, he or she may, over time, recover some of that lost equity.

Now consider the same project, only instead of gaining 20 percent in value, it loses 20 percent of its value. For the developer who only borrowed 40 percent, his equity drops in value from $6 million to $4 million, a loss of 33 percent. The developer who borrowed 60 percent sees his equity drop in value from $4 million to $2 million, a loss of 50 percent. Neither of these developers or their investors will be happy with this outcome; however, they still own and control their buildings and they still have some amount of their equity remaining. They can also hold on for a longer sell-out period or they can pause and try to reposition the project or raise prices later. In the case of a rental property they can survive a longer lease-up period and—if they hold on to the building—wait for the market to change and for rents to increase. It could take a long time but if they can afford to be patient they are likely to get some or all of their equity back and they may even earn a good return at some point in the future. This is called "negative leverage."

But what about the developer who borrowed 95 percent of the project cost? Like the other two, his equity has dropped in value by $2 million, but since he only contributed $500,000 to begin with, he is now "upside down" by $1.5 million. In other words, he has lost his $500,000 in equity and is unable to repay himself and his equity investors, who may think twice about investing in the developer's projects in the future.

But he has another, much bigger problem: he still owes $1.5 million to the bank. If he cannot come up with that money, the bank may foreclose on the property and then, in order to recoup some of its losses, come after the developer's personal assets if he signed a "personal guarantee." In this case the developer may find himself in a "work-out session" with the bank, which will seize and liquidate his first and second homes, planes, boats, cars, motorcycles, retirement funds, IRAs, children's college funds, and other assets that he pledged as security on the loan. Putting the homes in his spouse's name may help protect the developer somewhat and many developers do a thorough job of shielding assets, which is why some lenders consider personal guarantees to be virtually worthless. Still, it is no fun to be broke and have the bank come after everything you have that isn't nailed down for the next ten years.

During the housing boom of the 2000s, effective loan-to-cost ratios rose as high as 95 percent, as lenders offered combined packages of, for example, 75 percent debt at one rate plus another 20 percent "mezzanine," or "mezz debt" piece, at a slightly higher rate. By 2011 loan-to-cost ratios were back to 60 percent or 65 percent at most, and even then banks were only willing to loan to developers who could guarantee repayment and who had a very strong balance sheet of assets as security for the loan. In 2005, however, so much capital had flooded the U.S. real estate market that money was looking for projects, underwriting standards had dropped as demand and supply became disconnected, and almost anyone with a half-baked idea could get a loan. What Anthony Downs called "perverse incentives" led to the overbuilding of real estate that was driven by financial markets and the supply of money but that far exceeded actual market demand.[11]

The easiest way to think about leverage is that if a project is a screaming success—if it hits the market at the right time, toward the end of a cycle but not too late and sells out quickly at pro forma or better prices—then a highly leveraged deal will generate huge returns to equity, and profits for the developer. This is what happened at Ten Museum Park, where Gregg Covin and his partners benefited from positive leverage. There is little margin for error, however, so if a project misses the market, then the chances are pretty good the developer will lose his entire investment and have ongoing liabilities.

On the other hand, the lower leverage deal doesn't yield such large returns but it is a better hedge against the vicissitudes of the market and gives the developer more control over a longer time frame. So, positive leverage is great, negative leverage is not, but more important, as Downs and Minsky point out, leverage risk is directly related to market timing.

Timing, Timing, Timing

"In the Old Testament," says Buzz Ruttenberg, "Joseph read the Pharaoh's dream about seven fat cows being eaten by seven skinny cows and seven plump ears of corn being replaced by seven shriveled ones. He interpreted the dream to mean that there would be seven good years followed by seven bad years, so in the good years you must stockpile for the bad years to avoid famine and great suffering. Things haven't really changed since then, and a lot of what happens is human nature and psychological. So it is odd, but seven years seems to be a real cycle."[12]

Ruttenberg offers the commercial office building boom-and-bust cycle of the 1980s as an example of how the kind of human psychology that Downs and Minsky describe creates a boom-and-bust cycle. In the late 1980s, the market started to cycle downward and then, on October 19, 1987, "Black Monday," the stock market crashed and the Dow Jones Industrial Average lost 23 percent of its value. But institutional investors in real estate—the life insurance companies—didn't see the value of their investments drop because real estate had traditionally been countercyclical to the stock market, so they pushed more money into real estate. This led to a finance-driven rather than a demand-driven buildup in speculative office building development—similar to the finance-driven housing boom of the 2000s. By the early 1990s commercial office vacancy rates had soared. According to a 1989 Solomon Brothers report, there was so much commercial office space in production that vacancy rates for central business districts could be as high as 20 percent through 2010. "Then," says Ruttenberg, "in 1991, the 'mother of all wars'—the first Gulf War—broke out, which had the psychological effect of further reducing investor confidence. In the wake of the office over-building boom, banks became less eager to lend for real estate because they had gotten in trouble. And finally, in 1991 Donald Trump filed for his first bankruptcy," which fed the popular perception that the real estate market was in a downturn.[13]

"So we see these boom-and-bust cycles that start when one person has a good idea, and that's a good thing, but then when ten other people copy it that is not such a good thing. The first guy in, who is usually a cautious risk taker, is going to make money but then everyone enters the market and whether it is developers, bankers, or car dealers, they go to the other extreme. As Warren Buffett likes to say, 'The time to be fearful is when everyone is greedy; the time to be greedy is when everyone is fearful.' But it takes discipline to not be a part of the herd instinct—it is a hard choice. So an important point about development is that you have to check your ego at the door, which is difficult for some people who think, 'If I am going to take the risk, why not thump my chest?' "[14]

Knowing When to Get Out of the Pool

The developer John Carroll offers a similar observation on the housing boom-and-bust cycle of the 2000s. "The reason the real estate market is where it is today," said Carroll in 2010, "is that a lot of people who did not understand the business jumped in." Carroll offers the example of an unsuccessful, several-hundred-unit midrise condo project built in the Pearl District in Portland, Oregon. "The only prior experience the developer had was with a small townhome project in the suburbs." The reason that the developer was able to make the leap to a large urban project was because financing was so plentiful and cheap. "The banks were going crazy too. We always borrow 65 percent loan-to-cost at the most and we still did that even when we could have gotten 85 percent. I look at the downside scenario and always run the numbers because I just always want to be sure I can pay the equity back to the participants. But everyone else started abandoning models that really do reflect the risk."[15]

From Carroll's viewpoint, plentiful capital and increased competition created two problems. First, the products these other developers were building were questionable, and second, they were being built in questionable locations. "We saw a lot of stuff that just didn't make sense and yet we had to compete with it." Another big mistake a lot of developers made was looking for opportunities in other markets. "I had so many opportunities to go to Denver, San Diego, Los Angeles, but you have to remember that you must know the local politics and if you don't you are at a huge disadvantage. So everyone was getting into the business, opportunity was going away, risk was increasing, and you could not differentiate yourself in the marketplace anymore."

One day Carroll received a call from an associate at a sales center for one of his projects that was about to open. "The message was 'We are going to open in an hour and there are already people lined up around the block,' and this scared the hell out of me." At the same time Carroll had been taking flak from other developers who thought he was pricing his product too cheaply. "They told me I could be getting another $20 per square foot but I wanted to manage my risk and make sure that whoever buys from me has an opportunity to make a little money. We offer a quality product at a good price, we don't gouge our buyers, we have a good management company, and we take care of our properties. We have sold seven hundred units and I want seven hundred salespeople."

In 2006, Carroll spent the weekend with his wife in a town called Camp Sherman, near Sisters, Oregon, and he read a local, five-page, foldover weekly newspaper called *The Nugget*. "There was an article about how it looked like there was going to be a problem with 'subprime loans,' and I decided then and there that things were going the wrong way and the next week, when I got home, I shut off two projects. And now, in 2010, we have zero units on the market, zero debt, we have cash, and we are still involved in development."

Ruttenberg's and Carroll's stories both underscore another key issue related to timing. As risky and uncertain as it may feel to start a development project early in a market cycle, risk only increases with competition, so when everyone starts jumping into the pool it is probably time to get out. Timing affects profits in one more important way. While a developer may make a large profit on an individual project, to avoid capital gains taxes she must reinvest that profit in another property within a certain period of time. And while the tax code creates incentives to reinvest in real estate, the entrepreneur also wants to start her next project. So rather than accruing profits over the years as each project is complete, many developers reinvest a large share of their profits as equity into the next deal. And this is all fine and well until the last deal does not go according to plan, and a large share of the profits from previous projects is lost on the last project.

Because developers are such eternal optimists, they also have a hard time adapting when things take a turn for the worse and realizing when the ground has shifted under their feet. "I got out of the Pearl a little early," says Steve Rosenberg, who has been a successful equity investor in many projects in the Pearl District, including several with John Carroll. Despite his regrets, however, getting out a few months early is far better than getting out one minute late. Rosenberg has two simple rules for real estate investing. First, "there is no bad real estate, only bad prices," and second, "it doesn't matter how much you have in the deal." When the market changes and property values drop, Rosenberg often hears developers saying, "Yeah, but how much have I got in it?" And his point is that it just doesn't matter how much you have got in it—it means nothing—what matters is what it is worth today.[16]

The Third Fist

In addition to all of the usual risks such as construction cost escalation, interest rates, and market timing, there is the type of unforeseen risk that Nicholas Taleb calls a "black swan" and the architect and planner Andrés Duany likes to call "the third fist."[17]

Duany's father was a developer and Duany can remember his father talking about it. The idea is that you can always watch and guard against your opponent's two fists, which are in front of your face. But you cannot protect yourself from a third fist coming at you from beyond your angle of vision. The point is that in development you can do everything to manage risk but still fail to protect against things that are unforeseeable. "For example," says Duany, "the developer of the City of Coral Gables, a suburb of Miami, later went bankrupt—because of the unforeseen, devastating Hurricane of 1926. Had he planned for the possibility of a hurricane he might have been more careful with his debt load and perhaps he could have survived a two- or three-year hiatus. The strategy is that if you anticipate the possible third fists, they cease to be threats because they are in front of you where you can watch and guard against them."

A mixed-use development outside of Washington, DC, offers a more recent example. The Kentlands was one of the first successful, large-scale examples of the planning that has come to be known as New Urbanism. The Kentlands combined a mix of uses—residential and retail—with dense development and traditional space, making a more livable and walkable community.

The developer of the Kentlands knew that he would be able to obtain zoning. With this knowledge, he paid $43 million for 320 acres. He consequently entered into a contract with a mall developer called the Simon Group who agreed to pay $20 million for seventy acres on the corner of the site. The remaining 250 acres would then work financially at $23 million.

Simon paid a deposit—$2 million—but then, out of the blue, a Canadian "raider" called Robert Campeau, using a lot of leverage, bought Federated Department stores and drove them into the ground. The developer of Kentlands had his deposit, but Simon had to say, "I won't be able to build anchor stores for many years, so keep the $2 million."

"The third fist got him," says Duany. The Kentlands developer was $41 million in debt rather than $23 million," effectively doubling the cost of the land for the residential part of the development, "and no matter how well it sold—and it did well—he couldn't get ahead of the debt." While the Kentlands has since been completed by the bank and has become a prominent and successful example of the principles of New Urbanism, its original developer did not fare as well. Says Duany, "We had not anticipated that third fist."

Rome Wasn't Built in a Day

In 2010 the Southeast Florida chapter of the Urban Land Institute (ULI) honored a man named Tibor Hollo with its lifetime achievement award. Hollo was eighty-two and his company, Florida East Coast Realty, had been in constant operation since 1956. Hollo built the first high-rise on Brickell Avenue in Miami, and in 2010 he planned what would be Miami's tallest building, the $1.8 billion One Bayfront Plaza, on Biscayne Boulevard. Having successfully weathered nine market cycles over the course of a fifty-five-year career, Hollo had a long view of how to think about leverage and market timing.

Born in Hungary in 1928, Hollo moved to France when he was six. After surviving a German concentration camp during World War II he completed his schooling in architectural engineering—what is now called structural engineering—in 1946. He moved to New York City in 1948 but the market was terrible and he was unable to get a job as an architect. "Usually they say, 'Don't call us, we'll call you,' but back then it was so bad they just said 'No.'" Hollo took a job working for a contractor and a year later, in 1949, he was able to go into business on his own as a contractor, working at first on small projects. But his company grew very quickly and he opened offices in Detroit and on the West Coast. Hollo recalls that in a 1956 *Fortune Magazine* survey his construction company was ranked tenth largest in the country. That year was also Hollo's best year financially but by then he was burned out and had decided that he did not want to be a contractor anymore. "So I had in front of me two possibilities: either be an architect, because by that time I could get a job in architecture, or be a developer. I chose development because I could pick my own venue—a contractor has to go where the job is. So in 1956 I moved to Miami and became a developer.[18]

"I wanted to do fun things and things that go well with the land—the types of developments that are befitting of the property. I won't say that I wasn't motivated by money, because that is a stupid statement, but money was not the only motivation—I wanted to do good things. Some people build thirty or forty buildings a year but I knew that I didn't want to do that. So the business matrix I set forth was that I wanted to do one, maybe two projects at a time at most. This is because I wanted to be able to control what I was doing, I wanted to be able to give it what I had, and I wanted to be comfortable—both financially and in terms of my ability to control my work—and to do that I knew that I couldn't do more than one or two buildings at a time. And finally, I never wanted to borrow more than 40 percent of cost, and I knew that I could only do it if I only did one or two buildings at a time but not if I did more. So it was very comfortable for me to do it that way."

From "Location, Location, Location" to "Timing, Timing, Timing"

Hollo attended a Jesuit school in a small village in France, where he learned a Latin proverb, "Contemporem Mutandis," which means "In time we too change." In New York in the 1950s, Hollo became friendly with a real estate appraiser who had offices in the Flatiron Building and who went on to become a big developer in New York City. His name was Harry Helmsley. "Once, many years ago, Harry was receiving an award from the ULI—the Urban Land Institute—and I was sitting next to him at the award luncheon, when a reporter approached Helmsley and asked, 'Mr. Helmsley, what are the three most important ingredients to a successful real estate development?' and Harry said, 'Location, location, location.' I have thought often about what he said then and it was valid at the time, but times change and we change. If someone asked me that question today, I would say the three most important ingredients are timing, timing, timing." But how has timing become more important than location?

Between 1968 and 1971, Hollo assembled fifty-eight parcels of land in the City of Miami and began to develop projects on that land. In 2011— forty years later—he started development work on the last parcel. "I have waited a long time to see my money come back out of that land," says Hollo. "Real estate is an interesting business and it can be very rewarding if your timing is good but the only way you can make sure your timing is good is to think in terms of the long haul and the idea that Rome wasn't built in a day." Thinking long term also offers advantages when working with the community, says Hollo. "Instead of being dictatorial and shoving something that you want down the throats of your buyers, if you have the time you are able to have a dialog with the community and to listen to what they want, not just because they are the neighbors but because they reflect what the market wants."

Thinking long term also helps when it comes to financing and Hollo's most important rule: "Don't overborrow." A lender approached Hollo and his son in 2007 and told them that he would like to loan them money for a project they were developing. "We told him that we would like to borrow 40 percent of cost and that was all we were looking for but then the lender said, 'Why would you want to do that? We will lend you 75 percent of cost and then we will lend you a mezz piece for 20 percent more so, essentially, you don't have any money in the thing.' So I said, 'But I want to have money in it.' And so a little discussion ensued and the lender explained that 'the reason we do it is because we need to make a certain yield and we cannot make enough money on the yield by loaning you just 75 percent, so we can get a higher yield by loaning 20 percent more, which is why you need to borrow 95 percent.' We didn't do business with them," says Hollo, "and they could not accommodate us because they wouldn't lend us 40 percent."

The problem, says Hollo, is that "if you do thirty or forty buildings, you must borrow 90 percent, and then you will be robbing Peter to pay Paul and you will have to develop an organization that must constantly produce, and produce big in order to service that debt."

Proven Axioms

Hollo's initial business plan and a handful of proven axioms have served him well. Between 1956 and 2010, Florida East Coast Realty developed nearly sixty million square feet but, more important, Hollo found the comfort zone he had been seeking when he first began to draft his business matrix in 1956. He is proud to have had eleven people retire from his company after working for him for thirty years. He has sons and grandsons working with him and in 2010 he began passing control to the next generation. In sixty-one years in business he had only three secretaries and the latest worked for him for thirty-five years. And he never borrowed more than 40 percent of project cost and in some cases he did not borrow at all. "Because we never borrow more than 40 percent, nobody can hurt us. We can abridge the timing, so that if we happen to finish a building in a poor time we can wait with it."

Hollo's axioms also help to explain why he has managed to weather nine market cycles over the course of a career that has spanned six decades. "You can't really time yourself," says Hollo. "We have had eight-year cycles and three-year cycles, and some cycles have lasted only three months while this one has lasted three years. And one thing you develop when you go through a few of these things is a sense that it is happening. It is not a sixth sense—you just start seeing signs that you are accustomed to. So late in December of 2007 I felt it coming and I pulled in my horns and stopped pushing as hard on some projects. I can do that but the problem for firms that are doing ten buildings is that you have got to keep doing it—you cannot just come in one day and say, 'Everybody is fired.'"

Hollo offers an illustrative story from a previous cycle. "In 1979 there was a big slowdown and the *Miami Herald* ran a cover story in sixty-point red letters that said '20,000 Unit Condominium Overhang—It Will Take Ten Years to Absorb.' The next day the head of real estate at Irving Trust in New York called me up and said, 'Ted, you have to come to New York tomorrow—our chairman and the board want to see you.'" Hollo had borrowed from Irving Trust in the past but had recently finished a building and paid them off. He thought, "Oh my gosh, what can it be?" He asked why and was told, "We can't tell you, you just have to come in." "So I checked with my controller and asked, 'What is going on, do we owe them anything?' and he said no, we have paid everything back. I was genuinely concerned but there was nothing to do so I flew to New York and walked into the boardroom—which is very intimidating and something like eighty feet long—and I saw all of them looking very stern and they each had a copy of the *Miami Herald* from two days before sitting in front of them, with the sixty-point red letters predicting a ten-year disaster. So the chairman introduced me and the first guy sitting right next to him said, 'Mr. Hollo, what do you say to this?'

"So I said, 'I don't see twenty thousand units—I think that is somewhat of an exaggeration and exaggerations sometimes sell newspapers. In my opinion there are maybe five thousand to six thousand units on the market and 6,500 at the most.' Then the man asked, 'How long will it take to absorb?' and I said, 'Probably three years, maybe three and a half years.' You could see the whole group relax, from one end of the table to the other. They wanted my opinion because I didn't owe them any money and had no agenda, so I was the most plausible mark to call in to talk to them. So they were all relieved, we had a nice lunch, and I flew back to Miami. About a year later I received a little note from the chairman of Irving Trust, and all it said was 'Dear Ted, I am happy to say that you were wrong.' It was over in just eighteen months, not three and a half years, as I had predicted, and certainly not ten years."

What Does a Real Estate Boom-and-Bust Cycle Really Look Like?

Booms start when leverage begins to go up and more capital begins to flow into real estate, encouraging more people to enter the market. As competition increases, the costs of differentiating oneself and one's project in the marketplace rise as well. These costs include everything from land prices and design fees to construction quality and sophisticated marketing and sales programs. During the housing boom of the 2000s, increased competition required the hiring of more prominent and famous "starchitects" who charged higher fees and whose buildings cost more and took longer to build. They also required million-dollar sales centers and launch parties replete with celebrities to attract the attention of the market. At the beginning of a cycle, on the other hand, the first few developers who enter the market have the field to themselves and can take a more cautious and economical approach. And because there is pent-up demand for new product and a shortage of supply, buyers are not in a position to be choosy and developers can keep both costs and prices lower.

Time is money and as competition increases, it becomes increasingly difficult to deliver a project on schedule for a variety of reasons. These range from overworked city planning staff taking longer to complete approvals processes to the ability of consultants and contractors to perform fully on their increasingly bounteous but overwhelming workloads. The market's expectations increase unreasonably too. For example, during the condo boom, early projects offered enamel-finished appliances and plastic laminate countertops, with stainless steel and granite as upgrades. By 2007, however, everything on the market had become a "luxury" product and buyers expected stainless steel appliances and granite countertops as standard.

As total costs increase, so do dollar-per-square-foot costs, so developers must reduce unit sizes to control unit prices. This means that the latest products cost the same or more than larger units completed two or three years earlier. Most buyers are unsophisticated and unable to differentiate between products, so they use the easiest proxies: unit size, dollar-per-square-foot cost, total price, and, of course, what they can afford to buy. Finally, over the duration of a boom cycle, material costs rise as demand increases, so everything from metals and gypsum wallboard increase at rates beyond normal escalation. Prices must ultimately rise with costs while, paradoxically, overcommitted consultants and contractors produce increasingly shoddy work.

At the peak, there are too many developers in the marketplace, promoting too many projects of increasingly poor quality that have become too costly to build, too pricy to sell, and that have outstripped demand from a dazed and saturated marketplace. Developers have used increasing leverage, engaged in too many projects to execute well on, and grown their organizations to manage the work. Buyers have become speculators, more units have been built than are required for people to actually live in, and everyone, including your next-door neighbor, has become a licensed real estate sales agent.

When the music stops, as Minsky predicts, lenders have made too many dubious loans, borrowers cannot make their payments, banks become unwilling landlords and at the same time shut off lending, and economic recession ensues. This is a well-worn path and it is where the market ended up in 2007–2008. But one problem was that the last really big real estate boom-and-bust cycle happened twenty years before, in the late 1980s, and was a distant memory. Many of the people who were around for that cycle, which was caused by the overbuilding of speculative commercial office buildings, did not see the parallels. Many others were not alive or were too young to remember. And almost everyone seemed to abandon the fundamentals for the widely held belief that appreciation in home prices had no limits.

Why a Failed Project for a Developer Can Still Be Good for the Community

As we saw in Chapter 2, developers are very confident and often overoptimistic. They may also become emotionally connected to a project to which they have committed their own and others' cash and several years of their lives. The combination of confidence and that connection may make it more difficult to know when to quit. Many developers like to say, "The biggest mistake you can make is falling in love with a deal," because when that happens, objective decision making goes out the window. So they often proceed with construction during a boom even when in the cold light of day it has become clear that abandoning the project and taking the loss may be the better choice. The last thing that goes wrong, which Minsky also predicts, is that overconfidence leads people to proceed with projects where the risk has increased to unacceptable levels.

But from the community's viewpoint, what does a failed development deal look like and what is so wrong with a developer falling in love with a deal? An unfinished concrete frame is a blight on the community and can remain so for years and even decades, but this is extraordinarily rare. More common is a finished project that has not sold out or leased up fast enough. If the building is half-vacant it may look forlorn when most of the windows are dark at night and it could begin to detract from the neighborhood if there is not enough income to adequately maintain the grounds and landscaping.

The project's original investors may suffer, but this is often invisible to nearby neighbors and community members. Condo buyers may suffer, particularly if the project does not fill up enough to generate the homeowners association dues required to support the operation and maintenance of the building. In the worst case, which is rare, the bank forecloses, takes possession of the building, and sells the remaining units at a deep discount, devaluing the units purchased by the original buyers. If those buyers find themselves "upside-down," with mortgages that are greater than the current market value of their units, they may choose to mail their keys back to the bank and default, further lowering property values. But over time, demand will return and prices will adjust upward to reflect the long-term trend of population growth. And what does the community get when this happens? A failed deal can be a devastating loss for the developer and her investors, the bank, and in some cases, the early buyers. But if it leaves behind a good building, it can become an asset to the community in the long run.

Which brings us back to Jorge Pérez's Icon Brickell. That building was very large, late to the market, and slow to fill up. Ultimately, the bank took it back in a "friendly foreclosure" and sold off the units at a discount. Then, the building began filling up—mostly with renters—but filling up all the same. Once its unit prices have risen to reflect the market's view of the project's value, it should become a highly desirable residential address, not just for renters but for future condo owners as well. More important, the Icon Brickell's beautiful architecture and interior design, stunning views, and plush amenities should make it an important asset to Miami and the Brickell community for decades to come. True, it didn't work out well for Pérez and his investors but it may still work out for the larger community. There are countless other examples of developers who lost large sums of money but whose projects became successful in time and contributed to their communities.

The financial rewards that flow from real estate development can be great but the risks can be equally great as well, so entrepreneurial developers must have both a high tolerance for risk and a desire for large profits. But is money the only reason they do it or do some developers have other motives and interests? And why does someone like Jorge Pérez decide to "go all the way" on design, material quality, and artistic beauty for a project like the Icon Brickell?

Chapter 8

Profits, Values, and a Sense of Purpose

Visionary companies pursue a cluster of objectives, of which making money is only one—and not necessarily the primary one. Yes, they seek profits, but they are equally guided by a core ideology—core values and a sense of purpose beyond just making money. Yet paradoxically, the visionary companies make more money than the purely profit driven companies.

—James Collins and Jerry Porras, *Built to Last*[1]

On the face of it, shareholder value is the dumbest idea in the world.

—Jack Welch, former CEO, General Electric[2]

The Leaning Tower of South Padre Island

One day in 2005, a loan officer in the Midwest took a call from a broker about a proposal for a twenty-five- to thirty-story high-rise condo tower on South Padre Island, off the Gulf Coast of Texas. The broker was pushing the deal hard but the loan officer was uneasy. The financing request was very aggressive, but what really gave the loan officer pause was that the development team seemed to lack relevant experience either working together or working on this type and size of project. The bank passed on the deal but the developer was able to secure financing through another lender.

Ocean Tower broke ground in 2006. Its concrete frame, exterior shell and windows, and the fitout of all of the units were completed by 2008, by which time the developer had sold 100 of the 150 units that had been priced at an average of $2 million a piece. But soon the building began to tilt and construction was halted. The thirty-one-story tower was connected to an adjacent four-story parking garage, which is typical for a high-rise project. What wasn't typical was the design of the project's foundations. Because they would be different heights and therefore carry different weights or "loads," the foundations for the tower and the parking garage should have been designed as separate systems with a joint between them to allow each building to settle independently of the other. But the structural engineer for Ocean Tower had designed the project with a single, connected foundation system. As the taller and much heavier tower began to settle more deeply into the sand of South Padre Island than the smaller, lighter garage, the whole connected complex began to tilt. The building was never occupied, and the developer, Antun Domit of Ocean Tower LP, had to return deposits to the one hundred buyers who had signed contracts.[3]

At 9:01 A.M. on December 13, 2009, Domit had the dubious honor of pushing the ceremonial detonation button, setting off a series of explosions that reduced the tower to a pile of rubble in about twelve and a half seconds. At 376 feet high, Ocean Tower set a record for being the tallest reinforced concrete structure ever imploded in the world, requiring 1,550 pounds of explosives and two and a half miles of detonating cord and leaving behind 55,000 tons of debris. Prior to demolition, the building was stripped of finishes and fixtures—all sold for whatever minimal salvage value could be had. The demolition of Ocean Tower attracted more than two thousand spectators but it was also the culmination of a public relations campaign created to deflect interest away from the $125 million lawsuit that Domit and Ocean Tower LP had initiated in 2008 against the project's geotechnical engineer, structural engineer, and contractor.[4]

In the lawsuit, Domit claimed that the geotechnical engineering firm had made representations that its engineers were familiar with the soil characteristics of South Padre Island but that their work did not reflect this knowledge. Specifically, there is known to be a layer of "compressible clay" between 120 and 190 feet below grade on South Padre Island, but the geotechnical engineers drilled and tested soils only to a depth of 100 feet. They never encountered the clay, so their recommendations to the structural engineer for the foundation design did not take it into account. Next, Domit claimed that the structural engineering firm designed a foundation system that was bound to settle unevenly because the two buildings were

connected. This would have presented a problem under the best conditions but the compressible clay exacerbated it. And finally, Domit claimed
that the construction company's workers began to notice deviations in
measurements—as the tower began to tilt—while pouring the concrete for
the seventh floor, but that, instead of stopping work, crews continued
building up to the thirty-first floor and the company continued collecting
monthly payments. Domit claimed that all three parties engaged in fraud
by knowingly and recklessly making false representations and by making
positive assertions when they did not know the facts. Domit also claimed
negligence and gross negligence. Ocean Tower LP later determined that
there were no construction defects that caused the tower to lean, and the
construction company was dismissed as a defendant in the lawsuit.[5]

We will probably never know exactly what happened at Ocean Tower
but one thing seems clear and it was clear to that loan officer in the Midwest
back in 2005. While all of the members of the development team may have
had the desire to take on a very large and potentially profitable project, they
may not have all had the experience required to successfully complete it.
Ocean Tower offers a rare and stunning example of a failed project and, as
we saw in the last chapter, many other things can and do go wrong on
development projects every day. But what must happen for things to go
right?

People choose development as a career in part because they want to
earn large profits. But are profits the only motive for developers? How do
developers think about the quality of the products and services they provide
or their broader purposes and goals? How do they make business decisions
that lead them toward achieving those goals and how do their other motives
influence their success? Does experience matter and how far can a developer
reach—in product type and scale—from one project to the next before he
has reached too far? Do the answers to these questions offer any clues as to
why one developer might be more or less successful than another?

The Profit-Seeking Paradox: Why the Desire for Large
Profits Alone Won't Lead to Large Profits

The stereotypical developer and entrepreneurs in general are thought to
be in business only for the profits, but recent research suggests that this
assumption is simplistic and that it discounts how other motives influence

profitability. In his book *Obliquity*, John Kay, an economist and business consultant, concluded that companies that emphasize profit seeking alone are less profitable than those that focus on other core values and purposes. He finds instead that "returns and goodness seem to be inextricably entwined," a phenomenon he calls the "profit-seeking paradox." Kay attributes this paradox to the way people in the real world actually make business decisions as opposed to how, until recently, long-standing but inadequate theories have attempted to explain decision-making behavior.[6]

The main point, argues Kay, is that it is impossible to drive directly at a big goal like "increased profits" because it is just too vague and difficult to think about in terms of day-to-day work. Rather, the best we can do is to take an oblique approach, focusing on smaller steps and decisions, constantly adapting, and feeling our way through a murky and ever-changing business environment as we grope our way toward that bigger goal.[7]

According to Kay, the growth and success of the physical sciences in the second half of the twentieth century led to the proliferation of the idea that there can be "a science to decision making" and that if it were "decoded" everyone would arrive at the same right answer. This "rational model of decision making," which held sway in the social sciences until only recently, is based on a process of problem identification, development of options, weighing the costs and benefits of each, choosing the best option, and then implementing it from the top down.[8]

The rational model also reflected a modernist optimism about humankind's ability to completely understand and solve even the most difficult public policy problems, such as poverty, drugs, crime, and, most recently, terrorism. This approach led to big failures in areas ranging from urban planning to foreign policy. Most social scientists have come to accept the limits of the rational model and the intractability of those so-called wicked problems for which there are no simple solutions, but not, however, before optimism and confidence led decision makers who "thought they knew more about the world than they did" to do a lot of damage. Kay offers a broad range of examples, including planners who replaced well-functioning urban neighborhoods with crime-ridden, modernist high-rise projects; architects whose idealistic plans for modern cities created soulless wastelands when actually built; political leaders who prosecuted disastrous and costly wars in Vietnam, Iraq, and Afghanistan; and the bankers and financial leaders whose enabling of the expansion of credit led to a global financial crisis in 2007–2008.[9]

Decision Making: How We Really Solve Problems

These failures should come as no surprise, says Kay, because the very idea of a science of decision making is an unattainable abstraction. Rather, says Kay, "Our objectives are complex, multi-faceted, imprecise, and they change as we move towards them." Decision making occurs not within a static and closed system but within a boundless and fluid environment where there are many moving parts, variables, and unknowns, and a temporal dimension—everything is changing all the time. Our decisions are also influenced by how others respond to the actions and steps we take and on how we anticipate them responding—actions leading to reactions that cannot be predicted. "The world is complex, imperfectly known, and our knowledge of it is incomplete," says Kay, "and this will remain the case no matter how much more we learn and how much we analyze problems."[10]

Rather than using a scientific approach to decision making, Kay explains how "we solve problems obliquely with an iterative and adaptive approach." In reality, we must choose from among a limited set of options and act with incomplete, imperfect, and constantly evolving information. Rather than a single right answer, different people will arrive at different answers based on their individual viewpoints and the unique information sets that they possess at the moment they make their decisions. There is no one right answer and even if there were one it may not be discoverable. Further, Kay reminds us that "a good decision can lead to a bad outcome and vice versa, while a successful outcome may have little to do with either the original decision or the capability of the decision maker." Kay concludes that the very notion of a "best solution" is misconceived and that "the skill of problem solving lies in the interpretation and reinterpretation of high-level objectives."[11]

Rather than comprehensive solutions, Kay's oblique approach emphasizes an ongoing process of iteration and experimentation where what matters most are practice, skill, knowledge, and experience. Through this approach we learn about the nature of the problem as we solve it. Rather than relying on a single, simple method we use a toolkit of models and narratives, adapting constantly to new information. Solutions to problems come from "oblique" directions and often lead to solutions to problems we did not know we had. Flexibility, rather than omniscience, is the key to this process, which is based on reason and evidence rather than a "rational" process of identifying objectives, evaluating options, and modeling consequences. "The way you solve a problem or approach a daunting task," says

Kay, "is not by envisioning the solution and planning on how to get there, but by doing something, taking a first step, and doing something that seems relevant." But how does Kay's oblique approach apply to decision making in business?[12]

Core Values Lead to Profits

Kay developed his theory of obliquity by comparing pairs of U.K. companies in the same industry that experienced vastly different fortunes and by examining cases of industry leaders who lost their way when they went from core purposes with an indirect emphasis on profitability to a direct approach.[13] Kay's research reinforces the work of Collins and Porras, who, in their book *Built to Last*, studied pairs of industry-leading companies in the United States, with each pair consisting of a company that was considered to be "great" by CEOs of peer companies and a similarly sized but not-so-great competitor. Pairs included Hewlett Packard and Texas Instruments, Proctor and Gamble and Colgate-Palmolive, and 3M and Norton. Collins and Porras determined that the difference between the "great" companies and the other companies was that great companies focused on "core values" while the other companies focused on individual technologies, products, and profits. And the proof is in the profits: The great companies in the study were six times more profitable on average over the long run as compared to their competitors.[14]

Kay illustrates this point with the story of Boeing, a company that tried both approaches. From 1945 to 1968, its CEO, Bill Allen, emphasized that Boeing would "eat, breathe, and sleep the world of aeronautics." When Boeing merged with McDonnell Douglas in 1997, the new CEO, Phil Condit, redefined the company's mission by saying, "We are going into a value-based environment where unit cost, return on investment, shareholder return are the measures by which you'll be judged. That's a big change." Apparently it was, as Boeing retooled its strategies to match this mission statement and quickly lost market share to its rival, Airbus. Condit's successors reemphasized the mission of civil aviation and Boeing soon regained its lead over Airbus. Kay concludes that at Boeing and many other companies the greatest shareholder value was created when it was sought obliquely.[15]

Based on this understanding of how decision making works, the business environment is not one where successful businesspeople are able to profit by accurately predicting the future. Rather, they continually match their organizations' skills and capacities to a constantly changing market environment where, as Warren Buffett and George Soros have said, "The test of financial acumen is to navigate successfully through irresolvable uncertainties."[16]

Oblique Decision Making in Real Estate Development

Kay's theory of obliquity builds on previous theories from thinkers such as Charles Lindblom, a political economist and leading proponent of "incrementalism" and "gradualism" in public policy decision making. In 1959 Lindblom wrote a groundbreaking essay that offered an alternative to the rational model and that he called "the science of muddling through," where complex problems are solved through incremental steps and constant adjustment rather than with comprehensive solutions. In his 1999 book *Sources of Power,* the psychologist Gary Klein used a study of how trained experts like firefighters and paramedics really make decisions to further undermine the rational model. In his theory of "naturalistic decision making," Klein found that a person's experience, knowledge, and instincts combine to produce a single option—there is no objective consideration of alternatives. In 2005, Malcolm Gladwell popularized Klein's conclusions in a book with a title that said it all: *Blink: The Power of Thinking Without Thinking.*[17]

In previous chapters, we heard developers describe their own versions of oblique decision making. Buzz Ruttenberg's story about how he earned an instant 30 percent return from a single transaction by valuing a portfolio of assets very differently than the seller is an example of how decision making is usually based on incomplete information and different mental frameworks. Obliquity argues against the value of detailed planning, and. indeed, as Jerry Fogelson said of his career, "It wasn't some brilliant master plan— that is just the way it evolved." The most important trait a developer can have is flexibility and adaptability. As Jorge Pérez said, "The way you survive is by adapting to what the market gives you." Successful developers start by using their experience and taking a first step, adjusting, and then taking another step. As John Carroll said, "You don't want to keep running into a concrete wall—so instead you go two or three degrees to the left or the right."[18]

In applying the ideas of oblique decision making and the profit-motive paradox to the business of real estate development, we would conclude that developers prioritizing profits over purpose would be less successful than those who work hard to make a good product as the route to large profits. These process-oriented developers would also be the same ones who were hands-on, tinkering away, and trying to figure out how to develop the best possible product, constantly observing, learning, adjusting, adapting to new information and influences, and, as Buzz Ruttenberg said, "honing their craft." And developers learn and grow over the course of their careers, or as Tibor Hollo said, "In time, we too change." But how do these conclusions help us to separate those developers who understand that success comes from a focus on core values and purposes from those who are in it for the profits alone?

Good Developers Still Prioritize Profits but They Care About Other Things Too

When you ask them to talk about what they do, sooner or later, most developers will make a distinction between what "good developers" do and what "bad developers" do. They also express frustration that the public does not understand or believe that "the good ones" really do care about place, community, happy tenants or residents, and the creation of a lasting legacy. As the developer Collin Barr said, "For the good ones, it is not about greed first."[19]

When you ask developers what their goals are—why they do what they do and what they hope to achieve—most will tell you that profits are very important but that they are also interested in good design, quality products, excellent service, happy customers, good reputations, place making, community contributions, legacies, and enjoyment in their work.

On the other hand, a developer who ranks profits first and considers these other things as secondary or unimportant is less likely to be successful. Driven purely by the profit motive, this type of developer might seek to enhance returns by cutting corners, doing shoddy work, and reneging on obligations to vendors, consultants, contractors, buyers, and tenants. In the worst case, an obsession with profits can lead to outright fraud or attempts to dodge the Internal Revenue Service. Certainly, this developer is not in the business because he cares about place making or the community. Rather, these developers are mere speculators who enter the business during a boom because they have access to cheap capital and see the promise of outsized profits and hope to make hay while the sun shines. These are the inexperienced and hands-off "fly-by-nights" and "johnnies-come-lately" that plentiful global capital created during the 2000s and who helped to cause the housing bubble.

But at the same time, there is nothing wrong with a good developer—a developer who does care about place making—who ranks profits first too. Indeed, one major difference between a bad developer and a good developer is that the good developer recognizes that he will increase his returns if he does a good job of managing the process and taking care of the many other concerns, tasks, and details—the nuts and bolts of development. Over the long run, he also knows that by committing his career to the business, gaining experience, and developing his expertise, he will only increase his chances for financial success in the future.

Developers are careful when they talk about good and bad developers but they do share a few common opinions. Summarizing these opinions, Robert Engstrom, a life trustee of the Urban Land Institute and a developer with nearly fifty years of experience in the industry, said, "I can't say exactly how, but I think the difference between good developers and bad developers has a lot to do with design." Engstrom points out that "development is a business like any other and people go into it to make money first." At the same time, while returns are still the first priority for a developer, good developers know that "good returns are the product of doing everything right, from the vision and design to the construction quality and client satisfaction."[20]

Unfortunately, according to Engstrom, bad design can be an act of either conscious commission or unconscious omission, that is, willful neglect or just a lack of understanding. "Bad design can be from lack of caring or just from lack of design sensitivity, and some developers are just oblivious to the idea of good design." Engstrom identifies another paradox when he points out that, while design is an important factor, it does not necessarily explain all profitable development. "Bad design sometimes gets built and succeeds from the standpoint of returns," says Engstrom, "so bad developers can get lots done without knowing that they are doing poor stuff." This can happen in different ways, but one typical way is that a developer who is early in the market cycle can develop an average-quality product that sells well for sheer lack of supply.

But when it comes to separating good developers from bad ones, Engstrom has a much simpler question: "Is he a bad guy?" Engstrom recalls, "Once I was in a meeting with a developer and a capital person from somewhere, and after he left I said to the developer, 'He's a bad guy.' The developer went ahead anyway and indeed the financier turned out to be a bad guy." But how can we tell the good guys from the bad guys? According to other industry experts, it has to do with a combination of ego, experience, salesmanship, savvy team members, and knowledge of one's own limits.

A Gut Feeling

Ardyth Hall has worked with developers around the country for more than twenty years, first on the lending side as a loan officer for a bank and later by representing institutional investors. Her experience has taught her to look for a few things when sizing up a potential partner. First, Hall likes to meet the developer in person. "I want to get to know them a bit, see them in several different business settings, socialize with them over dinner, and learn what their personal interests are. First impressions matter, so do they look you in the eye? Does he seem like a bad guy?" Through all of this, Hall is trying to figure out one simple thing: "If things go bad, which they sometimes do, will this developer fight me or work with me?"[21]

Second, Hall wants to meet the rest of the team. The developer is the visionary but he does not have all the skills required to complete the project successfully, so Hall wants to know who is actually going to be doing the work. "I want to meet the developer's staff, the architect, the construction person, and the finance person." She also wants to spend time with the architect—whom she believes is critical to a project's success—and with the architect and the developer together to see if they get along well, have a good relationship, and have any kind of chemistry. When she meets the rest of the team, Hall asks herself, "Are they the right people, are they knowledgeable, and do they have the power they need to do their work?"

Finally, she wants to know about the developer's prior experience with the project type, so she asks herself, "Have they done this kind of thing before and, if not, have they done something similar enough?" Just because a developer has not done a high-rise condominium before does not mean that he cannot do one. If he has successfully done a high-rise apartment building, then he has probably learned enough to be successful. On the other hand, if he has only completed a few townhomes and has never done a high-rise of any kind before, that should raise a flag. In the case of a new developer, Hall wants to know if he has done the same kind of project before successfully for another company. Hall recognizes that because tastes, markets, and product types are constantly changing no one has ever done exactly the same thing before, so developers must be constant learners. "The question is, have they learned enough to be able to make the jump to the next project, and to answer this, you must dig and find out what the developer's real capabilities are."

Over the years, Hall has developed a list of traits that distinguish good developers from bad ones, and a lot of those traits have to do with ego. "Most developers have big egos, but the good ones know how to control themselves. It is a fine line because a developer must control the entire process but the good ones do not micro-manage. Instead, they understand and accept their own limits and weaknesses and bring in the right people and give them power."

While the good ones can manage giving up a little bit of control, the bad ones cannot. "They have ego problems and they don't trust their people to do their jobs properly. They are also the ones who always have to do the tallest buildings, the greatest number of units, and will ignore advice when the market is turning because their name and legacy become too important to them." For these developers, "It is all fun and great when things are going well but when conditions change they are not prepared."

"The good developers are salesmen extraordinaire," says Hall, "and they have the power, presence, and ability to sell anyone without being greasy or schmoozy—you know you are being sold, but you kind of enjoy it." And personality matters. "With good developers, you enjoy their company. They are intellectual, knowledgeable, and can answer questions on a variety of subjects. They also know their city, from the history to the politics to the social dynamics. They are Type A personalities who are competitive and driven to do well in everything they do, including their outside interests, whether it is racing sailboats, golfing, cooking, or competing in triathlons. And they are entertaining and interesting people to be around.

"Less successful developers, on the other hand are pompous, egotistical, and slimy—more like the stereotypical developer in Tom Wolfe's novel *A Man in Full*." Wolfe's story is about a man named Charlie Croker, whom Wolfe reportedly created from a composite of three real developers. For Hall, Croker epitomizes the worst traits of the stereotypical, ego-driven developer. Hall said, "[Croker] reminds me of one developer in Baltimore who had to be able to point to the phallic high-rise that was the tallest building in the city and say 'see what I did.' Unfortunately people point to someone like that and say, 'That is what a developer does,' and this type of image obscures a lot of other good developers who work in neighborhoods and elsewhere and are more below the radar."

But like Bob Engstrom, in the end, for Ardyth Hall it all comes down to that initial gut feeling she gets. "I remember once feeling that the guy was a bad guy. We did the deal but I was right, he was a bad guy, the deal went bad, and in retrospect I saw it coming from the moment I met him."

Attributes of Successful Developers

If, as John Kay tells us, returns and goodness are inextricably entwined, then we should expect a successful developer to be one who is not just focused on making a lot of money but who is focused on getting everything else right too. This includes quality of product and service; design quality; the needs and desires of potential buyers and tenants; relations with architects, engineers, builders, and other team members; and partnerships with neighbors, city officials, investors, and lenders. In development—and in business in general—success follows when the interests of the many parties to a project are in alignment.

Developers who remain in business and are successful over the long run have some things in common. They often work with the same people— from investors and lenders to architects, engineers, and contractors—over and over again, for years, if not decades. These team members become the developer's brain trust over time and while few developers have a procedures manual, when they call and say, "We are going to do this," their team members understand their objectives. When successful developers choose to work with new team members it is more often because they are trying a new product type that requires a different kind of expertise. Conversely, a developer who works with different people on every project is often one who is too greedy and who leaves little opportunity for his team members to earn a profit of their own. This comes at a cost, as the developer has few trusted advisors who know how to work with them; as a result, their projects end in poorly designed products that are badly built, late to market, and slow to sell or lease up. In some cases this is followed by nonpayment of consultants, contractors, and vendors; acrimony; and litigation.

Despite the famous statement by Gordon Gekko, the lead character in the 1980s movie *Wall Street*, that "greed is good," smart developers also know that Warren Buffett is right when he says, "When people are greedy, be fearful." Experienced developers know that market cycles are real, as we saw in the last chapter, and while going first with a new product early in a cycle is risky, there may be greater risk in being one of the undifferentiated horde that goes last—and misses the window. Successful developers know that they can't time the market but that by going in early they can still make a good profit, minimize their risk, and stay in the game for the long run across multiple market cycles. They also know that selling at a price that generates a good profit while also allowing buyers to make a little money from appreciation is one way to increase the chances of selling out quickly and ensuring a successful project, a good reputation, and happy buyers who will promote their brand.

Some developers may succeed for a while despite a lack of understanding, as Bob Engstrom said, but when the market becomes more competitive and quality goes up, they will face challenges. More important, developers who pay attention to the details and try to get everything right—not just the profits—are likely to be successful over the long run. These are developers who live the project and bring everything they have to their work and for whom, as John Carroll said, "Each project is a big life story making its way into the building." The next developer we will meet exemplifies this idea, and his projects illustrate how the ideas of obliquity and the profit-motive paradox can be applied to real estate development.

Substantial Transformations

Craig Robins was born in Miami Beach at a hospital that would one day become the site of one of his own development projects. The son of a developer, Robins attended the University of Michigan and then studied art at the University of Barcelona before returning home to earn a law degree at the University of Miami. "When I was graduating from college I was not sure if I wanted to be an art dealer or a developer, and I think that says a lot about who I am. Art was exciting and interesting but impractical, and real estate and the idea of building strip malls seemed just incredibly boring. So South Beach in the 1980s was a perfect place for me."[22]

Miami's South Beach was the product of a major speculative real estate boom that started in the 1920s. Through the 1950s developers built the many Art Deco and Miami Modern, or Mi-Mo, hotels. "The Beach" became a glamorous place for northerners and celebrities to vacation in the winter. Many northerners moved there later in life to retire, joining the many World War II veterans who had relocated there after the war. By the 1980s, however, South Beach was in decay. Populated by a large group of very old Jewish retirees from the North who lived on fixed incomes, Miami had become "God's waiting room." The recent arrival of Cuban refugees from the 1980 Mariella boatlift—when Fidel Castro put the most mentally ill and criminally insane of his population into boats bound for Miami—coincided with the growth in the cocaine trade, and Miami Beach became a "Wild West" soon made famous by the television show *Miami Vice.*

As Miami Beach's population aged, so too did all of its fantastic hotels, many of which had either become dilapidated old retirement homes or were just abandoned. In the 1980s a grass-roots movement succeeded in creating a historic Art Deco district to protect these buildings from the wrecking ball, and at the same time a handful of developers began to buy up the old hotels on Ocean Drive. One of the leaders was the developer Tony Goldman, who had previously played a major role in transforming New York City's SoHo and who saw a new opportunity in Miami Beach. Goldman's strategy was to buy a number of properties and focus on transforming an area and not just a single property. Goldman also gave Craig Robins his first opportunity as a developer and became his mentor.

Robins says, "I started out the way a lot of entrepreneurs start out— with a combination of a few incredible mentors, teachers, and partners, and by doing things myself." Robins initially wanted to have an art studio so that he could bring artists in to paint. "I found the perfect place but the guy didn't want to just sell me the studio, he wanted me to be his partner in the whole building, so I bought the building mainly because I wanted the studio and then I began to do all of the things that developers do." It was a sixteen-thousand-square-foot building, and Robins put $20,000 down, borrowed some money to do the renovation, hired an architect to do the design work, oversaw the construction, leased it up, managed the property, and refinanced it when it was done. Robins's partner was Tony Goldman, "and he ended up becoming a really important friend and teacher to me."

South Beach: Being an Art Collector and a Real Estate Developer

Since creating his development company, Dacra, in 1987, Robins has developed many properties and projects but he has concentrated his efforts on transforming three geographic areas. "We have done three good projects where we were either the sole contributor or the principal contributor," says Robins. "The first was South Beach and recreating that whole area—there were blocks and blocks of buildings and most of it was really important stuff. There were four or five developers and half a dozen key community activists but we all worked together and it was very collaborative. I was young but Tony and I were by far the largest contributors to that transformation. We owned all of the property on Ocean Drive from Casa Casuarina—Versace's house—to the Victor, Tides, Carlyle, Cardozo, Leslie, Cavalier, and Netherlands Hotels and we redeveloped most of that property." More important for Robins, "Buying all of those Art Deco properties was as much being an art collector as it was being a real estate developer, so I was incredibly lucky to actually be able to find a way to actualize my interests and desires at a very young age.

"That early period of literally transforming South Beach from a slum into an oasis was incredibly rewarding for me. The kind of holdings we had and the impact we had was just incredible. Tony Goldman was a leader and we pushed the envelope more, did more things, and were able to garner more resources. We still hold property in South Beach today and it is a vital and interesting place but it has been overcommercialized. There is not a lot of opportunity left there and for me it is over."

Aqua at Allison Island: Transcendent Ideas

Robins's next project after South Beach was the redevelopment of the southern tip of Allison Island, a long, thin island that runs north to south in a channel in Miami Beach that is crossed from east to west by a causeway that connects it to the rest of Miami Beach. The part of the island north of the causeway had already been developed with housing but the southern part was the site of an abandoned hospital—the same hospital where Robins had been born.

"Our objective is to always innovate," says Robins, "and we try on every project to innovate on different levels, always using art, architecture, design, and urban design." Robins frames each of his projects as an attempt to respond to both an important local condition and a larger national or international question that he also feels needs addressing. "If you can really be local and respond to the local market but you can also do something that is transcendent of what might otherwise be provincial ideas, then you are engaging in life and the business opportunity is potentially also very special."

The local issue for Robins was the proliferation of soulless high-rise condo towers throughout Miami Beach. "Everyone was building these architecturally unremarkable high-rises and they were turning Miami Beach into a suburban vertical neighborhood. Because they sat on top of pedestals of parking, these buildings were detracting from the neighborhood and they certainly were not adding in any meaningful way, aesthetically, artistically, or from the community sense. They worked as saleable real estate and they were bringing in affluent people, which is a good thing, but they weren't doing anything beyond that." So Robins wanted to demonstrate that developing low-rise and midrise housing with more architectural sensitivity and a greater focus on art and urban design could actually be more successful. "We wanted to prove that it is not all about the view from your shoebox-in-the-sky but that it is also about the place where you live."

At the idea level, Robins wanted to bridge what he thought was a pointless divide between modern architecture and New Urbanist planning principles. "My favorite architects are modernists and my favorite planners are New Urbanists, so for years I have been intrigued by the rift between New Urbanism and modernism. I understand that a lot of New Urbanism projects have used neoclassical architecture and I can understand how that could be a problem for an architect but as a person who has never been emotionally charged about the debate, it has just never made any sense to me. For me, New Urbanism is just good urban design."

So Robins set out to develop a project that would offer a compelling alternative to the shoebox in the sky by combining modern architecture and New Urbanist planning principles to create a unique type of community. "I wanted to do a project where I would get all modern architects working with the great Miami-based planning firm of Duany Plater-Zyberk—the inventors of New Urbanism—and do a project that was really about modern architecture and contemporary art with New Urbanist principles." With those goals in mind, Robins collaborated with Duany Plater-Zyberk, ten well-known modern architects, and two major international artists. "We created a project that I am very proud of."

For Robins, Allison Island was the ideal location in part because of its proximity to South Beach—another unmatched collection of modernist architecture in an urban setting. The site also presented a unique opportunity because it was a much larger piece of land than is typically available in overdeveloped Miami Beach. But disagreement with the surrounding community had put an end to the previous developer's attempts, so when

Figure 46. Robins combined New Urbanism planning principles and Miami Modern architecture to create the Aqua neighborhood on Allison Island. Photo by Steven Brooke; courtesy of DACRA.

Robins acquired it the Miami Beach Zoning Commission "told us to go work it out with the neighborhood, which we did." Most developers see working with the community as a big negative "but for us it was a fun process, we actually learned a lot from the neighborhood, and we used that tension to really perfect the plan. All really good plans involve a process of editing, and while a third party with more community-based interests may be less sophisticated and knowledgeable than the planners and developers, they also bring a perspective that is really valuable." In the end, and in part because of pressure from the surrounding community, Robins developed Aqua at a lower density than the zoning allowed. "There is no other developer who wouldn't have taken that land and done it at greater density and also put a high-rise or two on it, had the neighbors even allowed it, and there would have been a fight for sure."

Robins took a significant risk when he chose to use a for-sale real estate product as a vehicle through which to confront the larger issues of soulless high-rises and the gulf between modernist architecture and New Urbanist planning principles, but he never lost sight of the market. In Miami, views had become the most important selling point of any condominium, which is why the shoebox in the sky had proliferated and become the default product. This made Aqua—with its low-rise and midrise massing, increased density, and high design style—an exotic product, and in real estate "exotic" means "risky." Robins mitigated his market risk in two simple ways. First, and in part because of the nature of the site, Robins simply could not and did not build a lot of product. So, even though Aqua was different, "there was a perfectly adequate market for what we were doing, because there was a very limited supply of what we were producing and plenty of demand for it."

Robins did something else that was very important that he thinks most other developers would have missed. "Everything we were doing outside was radical but the one thing I wanted to do was to make sure that there was nothing about the interiors of those unremarkable high-rise units that we were not offering in our units." So Robins hired an architectural design consultant who had designed the interior units for many of the luxury condominiums in Miami and Miami Beach, and he made sure that everything that was being designed into those buildings was being designed into Aqua. "We wanted to have every single bell and whistle that was motivating those high-rise buyers incorporated into our project." A unit that will be attractive to the luxury market must have closets of a certain size, a certain type of bathroom design that includes a toilet and a bidet, a kitchen of a certain size and layout, and balconies. "Then, if you are not doing one of those things, it is because of a conscious and internal decision, not because you are unaware of what the rest of the market is doing." Robins always likes to have his architects design their own interiors, so in the larger midrise buildings at Aqua the architects designed the lobbies and the public spaces. But for the units in those buildings and the townhouses the interiors were plain vanilla. "We had a designer who did all of the kitchens and bathrooms and some of the townhouse interiors but the buyers could also hire their own interior designers if they wanted to. We were trying to merge scalable production housing with individuality, so the exterior spaces and public spaces were very personalized by the architects but the interior designs were nice and simple."

So, once Robins had provided an equivalent quality product in terms of unit design, layout, and "bells and whistles," the only decision for the potential buyer became the choice between the view and the community.

Figure 47. The view of Aqua from across the channel, with townhomes in the foreground on the eastern side of the island and midrises in the background on the western side. Photo by Steven Brooke; courtesy of DACRA.

"Everyone had to decide between living in Aqua or living in another boring high-rise, and certainly in the boring high-rises the view from your shoebox in the sky could be really spectacular. So the tradeoff was that you got to live in Aqua." Robins thinks that the planning and design strategies used at Aqua—and the emphasis on community—will only enhance the development's value well into the future as other more standard stock ages and loses its luster. "Aqua was very, very well received and the interesting thing," predicts Robins, "is that it is the only complex completed as a part of this real estate market cycle that will be even more respected and more highly regarded in twenty years than it is today. The only thing those other projects can offer is views and newness. The jury is still out, but I think there is potential for decades of rediscovery, continued appreciation, and higher respect for Aqua."

Robins admits that, like any other project, Aqua is not perfect. Alex Krieger, who teaches and writes about urban design at Harvard University's Graduate School of Design, hosted a seminar on the subject of Aqua. "One ironic conclusion," said Robins, "was that despite our best effort to create a New Urbanist community, we screwed up, because the fact that it was on an island meant there were fewer connections to the surrounding community." Worse, the residents required Robins to put up a guardhouse, which he did not want to do, effectively making Aqua a gated community. "We could have had ten thousand square feet of commercial development with restaurants and cafés that would have served the broader community but the residents chose to create an oasis instead and we couldn't do it. I pushed it," says Robins, "and you can only push things so far."

Aspirations for community and reality often turn out differently and, indeed, the reality is that Aqua can feel a little quiet and even uninhabited. As with other developments in Florida, many of Aqua's original buyers were not full-time residents but out-of-towners or, worse, speculators who never intended to live there. There does not appear to be much "community" and being on a small island separated from Miami Beach by bridges does not help. But if Robins is correct and Aqua is more timeless than the high-rises it competed against, there may well come a day in the future when it does feel more like a true community.

The Design District: A Center for Miami's Creative Community

In 1995, Robins began buying property in what has become known in Miami as the Design District. Here again, Robins sought a connection between the local situation and his own experience. "The Design District was an opportunity to really control an area instead of having this crazy overcommercialization that happened in South Beach." The Design District is on the mainland, north of downtown Miami and at the foot of the bridge that connects to Miami Beach. In 1995, Robins saw it as the next place where South Beach needed to grow. "Geographically, the commercial development locations in South Beach were over and done. But the growth had to go somewhere and the opportunity in the Design District was to improve upon what I perceived to be the weaknesses and the problems of South Beach." Specifically, Robins saw the development of the Design District as a chance to make a real creative center for Miami. But he also wanted to exert more control in shaping an integrated urban experience with a coherent brand. "It is really wonderful if every city can have one place where everything that happens is going to be great and where the aspirations are higher."

If the local problem was accommodating the expansion of South Beach, then the larger issue Robins wanted to tackle was the furniture industry in the United States, which, he felt, pointlessly restricted the general public's access to design. "As I got involved I learned that the furniture industry was operating with this arcane model based on 'decorator centers.' These were big, unattractive fortresses where the furniture was hidden inside and displayed in unattractive ways and in unattractive spaces, which didn't matter because there was no interaction with the public. The furniture industry was also kind of a racket, because the decorator centers would only allow the decorators in so you couldn't go there if you weren't with a decorator. The showrooms were giving the designers kickbacks, which they called 'commissions,' so a third of what you paid for a sofa was a commission for the decorator. When you compare this to all of the very public merchandising that goes into the sale of fashion and even art, which, arguably, should be more removed from people than furniture, it seemed completely backwards to us."

Instead, Robins felt that design should be moved out onto the street and that it should be really visible to the public, so he decided to challenge the entire furniture industry. One of his next steps was to commission an outdoor art installation by Roberto Behar and Rosario Marquardt called "The Living Room" that, when completed in 2001, literally put overscaled furniture on the sidewalk at a key intersection in the Design District. "There were a lot of politics working against us but we began to gain way

Figure 48. *The Living Room*, an art installation by Roberto Behar and Rosario Marquardt, which has become a symbol of the Design District.
Photo © Roberto Behar and Rosario Marquardt, R & R Studios.

and now I think the Design District is the most important single location for design in the country. We have the best brands in contiguous locations and this is the only place where it is all on the street, in an urban setting." The Design District has taken market share from competing decorator centers and in that sense it is a success, but that was not enough to succeed as a business model for real estate development. "Furniture design doesn't really bring people because you only redecorate your house every ten years—it is not like clothing that you buy for a few seasons or restaurants that you go to every week. So that was the first phase but we realized that we had to do more and so then it evolved."

Next, Robins collaborated with Art Basel, the huge international art show that happens in Miami every spring. He also founded a show called Design Miami in partnership with Art Basel. Over time, Robins succeeded in making the Design District into the cultural venue for Art Basel. The commercial fair—where all of the art is sold—happens elsewhere in Miami

Beach, but the Design District has become host to many of the parties, events, and exhibitions. "So in this neighborhood we took a totally non-commercial approach and this led to the best chefs starting to open restaurants and a number of high-end fashion boutiques opening up." Now the Design District is about great food, fashion, and design, and it has also become a place where a number of creative businesses have decided to locate their offices, which has diversified the tenant base and created more life in the area, day and night. "And although it has been tough, it is growing, even in this economy, and that is because the different market segments are growing."

By 2010 Robins owned six hundred thousand square feet in the sixteen-square-block area called the Design District and he had plans for the development of another one million square feet over the coming five years. "The Design District is a really interesting neighborhood," says Robins, "and although it is a part of South Beach in a way it is more sophisticated and not nearly as commercial. So we are balancing the need for growth and the need to drive traffic to make it the successful and vibrant place that it has started to become." The recession dampened growth but very soon the Design District would begin its next transformation and begin to grow again, and very quickly.

Things accelerated for the Design District in 2010 when Robins began talking to Michael Burke, president of Fendi, a brand owned by the Fortune 50 luxury brand conglomerate Louis Vuitton Möet Hennessy (LVMH). For many years, the Bal Harbour Shops, a retail mall at the northern tip of Miami Beach, had been the shopping destination for wealthy residents and tourists seeking luxury goods. But the mall required its tenants to sign a lease with an exclusivity clause that prohibited them from opening another location within a twenty-mile radius. A number of store leases were coming up for renewal at Bal Harbour and LVMH wanted the exclusivity clause removed because it felt the area was "understored" and that there was enough demand for other locations and larger stores than Bal Harbour could accommodate. But the owners were reluctant to eliminate the exclusivity clause so LVMH began to explore other options and chose to move to the Design District. While Louis Vuitton paved the way, other brands were soon to follow, including Christian Dior, Celine, Pucci, Hermés, and Cartier.[23]

But that is not all that LVMH did. After nearly a year of talks, LVMH and Robins entered into a partnership late in 2010, combining the best of

Figure 49. Orchids growing on the façade of the Christian Louboutin shoe store, one of the early luxury boutiques in the Design District. Photo by James Harris; courtesy of DACRA.

two worlds: Robins's vision for the area and the substantial resources of L Real Estate, LVMH's real estate fund, whose investors included European family trusts. Those resources allowed for the acceleration of development in the Design District. LVMH was the spark, said Burke. "It allowed a much more aggressive acquisition program, and gave credibility. It allowed for the Hermés and the Cartiers of the world to come in."

And come in they did. By the fall of 2013, a number of new luxury stores and restaurants had opened in the Design District, including Berluti, Dior Homme, and Prada. Another fifty shops are scheduled to open in 2015. In 2013 Robins said, "Our real focus now is to solidify the luxury retail offering, so that in addition to great design, art, and restaurants, you'll have the most comprehensive collection of luxury fashion and jewelry in South Florida."

In addition to acquisitions, L Real Estate helped fund significant public realm and infrastructure improvements in the Design District, including the creation of a four-block pedestrian promenade. Three hundred mature shade trees were added along the streets in the district, as were tree-shaded plazas, cafés, and more public art. The master plan for the district was by Duany Plater-Zyberk, and Robins recruited cutting-edge architects from around the world to design the buildings and stores.[24] In 2012 the Design District was certified as the first Leadership in Energy and Environmental Design (LEED) Gold Neighborhood in Miami-Dade County. And despite all of that growth, Robins has remained true to his roots and to his original partners in the Design District. He has continued to support furniture-design showrooms by working with his tenants, relocating them to other buildings in the district to make way for new buildings, and keeping rents at levels comparable to where they had been previously.

When complete, the Design District will include nine hundred thousand square feet of space in nearly twenty buildings. Dacra and L Real Estate together own approximately 70 percent of the property in the district, and both are happy with returns, with Burke claiming in 2013 that the financial results from LVMH's investment had already exceeded initial projections. Robins has done well too in his nearly twenty-year commitment to the Design District. In a comparison of property values, Dacra paid $23 per square foot for the Moore Building in 1994 while in the spring of 2013 a nearby property sold for $2,000 per square foot. And he has been able to continue following his interests. When asked in one interview if he saw himself more as a businessman, a prominent art collector, or a patron of

Figure 50. The Louis Vuitton store helped start the second wave of luxury boutiques in the Design District. Photo by Robin Hill; courtesy of DACRA.

the arts, Robins answered, "I am a curious man who is fascinated by creativity and who appreciates living in a time when rigid labels aren't needed."[25]

The Design District is a very big undertaking that Robins started working on after completing his South Beach projects but before he started Aqua. "It has been a really fun project and it has evolved and gone through phases. There have been these iterations over time. From furniture to a

Figure 51. The Design District's main street, 40th Street, lined with new trees. Photo by Robin Hill; courtesy of DACRA.

larger idea of fashion, culture, and design, to Art Basel and the cultural center of Miami's creative community, and now to a luxury shopping destination." But a big part of the Design District's success—not surprisingly—has always been design.

Architecture, Urban Design, and Public Art

Since the beginning, Robins has been a strong advocate of historic preservation, where appropriate, and he has also used art, architecture, and design to enrich the places where he works. "And fundamental to all of this is learning about, understanding, and focusing on urban design, because urban design is really the foundation for everything we do. Rigorous attention to urban design creates the platform upon which to make a neighborhood work. What urban planners argue for from an architectural standpoint is fundamentally our business model and everything else flows from that, so we think about use and scale and all of those kinds of things the way a planner would instead of the way a real estate developer would."

Finally, Robins's background and interest in art continue to influence all of his projects. His headquarters in the Design District hosts a large collection of contemporary art but he has also integrated public art pieces into all of his projects. At Aqua, the artist Richard Tuttle created a work called *Splash* that is made up of more than one hundred thousand colored glass and white ceramic tiles installed on a ninety-foot-high, blank white sidewall of one of the midrise buildings that faces the swimming pool. The Argentinian artist Guillermo Kuitca created a terrazzo tile sculpture of Allison Island that serves as the bottom of a shallow fountain in the center of Aqua's entry court, St. Francis Square. In the Design District, Robins commissioned the architect Zaha Hadid to create a piece called *Elastika* for the inside atrium of the Moore Building, an old furniture store.

A Philosophical Shift

Most developers deal with just one property at a time so they think in terms of the highest and best use for that land but not necessarily the highest and best contribution to the larger neighborhood and community. Robins's business model is different. Like his mentor and friend, Tony Goldman, who always bought enough pieces of property to control a district, Robins likes to focus on an area or a neighborhood and to acquire more and more property in that neighborhood. "When you do that," says Robins, "a philosophical shift occurs in how you think about a property. Because when you

Figure 52. Zaha Hadid's *Elastika* art installation, inside the old Moore Building. Photo by Steven Brooke; courtesy of DACRA.

own a half million square feet of space in twenty buildings in one area and you are renovating a ten-thousand-square-foot building your focus is not on making the greatest profit possible on the one building, but on driving the value up on the other five hundred thousand square feet of space. If you can make the whole neighborhood worth more with that one building, then the multiple on your return is geometric and enormous. So for example, if the value of the ten-thousand-square-foot building increases by $50 per square foot, that is a meaningful amount of money—$500,000. But if the half million square feet in twenty buildings increases in value by $50 per square foot, that is $25 million."

Like other developers, good design is central to the successful marketing and sales of his real estate, but Robins offers another interpretation of its value. "Everything always has to have a bottom line but as long as it works financially, good architecture and design is worth the extra cost because it creates goodwill. And goodwill is valuable because it is your reputation and it is going to affect the pricing you can get, the financing you can get, and all kinds of other things that are going to help you in business. But what is unique about our business model that makes goodwill even more important is that we own all of the property around a project, so the goodwill is immediately transferred to the property next door and all of the other properties."

Robins points out how the use of good design in real estate development can create a challenging paradox where the real estate market prefers plain vanilla products. "Interesting buildings are not valued as much commercially as uninteresting ones so, for example, if you were going to build a house in Miami, a fake Mediterranean-style house is probably going to be most saleable in the market. But I would rather do things that reflect and advocate for the creativity of our own time. These things then become individual expressions that add more to long-term value and make a place more vital. It is even better if you can do that in a place where there is some historical context, and the Design District has both. In the end, my real focus is on my own desire to always stay connected to what I have done and to be truly who I am and transcendent, which is another way of staying focused on the local and trying to be international at the same time."

If John Kay's profit-seeking paradox is correct and Collins and Porras are right about the importance of purpose to success, then Craig Robins has created a company that is "built to last." Robins can clearly articulate his own ideology, values, and purposes. He cares about profits but he is also interested in bringing together art and real estate development. He likes to frame each project as a challenge that addresses both an international and a local problem. He takes a broader view of a development district that allows him to value individual projects and properties differently rather than trying to maximize the value of every single one. Like Pérez, Ruttenberg, and others, he strives to combine his personal interests in art, architecture, and urban design into each project. And perhaps most important, he tries to "stay focused on who I am and what I have done." With these kinds of core values, Robins and other developers like him are in a better position than their less engaged competitors to succeed and have a lot of fun making money in what is a very hard business.

Many developers provide basic tried-and-true products that serve market demands—from retail centers to housing and office space—innovating at the margins over time. Some developers, like Craig Robins, operate at a larger scale and with a vision that goes beyond individual properties, using art, architecture, preservation, and urban design to create whole new districts and cultural centers. Robins also envisioned the future direction of growth and then stretched geography, successfully making the case for the Design District as an extension of South Beach, even though it was on the mainland. In the next chapter we will meet another developer who not only stretched borders but also reshaped the urban environment by transforming an existing building type so much that it effectively became an entirely new real estate product.

Chapter 9

The Creation of Place and Culture

> Developers are always doing something that no one has ever done
> before, whether it is a place that no one else has gone yet, a price that
> no one else has achieved, or a product that has not been tried. Think
> about it: the only deals they can do are deals that others have not yet
> done.
>   —Herb Emmerman, Chicago real estate developer and marketing
>   consultant[1]

Paradoxical People

By now you have come to realize that any discussion of entrepreneurs, businesspeople, and real estate developers is riven with paradoxes. As we saw in the last chapter, developers must focus on a core purpose beyond profits if they are to avoid the "profit-seeking paradox." And while many developers are driven first by money, as they accumulate it their motivations shift and evolve. Once successful, they begin to define themselves through their personal interests in everything from art, architecture, and urban design to planning, sustainability, and dignified housing for low-income people. As they integrate these interests into their work and turn their life stories into buildings, they create our shared physical environment and subtly shape our culture.

All developers are visionaries at some level but most innovate at the margins, creating new and improved versions of their most recent projects. A few, however, succeed in making entirely new things. Like many other entrepreneurs, developers sometimes create products that we don't even know we need. From the suburban tract housing, office parks, and regional malls of the 1950s and 1960s to the mega-malls of the 1980s, the entertainment centers of the 1990s, and the high-rise luxury condominiums of the 2000s, developers have always created the places where we live, work, shop, and play. But there was a time when people did not know that they wanted these kinds of places. This chapter is about how some developers, while still innovating at the margins, go a little farther to create new products and how, in the process, they change our perspectives and shape our culture. To understand how developers do this, we must first consider two more paradoxical figures: the "rogue" in business and the "trickster" of mythology.

The Rogue: A Persistent and Original Thinker

In addition to the internal paradoxical traits that illuminate their motives, entrepreneurial developers also present themselves as paradoxes to the external world, from their role in society to their role in the creation of place and culture. Schumpeter, for example, underscored the ambiguous character of the entrepreneur as an independent individual who operates at the margins of society while at the same time creating the commercial foundations for society, which "depends upon entrepreneurs and, as a class, lives and dies with him." But how does the entrepreneur fit—or not fit—into the larger world of business?[2]

Robert Solomon begins his book *Ethics and Excellence: Cooperation and Integrity in Business* by systematically debunking a variety of harmful stereotypes about how business works. He dismisses the ideas that business is "war," that it is "a jungle out there," that you must "kill or be killed," and that "Wild West" and "cowboy" metaphors make any sense. Solomon argues instead that business usually means repeat business and that war metaphors are inconsistent with the prevalent concept of "corporate culture," which is social by definition. Indeed, Solomon proposes that business should be thought of more as a social system and that Aristotle's views of the ethics of personal behavior should serve as the foundation of this social system. But near the end of his book, Solomon steps out of this framework to consider the role played by a special character in business that he calls the "rogue."[3]

Hero or heroine, the rogue is a paradoxical but familiar figure that abounds in contemporary culture. The rogue is "likeable and good looking" but at the same time marginalized and often at odds with the law. In

Hollywood movies the rogue can be found in characters from Harrison Ford's portrayal of Han Solo, the shady but handsome swashbuckling space pirate in *Star Wars*, to the accidental criminals that Susan Sarandon and Geena Davis become in *Thelma and Louise*. They are good people who do bad things for good reasons—or at least good reasons relative to other characters in the story—and earn our sympathy, if not our affection.[4]

But rogues have a much longer and more honorable history in arts and culture. Solomon lists famous artists and intellectuals including Beethoven, Balzac, Picasso, Freud, and Jung, and their rogue-ish traits, which include bad manners, untrustworthiness, high living, constant indebtedness, moral eccentricities, rudeness, and inconsiderate behavior toward colleagues. Solomon points out that examples of the rogue abound in business as well, where successful people are known for being cheap, rude, crude, short-tempered, mercurial, pushy, dictatorial, micro managing, and "anything but saintly." But the important thing about all of these people says Solomon, is that "over time, all is forgotten and their status as rogues and heroes outlasts the gossip and slander surrounding them."[5]

Solomon concludes that the rogue plays an important role in society and business by reminding us that "acts of creativity and courage often consist in following one's own sense of integrity rather than in thoughtless obedience, and inspiring others rather than following them." Thus, says Solomon, today's hero is more likely to be "a persistent and original thinker who brings an idea to fruition" than simply "the most ferocious fighter." But more important, says Solomon, to conclude that the rogue is simply amoral would be missing a nuanced ethical point and would paint a "fraudulent portrait of business and ethics." Rather, for the rogue, following one's own sense of integrity is a highly ethical act itself, one that is more representative of the extraordinary virtues exhibited by heroes and saints than of the ordinary virtues of the common man. But while Solomon's rogue operates in the modern world, he or she is also a reincarnation of an even more timeless character known as the "trickster."[6]

The Trickster: A Disruptive Creator of Culture

In *Trickster Makes This World*, the poet and writer Lewis Hyde considers a cultural version of the rogue through a character that has inhabited the human consciousness through mythology since ancient times, whom he calls the trickster. Hyde begins with the ancient Greek story of Hermes, a

mortal who, through a series of tricks and deceptions, is able to make himself immortal and "deal himself in at the table of the gods." According to
Hyde, Hermes and other tricksters "work at the borders and boundaries
of life, between heaven and earth, gods and mortals, commerce and life.
Sometimes they create new borders or bring old ones to life, rearrange
things, and then come in to solve problems that they themselves created."[7]

The embodiment of the trickster is the coyote of American folklore
who, unlike other animals, has no single nature or "one way," which is an
advantage rather than a disadvantage because it allows him to have many
ways. Thus the trickster is versatile, quick to adapt, flexible, and willing to
shift ground rather than stand and fight.[8] The trickster also has an unusual
"plasticity" of mind that makes him smarter and more cunning than others, giving him the ability to form an image or representation of some sort
and "float it, detached, to be considered and shaped or changed before it is
either discarded or acted upon." Thus a trickster invented creative lying—
the art of using language to "draw his adversaries into his own uncanny
territory," where he can float his ideas. A trickster uses speech, words,
feigning, and fibbing in his "playful construction of fictive worlds," where
deceit and inventive speech are integrated.[9]

But in another paradox, a trickster's lies are not necessarily lies. It is the
trickster, says Hyde, "who invents the gratuitous untruth. He is a mediator
who works by way of a lie that is really a truth, a deception that is in fact a
revelation." The trickster remakes truth on his own terms and "tells lies
that tell a higher truth." Because tricksters help people see the essence or
the heart of things, they "have a touch of the prophet about them," says
Hyde, and "the prophet disrupts the mundane in order to reveal a higher
truth."[10]

Most important, a trickster is the ultimate opportunist. "He keeps a
sharp eye out for naturally occurring opportunities and creates them ad
hoc when they do not occur by themselves." He is a master at doubling
back and reversing himself, he covers his tracks and twists the meaning of
his words, and he is "polytropic," changing his skin, shifting his shape, and
presenting himself in different ways as the situation requires. The trickster
uses his cunning to seize an opportunity for himself or to block another's
opportunity.[11]

Last but not least, tricksters are lucky, but not in the traditional sense.
Rather, they make their own luck. Echoing Louis Pasteur who said,
"Chance favors the prepared mind," Hyde differentiates between dumb

luck and smart luck, noting that "what a lucky find reveals is neither cosmos nor chaos, but the mind of the finder." Thus a trickster relies both on knowledge and experience and also on being flexible enough not to get stuck in rigid thinking and frameworks that would prohibit him from seeing anomalies and opportunities that others cannot see. "We therefore get this paradox: with smart luck, the mind is prepared for what it isn't prepared for. It has a kind of openness, holding its ideas lightly, and willing to have them exposed to impurity and the unintended."[12]

Hyde's trickster is an opportunist who has not just "one way" but many ways. In the same way that the word "entrepreneur" means "to get in between and take," a trickster looks for opportunities at the borders, the intersections, the crossroads, and the joints. He uses language creatively to float new ideas and expose greater, unrealized truths. And he has a flexible and cunning mind—he gets by on smart luck. All of this leads to the production of culture, says Hyde. "In spite of all their disruptive behavior, tricksters are regularly honored as the creators of culture. They are imagined not only to have stolen certain essential goods from heaven and given them to the race but to have gone on and helped shape this world so as to make it a hospitable place for human life."

Solomon's rogue and Hyde's trickster offer two similar and complementary perspectives on entrepreneurial people who follow their own paths and instincts, using cunning and flexibility of mind to identify and exploit opportunities that others cannot see, and in some cases creating problems that they can then solve. And with the trickster in particular, Hyde illuminates an important aspect of the entrepreneur in the creative use of language in the floating, shaping, and promotion of ideas. But what can rogues and tricksters tell us about real estate developers?

A Robust House of Cards[13]

> The architecture is, of course, exquisite. The decks taper to a slender edge, V-shaped columns create a dynamic, extraordinary profile that seems to refer to the sculptural concrete canopies with which Lapidus decorated Lincoln Road. The perspectives on the city from each deck are increasingly theatrical, and, from the very top, it is filmically panoramic. A rhythm of compression and release in the heights between the floors makes a

surprisingly engaging journey. It is intriguing, strange. This is a building very much in a modernist tradition of revealing function, of structural transparency, a building reveling in a curiously dated yet enduringly American autopia, an ambiguous vision of the ascendancy of the machine over the city. But it is also engaging, both sculptural and compelling, referring obliquely to the wonderful tropical concrete of Lina Bo Bardi and Paolo Mendes da Rocha. 1111 Lincoln Road addresses a forgotten typology and uses the planning and usage restrictions that would have otherwise choked the site to create value from seemingly nothing.
    —*Edwin Heathcote, architecture critic*[14]

It's not just a building—it's more like a performance piece. It is an urbanistic, friendly, connected building . . . a public place for anyone who wants to enjoy the city. It is also a cultural building where people can have an experience that mixes program in unique ways—ways people have not seen before. It's about twisting your sense of who you are. It's about putting you in a different perspective, shaking things up, putting you where you haven't been before.
    —*Robert Wennett, Miami developer*[15]

It may be difficult to believe, but these descriptions are of a parking garage. 1111 Lincoln Road, in Miami Beach, however, is not just any parking garage and its developer, Robert Wennett, who calls his latest project a "parking sculpture," is not just any developer. Indeed, how Wennett went about developing this project does not lend itself to a single narrative explanation but rather many. One narrative is about how Wennett assembled his team and then how together they framed and solved a complicated urban design problem. Another is the story that Wennett weaved about art, design, fashion, culture, place, and urban transformation, a story that helped to explain—and sell—a very unconventional project to a broad array of constituents from city officials and the general public to investors, lenders, tenants, and their customers. Yet another narrative is about the real estate deal and how Wennett saw an opportunity invisible to others and how he used his skill and experience to exploit it by creating a project where the whole was greater than the sum of the parts. At 1111 Lincoln

Figure 53. 1111 Lincoln Road: A robust house of cars. Photo by Iwan Baan.

Road, these and other threads are entwined to create one story and one project that would not make sense—or work—without all of them. And what is most interesting about these individual threads and the twisted-together whole is how much they rely on paradoxes, dualities, multiple readings, and how much they challenge our thinking about everything we think we know. But it all starts with Wennett himself.

A contemporary art collector with additional interests in fashion, design, and the counterculture, Robert Wennett shrugs off the label of developer. "I am motivated by drivers that are different from those that motivate other developers and I am driven by a passion and inspiration that comes from the creative field and an ability to see things that others don't see." Wennett traces these interests—and his unique approach to development—to his first job.[16]

Wennett grew up in Boston with his father, a lawyer, and his mother, a real estate broker. In the late 1970s, at around age eighteen, he started selling real estate in the South End of Boston. "Nobody else wanted to sell there at the time because the entire area was completely boarded up," remembers Wennett, "and the only people who were buying were the avant-garde and people to the left who were buying shells for $20,000 and renovating them." Selling in the South End was Wennett's first introduction to gentrification and seeing people who were investing in an area that, on the surface, looked like it offered little if any opportunity. "And obviously," points out Wennett, "those houses are worth, $2 million, $3 million, or even $5 million today."

Wennett earned a bachelor's degree in liberal arts from the University of Pennsylvania but eventually went into investment banking. He quickly became restless and decided to make a change. "I had to do something that spoke to me. I had a fairly traditional background—I went to Penn, then Columbia for my MBA, and then into investment banking—but none of it interested me because it was not who I was and I had a hard time relating. Instead, I gravitated towards things that were being explored by counterculture people, involving fashion and design."

Buying Old Shopping Centers—in Cool and Interesting Locations

Wennett had always excelled at selling and buying real estate but at this point in his career he also knew that he was beyond just being a broker. A break came in 1986, when he attended a conference in Washington, DC, where he met the president of one of the companies that had presented. Shortly thereafter, he accepted an offer to work for the company, Federal Realty Investment Trust (FRIT), a publicly traded real estate investment trust (REIT) based just outside of Washington, DC, in Chevy Chase, Maryland. REITs were growing in popularity at the time and this company was worth "a couple hundred million dollars" when Wennett started as an acquisitions officer. FRIT concentrated on acquiring, renovating, and repositioning tired old shopping centers in first-tier suburban communities adjacent to major metropolitan cities. This was Wennett's first exposure to retail real estate and buying large undervalued properties. He was attracted to it because it combined both his creative expression and the property type that was most interesting to him. "The main reason retail was the most interesting property type to me was because I could relate to the retailers and their sense of creativity so I understood things both from the retailer's and the developer's perspective.

"When I bought shopping centers I would become familiar with the area and something would hit me; I could see that it was just a great area and that the property was being underutilized and underperforming with little creative thought or positioning. I would buy great pieces of land—the key was not to think about the purchase too much. The play was that you bought the land and buildings for less than replacement costs or the value of the land alone and then you had to figure it out once you bought it. If you waited too long, you might miss the opportunity altogether as the upside was what it could be, not what it was today." Wennett started buying properties in 1986 and he rarely purchased a property based primarily on a lot of market research. "We always had to do demographic research and market studies because someone—an investor or lender—always wanted to see it, but I never relied much on that canned research to make buying decisions, I always went on my gut and instinct on what something could be rather than what it was."

Wennett worked at FRIT for twelve years. "I would buy properties all the time and I would buy in places that I thought were cool and interesting locations and where the opportunity was to change the tenant mix and renovate the property." Wennett's last big projects working for FRIT involved assembling land for two urban developments called Bethesda Row, in Maryland, and Santana Row, in San Jose, California. "In both cases, everything I did was about a vision I had that no one else usually saw. For example, Bethesda was just a concrete plant and we built it into an urban town center. And when we acquired Santana Row in San Jose, it was just a vacant shopping center across from San Jose Mall. Now it is a large, urban, mixed-use town center community with residential, retail, and office."

Wennett became a senior vice president, and Federal Realty "became large," but by 1997 Wennett was in his midthirties and he had a "midlife crisis" and realized that he didn't want to do what he was doing anymore.[17] Although he had started out in suburban shopping centers, Wennett had become increasingly interested in urban areas, so he decided to raise capital for a fund that would invest in large, urban, retail, and mixed-use properties in major cities. In March 1998 he started Wennett/Urban Retail LLC at his dining-room table and he was the new company's sole employee.

Wennett started pitching his fund idea to potential investors with the goal of raising $10 million per investor for a total fund of $50 million. One of his first meetings was with Starwood Capital LLC, which decided to give him $100 million so he and Starwood agreed to create the fund together. They named the fund "Starwood Urban," and Wennett became president of the management company Starwood Urban Investments LLC.

Identifying Undervalued Property

"My knack has always been identifying which areas were going to become popular because these were areas where trend-setting artists and cultural people were living. My typical formula was to buy things that were in the hands of people who had held them for a long time and had made few changes. People used to joke that all of my friends were at least seventy years old, and in some cases it was true. The reason was opportunity. People who hold something for a long time view that asset in one way, so if you paid them a good price based on how they were looking at it, you could present the holder with a good opportunity. But you could also look at the property from a forward-looking perspective, identifying the property's future potential, and then the property would have a totally different value."

Wennett first started buying properties in the Meatpacking District in New York City in 1999, and in 2000 a *New York Times* article quoted local real estate experts saying that Starwood-Urban was entering the market too early and that the area would take a long time to redevelop. In retrospect, Starwood-Urban could not have done better in terms of timing. "Back in the 1990s the Meatpacking District distributed meat during the day and hosted prostitutes at night. Nobody was looking at it like it was a potential fashion destination. However artists and creative people were attracted to the area for its emerging qualities as well as avant-garde retailers as an alternative to SoHo's mall-like tenant mix. The Meatpacking District filled that void for the beginning of a countercultural movement of art, fashion, and design, so that's what attracted me to the area."[18]

Starwood Urban went on to buy properties in Washington, DC; Wellesley, Massachusetts; South Norwalk, Connecticut; and Coral Gables, Florida. "Cities embraced us, because we were viewed as a big investor that could come in and buy a significant amount of property, which helped spur rede-velopment in distressed areas. What all of these locations had in common was that each had a history of being a countercultural place."

Wennett bought properties between 1998 and 2004. "But then I looked at myself and I didn't like what I was doing again—it had gotten too big and I wasn't having fun anymore. That's when I decided to liquidate the fund." Wennett's timing in retrospect was perfect. In less than a year he was able to sell the entire portfolio in three transactions for somewhere around $500 million, doubling investors' initial equity and resulting in returns that exceeded 30 percent for the life of the fund. "It was one of the more successful retail ventures and everybody was happy," says Wennett. "The decision had more to do with who I was rather than timing the mar-ket. There was no question that the market was getting too expensive and I felt that once everybody was doing what I wanted to do it was time to get out."

It was the end of 2004 and Wennett wanted to do something different. "It was time to change my life again." By the time he decided to sell, Star-wood Urban owned multiple properties in Coral Gables, including a high-rise residential building that was still under construction, so it made sense for Wennett to move to Miami until that project was completed. Wennett had resided part-time in Miami Beach since 1995, but he had always won-dered what it would be like to move there and never have to leave. While he lived in Miami Beach, Wennett became captivated by an unusual piece of property at the western end of Lincoln Road, Miami Beach's famed pedestrian shopping street.

A Crazy Site

Carl Fisher, Miami Beach's founder and developer, started building Lincoln Road in the 1910s and named it after his favorite president. "The Road" grew rapidly during the 1920s and soon became known as the "Fifth Ave-nue of the South." However, after being home to department stores like Saks Fifth Avenue and Bonwit Teller and other retailers for a half century, Lincoln Road fell into decline in the 1950s. In 1960, the City of Miami Beach spent $600,000 to transform Lincoln Road into an eight-block-long pedestrian promenade—only the second in the country—that extended from Collins Avenue on the east side of Miami Beach to Lenox Avenue. Designed by Miami's famed midcentury modernist architect Morris Lapidus—the architect of the renowned Fountainbleau Hotel and many

other South Beach hotels—the mall's transformation spurred a turnaround
and Lincoln Road returned to economic health. By the 1980s, however,
Lincoln Road had slipped into decline but reemerged again as a vital retail
center in the late 1990s. By the 2000s Lincoln Road was lined with clothing
stores specializing in club wear—designer jeans, skimpy dresses—and restaurants catering mostly to tourists, but it was not known for its fashion or
unique stores. As for people watching, it was more about spectacle than
shopping, yet, at the same time, retail rents were still high.

Wennett had been puzzling over the SunTrust Building, a forlorn 1960s
office building at the western end of Lincoln Road that had been designed
by a team of once-prominent modern architects. Paul Goldberger, an architecture critic for the *New Yorker*, described the building as "a heavy-
handed, neo-Brutalist structure of precast concrete, the kind of bargain
basement knockoff of Le Corbusier that everyone loves to hate but that has
been gaining in popularity recently among people who pride themselves on
having cutting edge taste." At seven stories, the building also dwarfed all
the low-scale Art Deco retail buildings that lined the other eight blocks of
Lincoln Road. A replacement to a now-demolished office building that had
been located on the more prominent corner of Lincoln and Alton Roads,
the new building was located on the other half of the block—on the corner
of Lenox. The former office building site was recharacterized as a public
space. But like the rest of Lincoln Road, time had taken its toll on the
property. What most people saw when they walked by the SunTrust Building in the early 2000s was a shabby, concrete office building that was too
tall, ugly, and out of place on lower-scale Lincoln Road. Next to the building was a drive-through branch bank, and the public space on the corner
had long since been replaced with an inadequately surfaced parking lot.[19]

But after walking by the site many times, Wennett began to see something else—an undervalued piece of property in a prime location. "Every
day I would come by this site and I would think, 'My god, this is a crazy
site.' Lincoln Road is the most important pedestrian street in Miami and I
see this big piece of land: 'Something needs to be done here, because this
just doesn't make any sense.' There was an office building, a surface parking
lot, and a drive-through bank that, when combined, added up to 72,000
square feet of partially undeveloped land right in the middle of Lincoln
Road—an area where it is difficult to buy a 7,500-square-foot piece of land.
The site appeared to have little development potential at all since it was
basically an overdeveloped office building on this plaza." Worse, because

the building had no dedicated parking it could only attract Class C tenants—and rents—so its owners had little money left over for maintenance or improvements. Perhaps most important, at that time, the parcel fronted on a typical street with vehicle traffic. The Lincoln Road pedestrian mall ended just across the street to the east of the site, and so the property just missed being at the beginning of a high-rent, internationally known, eight-block-long retail destination.

Wennett also saw something in the old building that no one else saw. "Having spent most of my life in New York, when I looked at this building what I saw was a concrete frame building with fourteen-foot ceilings and I knew that creative people would respond to this kind of space. In the Meatpacking District, we didn't lease to retailers first but rather the creative office users—architects, designers, stylists—and then people wanted to be around them so the retail followed."

And Wennett thought Lincoln Road was beginning to suffer from the same mall effect that had driven counterculture people to the Meatpacking District. Lincoln Road was becoming popular to the broad middle market and increasingly dominated by stores like Gap and Banana Republic. "So, my idea," says Wennett, "was that Miami Beach needed a place that was more like Bleecker Street, the Meatpacking District, Saint Germain, and Melrose Avenue, and less like sections of Broadway. The challenge was how to bring Lincoln Road to a new level." Despite the proliferation of middle-market retailers and overpriced tourist restaurants, Wennett thought that Miami Beach was on the brink of something big happening and ready to embrace a more hip type of retail. "I try to understand what people are interested in and I have a very good sense of the population of Miami Beach and what they want, without needing to do an enormous amount of research."

Wennett also saw an interesting urban design problem—and an opportunity. The pedestrian part of Lincoln Road ended at the eastern corner of the site, at Lenox Avenue, when in the 1960s it had ended at the western corner of the site, at Alton Road. Wennett thought an opportunity existed to enclose the street and design a new entry plaza extending the Lincoln Road pedestrian mall in front of his project, to its former western edge.

Finally, Wennett saw that by using the right design approach and providing dedicated parking he could transform the office building from Class C to Class A. He also felt he could lease up the loftlike office space with its exposed concrete floors and high ceilings to creative companies, increasing the vibrancy and appeal of the retail space. Wennett envisioned converting another underperforming piece of property into a very lucrative investment. "And of course I believed it would take all of the knowledge I have in transforming undervalued real estate.

"It was a unique time for me. I was at the top of my career, I was forty-five, and I had made some money, so now it was more about what I thought things should be like. I didn't have any investors or constraints and I really wanted to make the project be all about what my vision is for the kinds of places people want to visit and hang out."

Cultural Coauthors

When it came to assembling his project team, Wennett took an unconventional approach. "Rather than the typical development team, I assembled a cultural team of coauthors who would work together to make the project vibrant and unique." His first step in assembling this team was to select an architect so Wennett interviewed ten firms before hiring the Pritzker Prize–winning Swiss firm of Herzog and de Meuron to design the building. Wennett asked his architects to create a civic building along the lines of a nineteenth-century train station. But after studying the site and their client's brief, the architects concluded that height restrictions would make for an insignificant building at an important intersection and, worse, that the new building would be unable to stand up to the presence of the existing SunTrust Building.

Miami Beach's code capped the height of any new structure on the site at seventy-five feet but in an indication of how much the city restricted the density of development, the code also allowed only about forty-five thousand square feet of new building area, or the equivalent of less than one floor if it were to cover the whole parcel. At the same time, however, there was a parking shortage in Miami Beach so the code did not count parking as building area as long as it was required parking for the uses of the project. Based on these restrictions, Wennett was allowed to build enough retail to front the new plaza, a relocated bank branch and drivethrough, a rooftop restaurant, and five residential units in addition to six floors of parking. The issue was this would all have to be within the seventy-five-foot height limitation, which meant that any new building would be dwarfed by the existing 114-foot-high office building. Despite the site's location on a pedestrian street lined with low-scale, historic, Art Deco retail shops, these conflicting code regulations would have driven the average developer to build a typical parking garage. Wennett's goal was not to build this type of garage, but rather to create a very new and different kind of place and experience. "If we had built it as a warehouse for cars it would have added nothing to the urban environment and would have been very unfriendly."

So Wennett and his team sought a variance that would increase the maximum height to match the existing building and, rather than adding more program square footage or levels of parking, Wennett proposed to increase the height between the parking levels, increasing the building's overall height to make it more open and sculptural. He knew that a more open building would be more attractive to the kinds of potential retail tenants he had in mind. Thus Herzog and de Meuron proposed to build an addition that would be large and tall enough to complement the existing building while also being able to stand on its own.

Parking Sculpture Versus Parking Garage

The project encompassed renovations to the existing office building, the construction of two new buildings—a relocated branch bank and the garage—and the insertion of a strip of ground-floor retail storefronts running the length of the block and uniting the old bank and the new garage. The first building to be completed was a simple yet beautiful white box on the back corner of the property that housed the relocated branch bank and four townhouse-condominiums on the second floor.

The second building—and the main event—was the parking garage. The structure comprises seven exposed concrete slabs supported on tilting concrete columns. There are six levels of parking accommodating just over 250 cars with bridges that connect the office building and the garage at each level. Unlike any other garage, however, the floor-to-floor heights vary dramatically from one floor to the next. As a result, the experience of driving up the ramp is one of constant surprise rather than repetition, and as you ascend the views out to the sea continue to expand until you reach the uppermost level. This cathedral-like space is twenty-eight feet high and sandwiched between two concrete slabs with wide-open views in all directions. The wheel stops for cars on this level were made to be removable and Wennett rents the space out most weekend evenings for weddings, parties, and arts events. On the top deck of the garage, Wennett built himself a 5,200-square-foot residence complete with sloping lawn, lap pool, and 360-degree unobstructed panoramic views of Miami Beach, the Atlantic Ocean, and Biscayne Bay.

Figure 54. The new parking garage balanced against the old office building and the continuous ground-floor retail and pedestrian plaza that unite the two and reconnect the building to Lincoln Road. Photo © Duccio Malagamba and MBEACH1 LLP.

Figure 55. The garden outside of Robert Wennett's home on the roof of 1111 Lincoln Road. Photo ©Vanity Fair/Todd Eberle/cncollection.com.

Known for designing beautiful "skins" for building exteriors, Herzog and de Meuron took a different approach for the garage and designed an open frame in exposed concrete. But like the rest of the project, this is not just any concrete garage. The floor plates taper to a razor's edge, the angular columns taper up and down, the building is open to the elements, and there is no skin at all. The only thing preventing a car from driving off the edge is a set of thin, nearly invisible steel cables that run through sleeves in the columns. The sprinklers are concealed and there is only minimal lighting because daylight penetrates to the center of the building. In fitting the building to its climate, the architects excluded heating and cooling systems in favor of natural sea breezes and as a result the building cost less to build and uses very little energy.

The existing bank building's 110,000 square feet of office space were given a light renovation and the retail space was designed to accommodate twelve unique retail stores and three restaurants, including one on the roof of the original bank building. The architects slipped a single crystalline glass cube between the concrete decks on the fifth and sixth levels of the garage that houses a concept boutique called Alchemist but the rest of the retail is located in a unified band of storefronts on the ground floor, running the full length of the block from Alton Road to Lenox Avenue, beneath both the parking garage and the original building, uniting old and new and providing a continuous front on the new public plaza that Wennett was beginning to envision.

In a testament to the strength of this design approach, in activist, anti-development Miami Beach, Wennett easily obtained the variances and approvals he needed from the City of Miami Beach's Design Review Board and Board of Adjustment in March 2006. Wennett succeeded in rallying the design community and having a Pritzker Prize–winning architecture firm doing the design work surely did not hurt. More than one hundred supporters attended the public meeting and only one person rose to speak in opposition to the project.

Wennett says the reason he succeeded in obtaining the height variance he sought was simple: "Most people are used to developers asking for variances for their own good but it was clear the building next door was too high and the zoning didn't make any sense. People realized this and that the height would really enhance the project." Paul Goldberger agreed, finding that the existing building was "so overbearing that it would have swallowed most new buildings," but, when paired with Herzog and de Meuron's addition, "the two structures are actually good neighbors, and the old one, next to its glamorous new spouse, looks stronger and more self-assured than it used to."

With his approvals for the building in hand, Wennett turned his attention to transforming the street in front of the project into a new public plaza. He hired another designer, the Miami-based landscape architect Raymond Jungles, to design an "urban glade" that Jungles said was inspired by Miami Modernism, the works of Lapidus, and "swimming pool vernacular." Then Wennett, working with the city and the design team, asked that Lincoln Road be extended one more block, past his building, to Alton Road. The city agreed and approved funding for the $6.2 million project. Herzog and de Meuron's inspired vision for the building was a large part of the reason why the City of Miami Beach was willing to convert the street into a plaza and extend the Lincoln Road pedestrian mall one more block.[20]

What his team of cultural coauthors was doing, says Wennett, "was programming and activating a building for a commercial purpose. It was a building located in the center of the best retail market in the country and

Figure 56. A continuous strip of ground-floor retail unites the old and new structures above. Photo by Iwan Baan.

Figure 57. 1111 Lincoln Road at night, with the Alchemist boutique in a glass box on the fifth level. Photo by Michael Stavaridis.

Figure 58. The Alchemist boutique on the fifth level, surrounded by parking. Photo by Michael Stavaridis.

all of the team members understood that their interests where aligned and agreed that this was something they wanted to do. Every single person we brought on the job was educated," says Wennett, and what they learned was "if you think about this as a parking garage then you are not going to be able to help capture the essence of what we are trying to achieve."

Wennett then engaged the sculptor Dan Graham, through a design competition, to provide public art for the plaza, and the artists René Buser and Monika Sosnowska created public art for the building itself. These designers and artists are not the typical project team members and most of them are not the kind of people who even work for developers but in Wennett they found a different kind of partner—one whom they could relate to and work with creatively. "We bring in people from the creative fields and we do it at a very sensitive level," says Wennett. "Herzog and de Meuron, for example, would not be the first choice of architect for most real estate developers and they typically don't do commercial buildings but they wanted to be a part of this. The sculptor, Dan Graham, who is one of the most important living American artists, also wanted to be a part of it.

It would have been hard to afford his work at the time but he saw the opportunity to be a coauthor too. Everybody had to decide they wanted to be a part of it and had to develop a strong emotional attachment to the whole project."

In addition to smoothing the path with the city approvals process, Wennett's coauthors also played a big role in promoting the project. These architects, designers, and artists were already prominent individually so Wennett let the prestige of his team members and the story of their collaboration drive the marketing for the project. "We had no formal marketing and branding, nothing was mass-marketed, and there was little in the way of advertisement. Instead we went out, told the story, and got people interested, and then we watched the columns come out of the ground." Finally, says Wennett, "we didn't use front men or leasing agents." Wennett himself led the project and was its face—with the team, the public, and, perhaps most important, his tenants.

Curated Retail

Wennett points out that when traditional developers attempt interesting and unique retail spaces for fashion and design companies there is usually a big disconnect. "The typical real estate developer does not understand and cannot relate to the tenant, the user, and the buyer. It is like two people talking—you need to speak the other person's language and most people cannot speak the language of Herzog and de Meuron or Taschen," one of Wennett's tenants. And that is where Wennett comes in. Because of his interest in fashion, art, design, and culture production and his experience in developing retail, "I am the type of person who relates to and understands retailers and their ideas, so I can bridge between the two spheres because I inhabit them both."

Wennett used this ability to think like both a developer and a retailer when he set about attracting the perfect mix of global brands to the project. Rather than the more traditional process of using commercial leasing agents, Wennett himself approached the executives of the major companies. Stressing "the power of the architecture to attract and excite customers," says Wennett, "I went and talked directly to all of the heads of the companies who I thought would fit with the project and who were trying to find a place that would allow them to realize their visions."[21]

Because the project was so unique and because it was coming online during a recession, Wennett received two very different responses. "There were those who were believers and those who were not. The nonbelievers said, 'You are leasing this project in the worst possible market ever,' and if we had been making a commodity product that would have been true. But we were not making a commodity product and the people we leased to were not thinking about that. For those people, I was appealing to their sense of emotion, not selling a commodity product, so their response was 'My god, this is exactly the opportunity I was looking for.' These were not the kind of people and companies that would have come to Lincoln Road before but they saw the vision and wanted to be a part of it."

Commodity retailers are located in basic "white-box" retail space but Wennett's primary focus is neither the commodity nor the physical space. "You can't put these kinds of tenants in a box, which is what most developers would try to do. Instead, we were giving them a design opportunity." Atmosphere and experience have become increasingly important in the era of online retailing. "Product can be sold much better on the Internet," says Wennett, so "the reason to take physical space is to create an experience." This emphasis too is different from more traditional developers because it focuses not on the building but on the total experience. "I always think of retail as an experience, not as a commodity, so I am more like a curator than a developer—I curate the atmospheres and create the experience."[22]

For Wennett, atmosphere and experience mean culture. "The most important thing about this project," concludes Wennett, "is that we are generating culture here, which is not something most real estate people talk about. We are interested in figuring out how people absorb culture. So it starts as a civic place, not as a typical 'mixed-use' project, which makes it a completely different product type, because we are coming at it from a totally different perspective."

And the tenants could not have agreed more. The German bookseller Taschen has only three other outlets in the United States—two in Los Angeles and one in New York—but the owner, Benedikt Taschen, decided to build a fourth, Philippe Starck–designed store in Wennett's project. "From all that I've seen worldwide, I think Miami is a world class destination," says Taschen, and as for 1111 Lincoln Road, "You won't find a place like this anywhere else in the world. At least I haven't seen one like this. A great hit." Frederic Levy, the North American president of Nespresso, the Swiss espresso and food bar company, says the company's newest flagship boutique at 1111 Lincoln Road "will do more to expose customers to the brand than any kind of advertising." The front of the store is an espresso bar that serves $4 coffee drinks in china cups—Nespresso does not offer coffee to go in paper cups and the company does not even pretend to compete with Starbucks. For Nespresso, rather, the experience of sitting and enjoying your drink matters and, more important, this luxurious experience leads you to the back of the store and the main event, a beautiful showroom that sells single-serving home espresso machines in countless sizes, models, and colors—a big candy store for grownups.[23]

Wennett let the leases expire for most of the existing office tenants and then he signed new or renewed leases with creative companies like MTV Latin America and "now the building is filled with "three hundred culture workers." Last but not least, Wennett succeeded in luring New York's Danny Meyer and his Shake Shack restaurant to one of the retail spaces on the ground floor of the office building. Shake Shack offers gourmet burgers and shakes and nothing on the menu costs more than $10. "Now people go to Nespresso for their daily fix," says Wennett, "and they eat at the Shake Shack three times a week."

The Deal

Wennett's story about the creation of 1111 Lincoln Road may be a lot about coauthors, counterculture, retail experience, the creation of a civic place, the production of culture, and many other things, but in the cold light of day it is a story about a real estate development deal. And at its most basic level, real estate development is the business of buying a piece of property and improving it so that its value is greater than the costs of its acquisition and improvements.

At 1111 Lincoln Road, Robert Wennett used a handful of basic techniques to improve an old, undervalued building and the land surrounding it. First, by rearranging the program elements onsite and moving the branch bank to the back, he was able to create a large, regular, buildable parcel along Lincoln Road and add a 250-car parking garage in an area where there was a parking shortage and clear demand. He also squeezed a little more revenue from the site by adding four for-sale condos above the branch bank.

New parking in combination with modest interior renovations to the old bank building allowed Wennett to reposition a tired, Class C office building as a unique, Class A building that could command Class A rents. It also attracted a different type of creative tenant that would, in turn, attract retail tenants. Further, because of the site's central location, Wennett's garage maximized parking revenue by operating twenty-four hours a day, seven days a week, serving not only his own office tenants and retail patrons during the day but also tourists and clubgoers on evenings and weekends.

Next, by building retail beneath the garage, repurposing the ground floor of the old bank, and running a unifying façade across both, Wennett was able to bring coherence to the project while adding an entire city block of new storefronts in a location where there are few other places to physically add retail space.

But perhaps most important, by providing a bold new vision for the space in front of the building, Wennett was able to convince the city to extend the Lincoln Road pedestrian mall one block west. In doing so he literally repositioned his building—geographically and perceptually—by stretching the existing border so that his property fell inside—rather than outside—of one of the highest rent retail districts in the country.

But that is just the beginning—rather than the end—of the story. Wennett's broader urbanistic approach, his insistence on high-quality design, and his recruiting of an internationally renowned and elite team of coauthors led to a uniquely integrated and incredibly sophisticated design. And this design helped Wennett obtain difficult approvals and also played a lead role in luring investors and lenders and attracting creative office workers and global retail brands. Wennett could attract these uncommon tenants because he knew both their business and his own, and he was able to offer a completely new and different product type that the typical retail space simply could not compete with. "These were not the standard-fare retail tenants like Kohl's and Ross who look at rents first," says Wennett. "These were visionaries who saw a unique opportunity to be part of something special and who wanted the building to be part of their brand."

Smart Luck

Good luck and timing influenced the approvals because the project followed on the heels of so many condominium projects. Its freshness, coherence, and strong design helped to garner broad public support—enough to obtain several major variances. "People had seen a lot of repetitive condo presentations and our presentation was so different that people accepted it and they went out of their way to defend it." But luck and timing also influenced the financing of the project. When it came time to negotiate the terms of a construction loan in 2008, financing was unavailable. But because Wennett had his approvals in hand most of the risk in the project had been eliminated: "In the end I was able to convince lenders to make the loan." If he had waited a year, on the other hand, the bubble would have burst, capital markets would have been frozen, and financing of any kind would have been much more difficult to obtain.

On the flip side the tough economic times brought Wennett some benefits by reducing his construction costs. "We broke ground in 2008 which was great, because the bubble had burst and construction prices had come down—maybe as much as 20 percent." Another benefit was that Wennett had his pick of contractors whereas two years earlier, when many high-rise condo projects were under way in Miami, he would have had to struggle to get the attention of any contractors, all of whom were booked up with condo projects.

Wennett made some of his own luck too, successfully hedging against a future economic downturn by using extraordinary design to ensure that his product stood out from the pack. So as the market began to soften after 2007, the high-quality architecture of the building made for a more robust product offering that was able to attract the kind of elite retailers who wanted to have a new presence in Miami when nonluxury brands were retrenching and the market was flooded with vacant traditional retail space. Indeed, Wennett had all but one of the tenant spaces leased up by the end of 2009 just before the project opened and at top rents of as much as $150 per square foot. Says Wennett, "If we had built a normal project it probably never would have happened."

A combination of good luck and good timing allowed Wennett to borrow and, as the bubble had burst, to build at a deep discount. But equally important, by taking a holistic view of the project, Wennett developed a property that was much more robust in the downturn than a typical real estate product would have been, which reduced his market risk. In terms of supply and demand, the market for global brands in Miami Beach was not bottomless but it was deep enough to fill Wennett's unique and limited space and he could hardly have gone wrong by adding parking in such a congested area. Finally, Miami Beach suffered less in the economic downturn than the rest of the country because it is an international market that serves as a gateway to the United States for wealthy Latin Americans and as a year-round destination for international tourism. When you think about it that way, Wennett's project seems a pretty safe bet.

How Much Does Each Parking Space Cost?

Wennett identified an opportunity in a place where anyone else without his unique experience and perspective would have seen only risk. "Even when people thought what I was doing was out of the box I didn't think it was out of the box because I understood the trends and what people were going to be interested in as well as the risk."

To illustrate the point, Wennett describes a typical conversation he has had over and over again. "The first question everybody asks me is 'How much does each parking space cost and how much per square foot does the building cost?' They say, 'You can build a parking garage with a little bit of design for about $35,000 a space but this one costs $100,000 per space and that cannot make sense.' First I say, yes, ok, if I could get the same thing for $35,000 as I could for $100,000 it wouldn't make any sense and you would be right. But you and I view things differently, because we are buying different things. It would be like a person who stands here and says, 'Here is a chair, here is a desk [he points at the high-design furniture in his office], and I can go buy the same thing for less.' But it is not the same chair, not the same desk, and it will not have the same effect. It is what I am investing in that is different from other people because I am not trying to just spend more money than somebody else—I am trying to do something that in the end should make more money.

"The most difficult thing about a civic building is how to activate it and bring people to it," says Wennett, "so what makes this building different is that it is not just a parking garage." Because the idea was to activate the whole building, the program is mixed together rather than being separated into different sections in a traditional mixed-use project. As for program and use, it is difficult to see or think of the building as broken up into the basic programmatic elements of office, parking, and retail. Instead, it is all woven together. *The New Yorker*'s architecture critic, Paul Goldberger, agreed. "You could call this a mixed-use building that happens to have cars driving through it." Rowan Moore, the architecture critic for *The Observer*, contrasts the building with the tendency of modern-era planning and design to arbitrarily separate integrated urban function like roads, shopping areas, and parking garages into discrete parts. "It's like making a soufflé

Figure 59. Not your average parking garage: Wennett regularly rents the upper level of 1111 Lincoln Road for everything from arts and culture events to weddings. Photo by Iwan Baan.

back into eggs, butter, and flour." Instead, 1111 Lincoln Road, concludes Moore, "tries to cook them back together again."[24]

Creators of Culture

The best attributes of Solomon's rogue and Hyde's trickster live on today in developers like Robert Wennett who use their experience and their wits to create new ideas and shape the culture and places we live in. These complex and paradoxical figures look for opportunities that others can't see, use language creatively to promote their ideas, and adapt easily to new information and changing conditions as they follow their own instincts rather than those of the herd. We are drawn to them because they are both attractive and provocative. Through their work, developers "create culture and make the world inhabitable." Most important, says Hyde, "like trickster, each of us must find those opportunities that are suited to our individual natures."[25]

Robert Wennett does exactly that by combining his interests in art, design, fashion, and culture with his knowledge of real estate and his ability to identify undervalued property and opportunity. But what should community members do when a developer like Wennett comes to the neighborhood meeting with their own plans to create culture and make the world inhabitable, right down the street?

Developers and the Community

That piece of land is not zoned "vacant"!
—Buzz Ruttenberg, Chicago real estate developer[1]

Understanding Real Estate Developers

I started this book with David Haymes's story from Evanston in the 2000s and followed with the story of Beacon Hill in Boston from two hundred years earlier. Comparing these two stories side-by-side illustrates how community members think about two types of developments in two different historical periods. We are comfortable and often even unaware of old developments that long ago blended into the community. But we are less comfortable with proposals for new projects that may change our community in ways that we cannot easily envision or appreciate.

We usually lack the expertise, time, and capacity as individuals and as volunteer members of community organizations to fully analyze a development proposal. Our concerns and biases may make us less able to objectively assess the positive and negative effects the project may have on the community. Even if we are able to remain objective we must work with incomplete information. We cannot possibly know, for example, all of the details of a private business venture and what the investors and lenders are willing and not willing to finance. Nor can we fully understand the fine points of the city's regulatory process, what exactly the developer is allowed to do per the code, and how the planning commission and elected officials are likely to evaluate and vote on the proposal. And none of us can predict what the market demand for real estate products will be two or three years into the future, when the project is actually completed and goes to market. Yet development is going to continue and we will keep on receiving proposals to review. So if we hope to have an influence on the new projects in our community we must take a pragmatic approach to working with developers.

Developers are entrepreneurial people who are capable of spotting opportunities that are unseen by others and of envisioning and creating new and different physical environments in the future. They are optimistic and have the confidence to push through and complete a project in the face of countless difficulties. Because they want to succeed, they are flexible, creative, open to feedback, and willing to constantly adapt their vision to reflect new information. And through that continual process of adaptation and refinement they skillfully sell their constantly shifting vision to a growing number of stakeholders, hoping to build a base of support for a project.

Developers create, produce, and sell products that we want and need, and they know that design matters but they also know that design must be reconciled with economics. And they know that good design is in the eyes of the buyer first and that a good design is a design that sells out. How a project sells, however, is directly related to when the product goes to market. Developers know that it is very difficult to "time the market" and that the best hedges against a turning market are lower levels of leverage and a good product that offers value to the buyer. They also know that when the marketplace becomes crowded opportunities disappear, risk increases rapidly, and it is time to get to the sidelines.

And all developers are in the business because they hope to earn large profits but successful developers know that profits flow from hard work and from bringing all of their knowledge, experience, confidence, and a larger sense of purpose to each project. Much of what we think of as real estate may look like undifferentiated stock product but developers know that no two deals are the same. Price, product, location, and timing are always different and each project is unique. That is why developers must tinker and innovate at the margins, going two degrees left or right, and refining the product with each new project. In some cases developers innovate enough to create new products and over time the sum of all of this innovation is what we know as our urban environment. In providing products that we want and need, developers influence and shape our society and culture and how we live, work, shop, and play.

These all seem like relatively positive outcomes so why does it seem that developers are so often at the center of controversy and conflict? Fear of change, mistrust, and the inability to envision the benefits that development will bring in the future are a part of the answer but another important reason can be found in the very different ways that developers and members of the community value property.

How Developers Value Property

In their 1988 book *Urban Fortunes*, Harvey Molotch and John Logan argued that scarce land in urban areas had both "exchange value" and "use value." "Exchange value" refers to goods that have monetary value and "use value" refers to goods that can only be valued for their intrinsic properties. In the case of urban land, exchange value is the market value of a piece of property in dollars, based on being developed to its "highest and best" economic use. Exchange value is influenced by the various planning and zoning regulations that determine how densely a piece of property can be developed and for what uses. Land is just one part of a development project but its cost must be an acceptable proportion of the total cost if the project is to compete successfully in the marketplace. Exchange value is also influenced by other market forces that tell sellers and buyers what it will cost to develop, design, and construct a project, how much demand there is for the product, and at what price the developer will be able to sell or rent the completed units. By considering this combination of factors a seller or buyer can easily determine the rough value of a piece of property in dollars.[2]

For example, a developer might determine that there is a market for condominiums and that if he builds a site out to its maximum envelope based on planning and zoning codes he could build a 20-story tower with 8 units per floor for a total of 160 units. If the condominiums cost $250,000 each to build on average and land should be about 10 percent of that cost, or $25,000 per unit, then the land is worth about $4 million (160 units x $25,000 = $4 million). The developer may offer $3 million; the seller, if she uses similar math, may counter with $5 million; and they will probably strike a deal somewhere in between those two amounts.

Another developer who is more optimistic, creative, and tuned in to the currents at city hall may believe that she can get the zoning changed to allow 50 percent more units on the same site. If she buys for $4 million and is successful in making her case to the zoning board, then the land is worth $6 million and she has just earned a paper profit of $2 million simply by upzoning the land. The developer can now fit 240 units on the same piece of land at a reduced cost of $16,667 per unit but she can still charge $25,000 per unit for all 240 units ($25,000 × 240 = $6 million − $4 million = $2 million). The unit cost for the land drops while the unit sale price stays the same so the developer pockets that $2 million as entrepreneurial profit. This is on top of whatever profit margin she expects to earn from unit sales, for example, 15 percent of the total project cost.

On the other hand, if the neighbors succeed in convincing the zoning board that density should be reduced on the site by 25 percent, the developer will have overpaid for the land by $1 million, reducing the overall profit on the project. Whatever the final density, the land cost has an important effect on the project's economics, whether it is measured in numbers of apartments, condominium units, hotel rooms, or in square feet of commercial office or retail space.

Land cost is based largely on the buildable envelope and for every square foot that goes unbuilt the developer leaves money on the table. Other inefficiencies, such as an oddly shaped site or inefficient site dimensions, can reduce the buildable envelope. Or the developer may choose to build less than the maximum allowable area to hedge against market risk and avoid supplying more product than can be absorbed at a certain price within a certain time frame. After factoring in these types of constraints, the developer otherwise has the incentive to do everything in her power to maximize rather than minimize the density of development on a piece of property. Developers must consider many other factors when planning a project, but this simple example illustrates why they see land in terms of its acquisition price in dollars and its future value in dollars once it has been developed. But what is the property worth to the people who live in the building across the street from this hypothetical development?

How Community Members Value Property

It is worth quite a lot to those people across the street but for different reasons. All of the dog owners in the building have been using the vacant, weed-strewn parcel as a dog park that would surely go away if development were to proceed. There is an old factory on the property that would have to be demolished to make way for a new building but it has some nice brick detailing, and the historic preservationist on the fourth floor knows that an important nineteenth-century architect designed it. While this is not one

Table 9. Value to the Developer: Profit

Land Cost Per Unit	Market Cost		Below Market Cost		Above Market Cost	
Max. Buildable Units	160	100%	240	150%	120	75%
Land Cost/Unit	**$25,000**		**$16,667**		**$33,333**	
Total Land Cost	$4,000,000		$4,000,000		$4,000,000	
Total Land Value	$4,000,000		$6,000,000		$3,000,000	
Profit (Loss) on Land	**$0**		**$2,000,000**		**($1,000,000)**	
Profit Per Unit						
Land Cost/Unit	$25,000	10%	$16,667	7%	$33,333	13%
Other Costs/Unit	$225,000	90%	$225,000	93%	$225,000	87%
Total Cost/Unit	$250,000	100%	$241,667	100%	$258,333	100%
Sale Price/Unit (Market)	$287,500	115%	$287,500	119%	$287,500	111%
Profit Per Unit	**$37,500**	**15%**	**$45,833**	**19%**	**$29,167**	**11%**

Note: The developer has an incentive to maximize density on the site and reduce the per-unit land cost of $25,000 as a way to increase profits and hedge against the potential need to lower prices in the future. If the developer can obtain approval to increase density by 50 percent, she can build more units on the same land at less than $17,000 per unit but still price the units based on that original cost of $25,000. The developer then earns $2 million—almost $8,000 per unit—in entrepreneurial profit; or if prices drop, she has a larger cushion. If, on the other hand, density is reduced but the land price stays the same, the developer's profit margin drops significantly and she has even less cushion against falling prices.

of the architect's most remarkable works, it is one of the few that remain standing and the preservationist thinks it is significant and should be saved. The environmentalist on the ninth floor has been using binoculars to watch the family of peregrine falcons that have taken up residence on top of the smokestack of the old factory and believes that their habitat should be preserved or that they should at least be relocated. The site is also located in a migratory flyway and the environmentalist knows that migratory birds have been killed flying into glass high-rise towers that birds cannot see at night and thinks that the building design should incorporate special exterior lighting. The environmentalist's partner has an interest in sustainability and storm-water management and believes that a green roof and a rain garden should be incorporated into the new project to manage the building's rainwater on site.

A planner who works for the city and lives on the third floor knows that the street was formerly a vital commercial corridor and believes that any redevelopment project should include a retail component, preferably a ground-floor grocery store. The developer, however, has commissioned a market study that found there is not enough demand in the surrounding neighborhood to support storefront retail, let alone a grocery store. The planner also thinks that all of the parking should be contained in an underground parking garage that is hidden from view, rather than in the proposed aboveground, structured parking garage, although the code allows it and the developer's architect has designed the exterior of the building so that it largely hides the garage.

An architect who lives on the sixth floor believes that anything built in the neighborhood should be designed in a historical style and use historical materials like brick and natural stone to blend in with the surrounding old industrial buildings. This architect does not approve of the developer's rendering, which shows a contemporary glass and metal "point tower" with some historical-looking details on the lower levels. The architect's neighbor on the seventh floor is an architect too but is a modernist who thinks the proposed design should be even more modern and reflective of current times and that the historical details are just phony looking.

A small business owner on the ground floor is worried that automobile congestion on the street is already difficult and that any new development will only make it worse. In particular, she is worried about her clients being able to find street parking when they come for meetings at the office she runs from her "live-work" unit. Worse, the intersection at the corner is already too busy and the site of periodic accidents, so the developer should pay for a new traffic signal in the business owner's opinion.

The financial analyst on the tenth floor heard that the developer is seeking a public subsidy for the project and believes that subsidies are unnecessary handouts and that the developer's profits should be capped if he receives a subsidy. All of the residents of the building currently enjoy a wonderful, unobstructed view of the skyline at night, but if something tall were to be built on one part of the site this view would be obstructed forever. They think the developer should locate the tower on another part of the site and make its floor plate longer and skinnier in order to preserve their views. The tower will also cast shadows over a nearby park even though the developer's shadow studies show that this would only happen for a few days in December. And finally, all of the neighbors wonder why the developer can't just be magnanimous and donate the whole parcel to the city for a park. Why not, he's already rich, isn't he?

This example, like the previous example of exchange value, is a simple caricature but it summarizes many of the arguments that are typically used when an urban real estate development project is making its way through the community review and approval process. The neighbors value this piece of vacant urban land based on how they experience it and use it every day. Indeed, almost everyone other than the developer evaluates the property using criteria that are based on use value. How can this divide between monetary value and intrinsic properties—between exchange value and use value—be bridged?

What, for example, will it cost to photo-document or otherwise "mitigate" the old warehouse before it is torn down? Can its façades somehow be incorporated into the new project and at what extra cost? How much will it cost to relocate the peregrine falcons and how much will the exterior lighting system cost? Is it reasonable—or even sensible—to ask the developer to incorporate a retail component into the project if there is clearly not sufficient demand? Can the original city streets handle the development of a vacant parcel that generated similar amounts of traffic when it was last in use as a factory or is congestion a real problem and not just a perceived one? Can the project bear the increase in cost of changing from above-ground, structured parking to underground parking, which typically costs about 50 percent more per stall? Who decides on architectural style and materials, both of which influence project costs as well as marketability? Are subsidies inherently bad and does capping profits help or hurt a project? What legal claim do the neighbors have to their existing views across another piece of privately owned property and is it reasonable for them to ask the developer to rearrange the site plan or make a less efficient and more costly floor plate? Where in the city code does it require developers to ensure that nearby parks remain 100 percent shadow-free 365 days a year? If the developer did agree to make all of these proposed changes, would the project still be viable? Would the product be competitively priced and attractive to potential buyers or would the demands of the residents increase costs so much that the project no longer made economic and financial sense for the developer? If the project did not go ahead because it no longer made economic sense for the developer, would that be a good or bad outcome for the community?

At a policy level, are the residents demanding that the developer provide a product of significantly higher quality and cost than their own? Could they afford to rent or buy into the building themselves and if not, aren't

Table 10. Value to the Community: Interests and Issues

Site Plan	Special Interests
Increased Traffic Congestion	Historic Preservation
Driveway Locations	Habitat Preservation
Structured vs. Underground Parking	Environmental Contamination
No. of Parking Stalls—Garage	Storm-water Management
No. of Parking Stalls—Surface Lot	Sustainability, LEED, Green Roof
No. of Stalls—Electric/Shared Vehicles	
No. of Bicycle Parking Spaces	**Building Envelope and Design**
Need for Street Improvements	Height, Massing, Density, Setbacks
Need for New Traffic Signals	Obstruction of Views
Paving and Sidewalk Materials	Shadow and Shading
Landscape Plan, Greening	Architectural Style
Dog Walk Area	Building Materials and Colors
Public Realm/Space	
	Economic Development Policies
Building Uses	Subsidy to Developer
Mixed Use	Grants of Money or Land
Ground-floor Public Uses	Tax Abatement
Grocery Store	Tax Increment Financing
Park/Green Space	Developer's Profit

Note: Exchange value, land price, and the developer's profit mean little to the neighbors, who care more about the positive and negative effects the project will have on their use and enjoyment of the community.

they just making the neighborhood more exclusive and pulling up the drawbridge behind them? Most important, how can neighbors who see only the use value of the property ever understand the position of the developer, who is not only familiar with the neighbors' arguments but also knows what the property is worth in dollars? Based on the example from Evanston at the beginning of the book, what is in the neighbors' best interests and what should they do to protect those interests and maximize the benefits of a development project to the community?

Design as Our Common Language

Unlike exchange value, use value can be very personal and very difficult to quantify. Yet it is at the intersection of exchange value and use value where most debates over urban real estate development occur. Developers must always keep an eye on costs and returns but most community members see project economics as the developer's problem. Moreover, because development projects are privately financed, the public rarely has access to enough economic and financial information to understand the project from an exchange-value perspective. This lack of a common framework for considering all of the interests surrounding the development process tends to move the discussion from the arena of exchange value to the arena of use value. The common language used in this discussion is the language of design and the key words include density, massing, height, articulation, setbacks, style, materials, colors, uses, historic architecture, environmental impact, sustainability, habitat preservation, congestion, parking, greening, and public space.

Like the idea of use value, these words are qualitative rather than quantitative and because they are based more on subjective tastes and opinions than on simple arithmetic they are also open to interpretation and purposeful misinterpretation. For example, the neighbors may argue that the design of a project is too dense or that its massing is inappropriate when the real issue is that their unprotected views will be blocked. In some cases they may hope to persuade the developer to redesign in a way that preserves some of their views. In other cases the neighbors may raise various objections as a strategy to scuttle a project entirely, sometimes hoping that they can gain the sympathy and support of the planning commission, the district council member, and the city council. A developer who hopes to profit from increasing density may turn the massing argument around by claiming the need for additional height because otherwise the building designed per zoning will look squat and unattractive. If the developer were allowed to go higher than code, he could add a soaring and majestic tower to the skyline that would reflect well on everyone involved and enhance the city's brand image.

In some cases these starting positions may lead to reasonable discussions and compromise: for example, a taller, thinner tower on a corner of the site that minimizes the obstruction of views and allows the developer to increase buildable area. Other arguments are simply Trojan horses for positions that community members know they cannot voice in public, such as opposing unwanted uses like affordable housing. And, ultimately, who really knows what would be the best course of action for enhancing the community? Can the neighbors trust the developer and their architect who together have designed many similar buildings but perhaps not in this particular neighborhood? Or should they rely on the opinion of that one resident who has not been educated in design but who has lived in the neighborhood all her life and is certain that the brick color should be a darker shade of red if it is to match other nearby buildings?

While these issues of design all matter, they can become distractions that obscure a bigger and more important question: If a development is going to happen on this site, what can you do to ensure that it is as good as it can be and that it will make a positive contribution to the community? Before we can answer this question, we must take a more sophisticated and pragmatic approach to engaging with the developer and the first step is to figure out exactly what kind of developer he or she really is.

Get to Know Your Developer

Different participants in the development process have slightly different but often overlapping ideas of what makes a good developer. Investors are concerned with returns and buyers care about the prices and quality of their units. Architects like working with developers who are strong leaders with vision and who value good design but also pay their bills. Elected officials want developers who can work with the community but who also perform and have the resources required to successfully complete their projects. And city planners prefer developers who understand the regulatory regime but who are creative and flexible enough to be able to integrate the city's regulatory regime and growth objectives into a proposal on a unique piece of property. But what are the qualities of good developers from the community member's perspective?

First, they have chosen real estate development as a career and they have usually been doing it for some time. Some good developers specialize in one or two product types and work primarily in one neighborhood, community, city, and region. Real estate development is an intensely local business, and success depends on an acute understanding of the local context, from history and geography to socioeconomics, demographics, political culture, and regulatory frameworks. Some good local developers with a quality product and the organizational and financial capacity are able to successfully expand into new markets. Other good developers work successfully in communities in a dozen or more states where they succeed by providing a specific type of product that they know how to do well, for example, student housing or tax credit–financed low-income housing.

Many good developers work on only one or two projects at a time and become deeply involved in all aspects of the work. They begin by establishing the overall vision for the project, from use, market, and design to financing, brand, marketing, and sales. Good developers also take the lead in discussions with city staff, elected officials, and community members. They follow through with the leadership of their design team, down to the details of the knobs on the kitchen cabinets, and throughout the marketing and sales effort. They focus intensely on making each individual project a success as measured by healthy sales and positive responses from city officials, the media, and the neighbors.

Good developers also work with the same architects, engineers, and contractors repeatedly, sometimes on many projects over years and even decades. They may change team members sometimes when, for example, an architect lacks experience with a new product type. These developers rely on their architects and other consultants who, in turn, come to understand their clients well and form a sort of brain trust. When the developer calls and says, "I have this property and I want to build X units of Y quality for Z cost," their team members already know enough about their client's other preferences to get a good running start. This type of collaboration leads to a more efficient and lower-cost pursuit phase than always having new team members who must get up to speed and get to know their client and one another for each new project. And because team members who have worked together before already "know the drill," as the project moves forward they can focus more on the details of designing a better project for the developer and their buyers as well as for the community.

And good developers know how to work with rather than against neighborhoods but they stand their ground when they need to protect their own interests so there will often be some tension and disagreement. They have healthy egos but they are not arrogant. They are good listeners and always looking for more opinions and feedback because they know that they can better serve their market—and sell their product—if they understand as much as possible what it is that people want before they build it. But despite the public perception of developers as risk takers, good developers respond to existing markets rather than try to create new ones, so they tend to be conservative when it comes to trying unproven products and strategies. Whether they have market data disproving an idea, a bad feeling, or both, they will avoid taking risks on strategies and uses that do not seem viable. This is why good developers often resist many of the suggestions that come from the community for uses such as daycare centers, restaurants, grocery stores, and ground-floor retail in general.

Last but not least, good developers are clearly the leaders of their projects and their teams. They represent themselves at public meetings and to government staff and elected officials. They may let their architects do some of the talking in some meetings—in part because the public generally trusts architects more than developers—but when they need to, they step in, lead, and make the hard decisions. Developers play the part of conductor, surrounding themselves with a variety of talented specialists, empowering them, and trusting them to do their jobs. At the same time they guide with a firm hand, from establishing the overarching vision down to realizing that vision through attention to the smallest details. We stand a good chance of being able to work well with developers who generally fit this description but there are several other types that we should be more cautious of.

Many new developers, for example, are undercapitalized and just one unexpected and costly problem away from running out of cash. New developers who get along too well with the community or let their architects drive the design may overpromise, overspend, and produce a nice building for the community while underachieving or failing economically. At the other extreme a more cautious and cost-oriented new developer may reject the suggestions of the community completely, doing only the minimum required to obtain approvals from the city. The same developer may also nickel-and-dime the architect and contractor as a way of keeping design and construction costs as low as possible. This lack of willingness to listen and invest may reduce the developer's chances of best integrating the project into the community and worse, for the developer, the effort to keep costs down could backfire. The product may not sell well because it is cheaply built and its design has not been refined to reflect input from its most likely potential buyers: the members of the community. All developers must start somewhere but a new developer doing his first project presents greater risks—to himself, his investors and lenders, and the community. Those who do succeed are the ones who attend every meeting, ask every dumb question, draft every spreadsheet, walk the site every day during construction, and immerse themselves in every detail before making their decisions. New developers who succeed are those who take that first project very seriously, know that the stakes are very high, and do everything they can to learn and gain experience as quickly as possible so as to avoid making mistakes.

New developers who are doing their first deals when the market is heating up face even greater odds. They hope to make a quick profit on the investment vehicle of the moment—real estate—but are professionally uncommitted and inexperienced. Rather than driving the project forward with their own vision, they will rely too much on their architects and other team members to tell them what they should do. They will not do the hard work required to understand the location, the community, the economics, the product type, and their potential buyers. Because they are latecomers, their projects will more likely be located on difficult sites for which they overpaid and will be poorly designed, over cost, overpriced, overleveraged, and late to market, so sales will be slow and the chances of failure even greater.

Similarly, developers who are making a big jump, either to a much larger scale or to a very different product type, face reduced chances of success because they don't have enough experience. Although they may have confidence they may not know what they do not know. Further, the fact that they are trying to make a jump may also suggest that they are overconfident and in development only for the profits alone. Smart developers grow incrementally, increasing in scale and complexity from one project to the next; like new developers, they concentrate on learning everything about their product type and market. When they try a new product type it is usually similar or analogous to something they have done before— they go two degrees left or three degrees right. But a developer who has completed a four-plex and is now proposing a high-rise should be a cause for concern, as should a developer who is switching from suburban warehouses to urban apartments. Like new developers, those who reach too far are more likely to produce ill-conceived projects that are late to market only to have them taken back by the bank. Or they may lose their invested equity but never get out of the ground, which is still a better option than completing a project that cannot generate enough income to repay the construction loan that they backed with their own personal guarantee.

Not surprisingly, new developers entering an overheated market who are developing a product that they are unfamiliar with at a scale larger than anything they have ever attempted while relying on high leverage face extraordinary risks. This describes many of the developers who help create boom-and-bust cycles but as we saw, Rome was not built in a day and attempting to time the market is a very risky approach, both for developers and for communities. Unfortunately, we do not get to choose which type of developer will be coming to our neighborhood meeting so we must arm ourselves by understanding everything else about how the development review and approval process works.

Understand the Review and Approvals Process

A first step is familiarizing yourself with the comprehensive plan and zoning code for your community and finding out what it says about the site that is being considered for a development project. Taken together, plans, codes, and zoning maps serve as a regulatory framework and articulate the city's objectives for land use and development. This framework also acts as a set of rules, telling developers—and the members of the community— what can and cannot be done on a piece of property and when a variance or other special approval is required.

The plan, code, and zoning maps together describe areas within which different uses are permitted and the buildable envelope, including height, bulk, density, massing, and sometimes floor area ratio (FAR). The code dictates site-plan requirements including front-, side-, and rearyard setbacks as well as fencing, trees, and landscaping along public streets. The code may also include design guidelines and minimum requirements for exterior building materials. Some cities require that parking garages in the downtown core be designed so that their façades screen cars from view. In other cities buildings in commercial districts are required to use clear glass in ground-floor retail stores to improve visibility and enhance street life. Many cities make their plans, codes, and ordinances available online and they are written to be accessible to the average citizen. When they are unclear it is the job of city planning staff to help interpret and explain these documents and the regulatory process to members of the community.

Development proposals are influenced by individual citizens, community organizations, citizen advisory panels, city planning and economic development staff, and elected politicians. But rather than taking a monolithic view of a project, these individuals and groups each have different interests and views of their own. Members of the planning commission and the staff who work with them, for example, are charged with looking at a project in terms of how it complies with plans, codes, and standards. The city council must place the project into the larger context of economic development, job creation, increasing the tax base, and other citywide objectives.

It is important to have a feel for how all of these individuals and groups interpret plans and codes and how together they influence the outcome of the review and approvals process. Perhaps most important is to understand how these groups have interpreted the plan and code in recent decisions on similar projects. With an understanding of both the letter of the plan and code and the softer politics of their interpretation, you should then determine what the developer is allowed to do on the site "as of right" and then begin to compare their proposal against that set of requirements and recent decisions.

If you care about development generally or a certain project in particular, then the most effective way to influence the process is to participate in the meetings of your neighborhood organization and get to know the planning staff and elected officials who represent your community. It is better to have a general understanding of the issues and positive relationships with key people before a contentious project review comes along.

If you hope to be influential then you must be prepared to attend public meetings of the planning commission, the historic preservation commission, the zoning and planning commission, and the city council. You may have to wait through a long agenda for your opportunity to speak for two or three minutes. Still, it is important to speak in public whether in support of a development, with or without qualifications, or against it. Speaking at a public hearing is one of the best ways to make your views known to planning staff, commissioners, and elected officials. It is also a way to build personal relationships and credibility with the people who will make the final decisions and with whom you may be working well into the future.

If you cannot attend a public meeting, then write a good letter or email and submit it to your community organization, city planning staff, and your council member. Both letters and remarks at public hearings become part of the public record. And if the project is very important then speak directly with your district council member. If the project is at all controversial they will want to know what members of the community think about it and they will welcome your insights. At the same time, you should listen because elected officials have experience with developers, and they may also have information or interpretations that will deepen your understanding of the process and the particular project. Your council member may also share his or her own opinion with you and may also offer suggestions for how to refine your arguments. Finally, if you want your words to have an impact then make sure that in all your communications you speak with a rational voice and present a sound and well-articulated argument. Opposition for opposition's sake based on a long laundry list of faults is a weak position to take in cities where elected officials have a sophisticated understanding of land-use politics and where growth and investment are key objectives.

And remember that politicians must also represent the interests of developers, contractors, real estate professionals, property owners, and other related businesses when weighing decisions about land use and new development.

Focus Your Feedback on Aspects of the Design That You Can Influence

When a developer presents her design proposal at the community meeting, pay attention to both the overall concept and the details. After the meeting, go "walk the dirt," just like the developer, and get to know the property. Try to fit the design ideas to the property and the requirements of the city's regulatory framework. Picture how the project responds to those requirements and look for places where there are gaps or oversights. If the developer is seeking a variance, try to understand what she is trying to accomplish and why. Is it to adapt the project to an odd aspect of the site's geometry or is the developer just trying to get permission to increase buildable area? Does the request seem reasonable and does it improve the project? If granted, will it cause any negative impacts for anyone? More important, imagine how the completed project will influence nearby neighbors as well as the larger community for the better in the long run.

Next, be strategic about how you hope to influence the design and pick your battles when it comes to the big issues. List all of the items that you think should be discussed with the developer, beginning with the two or three things that give you the greatest concern. Also list those items that you may be able to live with if they were to be modified or if you received something else in exchange. Most important, focus on those areas where you can be influential, assume you may only get a couple of your demands met, and be prepared to horse-trade.

Be aware that the developer's resources are limited and that much of what she tells you will be accurate as to why she cannot do one thing or the other or why she can't make it out of the material you prefer. Developers are used to being in meetings where people say, "Can't you just . . ." and often when the developer says "no," she really means it. If the developer proposes ten stories and you say "Can't you just make it six?" you may not like the answer but you should not be too surprised. Better yet, instead of spending your limited political capital on something you won't get, like a reduction in height, focus on relocating the driveway so that it is farther away from the corner or more screened from the neighboring property. At the same time, remember that developers are charismatic, optimistic, and extraordinarily good salespeople and they will be selling to you when they explain why they intend to do one thing, why they simply can't do another, or how they have come up with an alternative that is just as good or perhaps even better. So pay attention and don't get sold on something that doesn't seem right.

At the same time, bring your own local knowledge to the table and try to help the developer improve the design of her product. The developer will listen to you if you help her to better understand the property, its context, and the local market. If there is an existing structure on the property or nearby the developer will want to know its history. Popular routes through the neighborhood and important amenities and destinations are important too.

Match your requests to the code, recent land-use decisions in your community, and the realities of contemporary construction practices. It costs an extraordinary amount of money to build a new building of any kind in the United States and it is also true that "they don't make them like they used to." This is in part because the cost of labor has risen more quickly than the cost of materials, which is why it is no longer cheap to have masons make buildings with solid brick walls. So instead of insisting that the developer use brick when the metal panels they are proposing are allowed by the code, focus your comments on the quality of the panel and the pattern, colors, and details.

Understand that developers often have an advantage over community members at least with respect to knowledge and resources. Developers know more about development, about the property, and about their own plans and they have greater resources at their disposal. They also have already taken a risk and invested money in the project so they will concentrate their resources to protect that investment, reduce their risk, and ensure a successful project. They have the money to spend on designs and studies to prove their points, while unfunded volunteer organizations rarely have the capacity to develop independent studies of their own. They also have paid employees working full-time on their projects and they have spent years building relationships with elected politicians and working with planning and economic development staff. Communities and even city staff often do not have the capacity to match wits with developers, particularly on big and complicated projects.

While developers can be cheap and create shoddy or inferior products, in twenty-first-century America they are regulated by government agencies and building codes, they must warranty their projects, and they face real risks and liabilities if they do not perform at a legally dictated minimum standard. Many developers also know that their reputations are important, that their political and social capital are central to their success, and that if they hope to keep doing business in the community they cannot repeatedly churn out inferior products.

Last but not least, remember that the developer has already spent time and money before coming to the neighborhood. He purchased an option on the land, spent money on design fees, and perhaps commissioned a market study. By the time the developer arrives at the neighborhood meeting he has already committed to doing something on the site and you can be sure he won't be going away after one hostile meeting. Remember, he knows his rights, and, as we saw in Chapter 2 he may be low on the "agreeableness" trait so it is hard to hurt his feelings.

Focus on Interests, Not Positions

Experts in the field of negotiation and conflict resolution recommend that two parties can both obtain better outcomes if they focus on understanding their own *interests* as well as those of the other party rather than by simply taking hard *positions*. The classic example is of two cooks who argue over who gets to use the last remaining orange in the kitchen. They agree to cut the orange in half, only to learn when it is too late that one cook wanted the juice of the orange for a sauce while the other wanted the peel for baking. By taking positions—"I must have the whole orange"—they cornered themselves into a false choice and obtained only half of what they wanted. If they had only understood one another's interests better, they could have each effectively obtained a whole orange.[3]

Here is the important question that next-door neighbors and other community members must answer: "Is this an appropriate project for our community and, if so, how can we do everything in our power today to make it as good as it can be and ensure its success in the long run—for the developer and for the community?" Finally, after coming to a better understanding of developers, we must put our feet into their shoes and imagine what they are thinking of doing in our neighborhood—and how they are thinking about working with us.

"Why Is It in Your Best Interest to Work with Me Today?"

"The hardest job for a developer is selling the community on the idea that 'that piece of land is not zoned vacant,'" says the Chicago developer Buzz Ruttenberg. "Everybody is used to looking at that lot and their dog regularly pees and poops there. So they say things like 'You are going to block my view,' 'There are people living here—where are they going to park,' and 'I like the fact that there is not so much traffic here now.' That is a difficult sale to make and there are always naysayers, so I would rather just meet them head-on. So after the day that I sign a contract for a piece of property, and long before we close on it or have definitive plans, I call up the one or two community groups in the area and meet with them."[4]

Ruttenberg says that on balance, over the years, "we have been blessed. We had an eye to the architecture and the community and better still, my dad was a very friendly guy and we had credibility because we had done so much work in the area and we lived in the community." Ruttenberg and his father both always represented their own interests directly to the community so they were known. "We never hired anyone to speak for us and we always started by saying, 'I live here, my children live here, my grandchildren live here. I did this one, you live in that one, you shop at this other one, and you know that we generally do good work.'" Because he lives in the community, Ruttenberg can say that "but you can't say that if you have been hired to speak for a developer or if you just flew in on a plane from someplace."

So Ruttenberg opens the communications channels early. "We let them know we are coming and usually the first thing someone says is 'We were going to make that vacant land a park,' so I say, 'Well, the city will have to buy it because it is not zoned vacant. Let us meet and discuss what would be good for the community.' I am being genuine and I am interested in their ideas and I don't have a hard drawing yet." Smart developers are careful not to bring overly developed drawings to a community meeting because it sends the message that the design is a fait accompli and they are just speaking to the neighbors because they have to. At the same time, the developer has to invest some time and money into a design to determine if the property is developable. "I do have a soft sketch or an idea because you cannot put a piece of land under contract if you don't at least have a soft drawing that shows you something that can work."

"The bigger issue," says Ruttenberg, "is that developers must know that today we are living in a state of anarchy, where the nonelected neighborhood watchdogs are trying to control the politicians. More often the only people who show up at neighborhood meetings are those who oppose the project and many negative people have some other personal agenda. They have not been successful in their own careers, they have the time, or they have a narrow personal interest. And they think they know more than I do, even though they have no experience in the development business, they have never signed their name on a construction loan, and they have never paid for someone else's mistake. But they know what housing is 'because I live in a house' and they know what a neighborhood is 'because I live in a neighborhood.'

"So ten or twenty naysayers show up but the one hundred or so supporters don't bother coming and if you invite them and they do come then you are accused of packing the house." Ruttenberg always starts by saying that he has lived in the neighborhood all his life and usually somebody snidely asks "how long is that?" and Ruttenberg tells them that he is seventy-one, although he looks energetic, youthful, and younger than his age. Ruttenberg used to bring his children along with him "because it is harder to unfairly pick on me if I have my children there," although that doesn't stop everyone. When Ruttenberg introduced himself at one meeting, a man said, "You are not David Ruttenberg—I know David Ruttenberg." Ruttenberg's high school–aged daughter was with him at that meeting and before he could say anything, "she stood up, pointed at her father, and said, 'I am his daughter and that is David Ruttenberg.'"

Other things matter too, from the arrangement of the room to personal appearance. "Whenever I am in a room, I do not make it appear like a church or school with rows of chairs and me in front or on a stage." Rather, Ruttenberg likes to make sure that people sit together around a table or in chairs arranged in a circle. He dresses casually like part of the community too. "I don't wear expensive suits and no one wears ties anymore anyhow. We take all of the peripherals away and emphasize that we are equals."

And they are equals, in a sense, because Ruttenberg needs their buy-in at some level. "The truth is you have to find a way to satisfy enough of the community to get their support." So Ruttenberg starts most meetings with the same question: "Why is it in your best interest to work with me today?" And then he answers the question. "Number one, that piece of land is not zoned vacant and once it is ten or twenty stories high it doesn't really matter how high it is because it is going to block much of the view anyhow. Number two, I am going to be putting housing there and when I am done, my units will sell for x dollars per square foot and the unit you bought for x minus one dollar per square foot is going to be worth more—your property value is going to go up." Then Ruttenberg listens to the neighbors and looks for a common goal that they can work toward solving together.

"One of the most important things is to check your ego at the door because you have to be a good listener. So somebody says, 'Tall, short, wider, fatter, this kind of unit, that kind of amenity,' and you listen to them. And the reason you listen is that the truth is, they are reflective of the market and you can learn useful things because the market is smarter than you are. So if people say they want more closet space or bigger bedrooms, those are things you want to know. And you would rather know sooner than later because in places like Chicago and elsewhere, where you can presell before you begin construction, you can learn a lot and then make changes." Changing a building after it has been constructed is costly and difficult, but "if the market says 'that doesn't work or sell,' then you can fix a drawing pretty easily, and that is why I would rather know early."

Ruttenberg has found that by identifying and working toward common goals and incorporating the feedback of residents into the design he can both improve the quality of the product before he goes to market and go some distance toward earning the support of the local community. And, at the end of the process, says Ruttenberg, it helps to be able to say, "As all of you know, I have met fourteen times with this committee and although we have not agreed on everything we have made twelve changes." "That," concludes Ruttenberg, "will generate some support and trust."

Conclusion

Much unnecessary unhappiness in our lives comes from people not doing what we expect them to do, or not doing what we think we would do if we were in their position. If we expect developers to act the way we would like them to, we set ourselves up for disappointment. But if we come to understand their entrepreneurial personalities, their processes and products, and their skills and motivations, then we are in a better position to advocate for the best possible projects for our communities.

Developers fulfill a necessary function by providing the products that we want and need. So rather than being fearful and distrusting when developers walk through the door, keep an open mind and try to figure them out. What other areas have they worked in? Have they developed elsewhere in your community and, if so, how did they get along with the neighbors on those projects? How important is reputation to them and are they planning to build again nearby? Do they have good relations with local elected officials and the district council member? How well do they seem to get along with their architect and other consultants—do they have good chemistry? What do the buyers in their previous projects think of the quality and value of their products? Do they seem to listen to what community members have to say or are they just paying lip service? Are they smooth or just slimy and do they have a big ego or are they just plain arrogant? And ask yourself, "Does he seem like a good guy or a bad guy?"

Last but not least, get them to tell you about their work, their personal philosophy, and how their latest project is their whole life story turned into a building. That should give you a pretty good idea of what they will try to do next door, down the street, and in your community. And with that level of understanding you may be able to find some common ground and the basis for a productive relationship.

Figure 60. Development becomes community: Families playing in the Jamison Square fountain in the Pearl District of Portland, Oregon. The whole area had been an abandoned railyard in 1996. Photo by Kirsten Force; courtesy of Ankrom Moisan Architects.

Prologue

1. Andrés Duany, Duany Plater-Zyberk & Company, interview by author, 7 July 2010, Miami.

2. David Haymes, interview by author, 30 June 2010, Chicago.

3. The City of Miami alone produced twenty-three thousand new condo units between 2003 and 2009, and Broward and Palm Beach counties, to the north, built or permitted another eighteen thousand during the same period. Lisa Rab, "South Florida's Housing Crisis Leaves Behind Ghost Towers," *Broward/Palm Beach New Times*, 18 June 2009, available from http://www.browardpalmbeach.com/content/printVersion/856231/ (accessed 9 February 2014).

4. Anthony Downs, *Niagara of Capital: How Global Capital Has Transformed Housing and Real Estate Markets* (Chicago: Urban Land Institute, 2007).

5. "What a Difference Four Years Make: U.S. Population Projected to Grow at a Slower Pace over the Next Five Decades," *Random Samplings*, the official blog of the U.S. Census Bureau, available from http://blogs.census.gov/2012/12/12/what-a-difference-four-years-make -u-s-population-projected-to-grow-at-a-slower-pace-over-the-next-five-decades/ (accessed 12 December 2012). I first heard the term "flight to the city" in remarks made in a meeting by Minneapolis Mayor R. T. Rybak in December 2013.

6. Alan Ehrenhalt, *The Great Inversion and the Future of the American City* (New York: Vintage, 2013).

7. Edward Glaeser, *Triumph of the City: How Our Greatest Invention Makes Us Richer, Smarter, Greener, Healthier, and Happier* (New York: Penguin, 2011).

Chapter 1

1. David Waronker believes that he first said this at a Moorestown, New Jersey, Rotary Club meeting in 2000 when, as guest speaker, he spoke on behalf of and as president of the Builders League of South Jersey. Email communication between the author and David Waronker, 10 February 2014.

2. Arlene Vadum, "A Short History of Boston's Beacon Hill," available from http://www .beacon-hill-boston.com/History (accessed 21 January 2013); Christopher Klein, "Where the Melting Pot Still Simmers," *Boston Globe*, 8 November 2009, available from http://www .boston.com/yourtown/boston/beaconhill/articles/2009/11/08/where_the_melting_pot_still _simmers/ (accessed 21 January 2013).

3. Vadum, "A Short History of Boston's Beacon Hill"; *Wikipedia*, "Beacon Hill, Boston," available from http://en.wikipedia.org/wiki/Beacon_Hill, Boston (accessed 21 January 2013);

Moshe Elmekias, "How Real Estate Developers Shaped Beacon Hill and America," 27 September 2012, available from http://blog.magrealestate.com/boston-property/how-real-estate-developers-shaped-beacon-hill-america/ (accessed 28 August 2014);

4. Elmekias, "How Real Estate Developers Shaped Beacon Hill and America."

5. Vadum, "A Short History"; Elmekias, "How Real Estate Developers Shaped."

6. Vadum, "A Short History"; Elmekias, "How Real Estate Developers Shaped."

7. The quote was attributed to Burnham after his death although there is no evidence that he actually said it. Charles Moore, "Closing in, 1911–1912," in *Daniel H. Burnham, Architect, Planner of Cities, Volume 2* (Boston: Houghton Mifflin, 1921).

8. The term "federal bulldozer" comes from Martin Anderson's book of the same title (*The Federal Bulldozer* [Cambridge, MA: MIT Press, 1964]).

9. About 60 percent of the land in the United States is privately owned but when Alaska and the Western states are excluded, this number rises to between 80 percent and 98.5 percent for the remaining thirty-four states. Ruben N. Lubowski, Marlow Vesterby, Shawn Bucholtz, Alba Baez, and Michael Roberts, *Major Uses of Land in the United States, 2002,* Economic Information Bulletin No. EIB-14, May 2006, Economic Research Service, U.S. Department of Agriculture, March 2006, available from http://www.ers.usda.gov/media/249896/eib14_reportsummary_1_.pdf (accessed 4 March 2013).

10. Gerald W. Fogelson, interview by author, 1 July 2010, Chicago; Gerald W. Fogelson and Joe Marconi, *Central Station: Realizing a Vision,* new updated ed. (Chicago: Self-published, 2007).

11. "Central Station a Product of Developer's Big Dreams," *Chicago Journal,* 1 November 2001, available from http://www.centralstationsouthloop.com/news_bigdreams.asp (accessed 20 January 2014).

Chapter 2

1. Quoted in Brad Tonini, *The New Rules of the Game for Entrepreneurs: Success Strategies for Anyone Starting or Growing a Business* (Melbourne: Wilkenson, 2006), 3.

2. Joseph A. Schumpeter, *Capitalism, Socialism, and Democracy,* 5th ed. (London: George Allen and Unwin, 1976), 131–134.

3. Michel Villette and Catherine Vuillermot, *From Predators to Icons: Exposing the Myth of the Business Hero* (Ithaca, NY: Cornell University Press, 2009), 18–19.

4. Schumpeter, *Capitalism, Socialism, and Democracy,* 131–134; Villette and Vuillermot, *From Predators to Icons,* 18–19.

5. Scott Shane and Sankaran Venkataraman, "The Promise of Entrepreneurship as a Field of Research," *Academy of Management Review* 25, no. 1 (2000): 218–224. Shane and Venkataraman's framework is based on a comprehensive review of the entrepreneurship literature that consolidates and summarizes fifty-nine other studies. For ease of reading, I have not cited those studies individually here but rely instead on the authors' summary of their findings. For those interested in looking more closely at the subject or individual studies, I can recommend no better single summary of the field than this article.

6. Ibid., 223.

7. Daniel Kahneman, *Thinking Fast and Slow* (New York: Farrar, Straus, and Giroux, 2011), 334–341.

8. Shane and Venkataraman, "The Promise of Entrepreneurship as a Field of Research," 218–224.

9. Scott Shane, *Born Entrepreneurs, Born Leaders: How Your Genes Affect Your Work Life* (New York: Oxford University Press, 2010), 151.

10. Ibid., 154–158.

11. Ibid.

12. Ibid., 158–168.

13. Ibid. Geneticists do not actually talk about the "novelty-seeking gene" but Shane uses a sort of shorthand to name genes based on the personality traits they influence.

14. Ibid., 151–154.

15. Villette and Vuillermot, *From Predators to Icons*, 102–103.

16. Ibid., 84–91, 115–118.

17. Ibid., 73–84.

18. David "Buzz" Ruttenberg, interview by author, 1 July 2010, Chicago.

Chapter 3

1. John Carroll, interview by author, 21 July 2010, Portland, Oregon.

2. Clayton M. Christensen, *The Innovator's Dilemma: When New Technologies Cause Great Firms to Fail* (Boston: Harvard Business School Press, 1997), xvii–xix.

3. Ibid.

4. *Wikipedia*, "Disruptive Innovation," available from http://en.wikipedia.org/wiki/Disruptive_innovation (accessed 4 January 2014).

5. [5] Harvey Molotch, *Where Stuff Comes From: How Toasters, Toilets, Cars, Computers, and Many Other Things Come to Be as They Are* (New York: Routledge, 2003), 97.

6. Pat Prendergast, interview by author, 20 July 2010, Portland, Oregon.

7. Portland maps, 2010 U.S. Census, available from http://www.portlandmaps.com/detail.cfm?action = Census&propertyid = R239129&state_id = 1N1E34BC%20%201900&address_id = 377770&intersection_id = &dynamic_point = 0&x = 7642768.468&y = 686772.724&place = 930%20NW%20 12TH%20AVE&city = PORTLAND&neighborhood = PEARL&seg_id = 112544 (accessed 28 March 2012).

8. John Carroll, interview by author, 21 July 2010, Portland, Oregon.

Chapter 4

1. David "Buzz" Ruttenberg, interview by author, 1 July 2010, Chicago.

2. Alan Lapidus, *Everything by Design: My Life as an Architect* (New York: St. Martin's, 2007), 73. According to Alan Lapidus, this was "the best piece of architectural advice that Morris Lapidus gave his architect son."

3. Dana Cuff and John Wreidt, eds., *Architecture from the Outside In: Selected Essays by Robert Gutman* (New York: Princeton Architectural Press, 2010), 31–42.

4. Louis H. Sullivan, "The Tall Office Building Artistically Considered," *Lippincott's Magazine* 57 (March 1896): 403–409; Herb Emmerman, interview by author, 30 June 2010, Chicago.

5. Collin Barr, interview by author, 7 May 2010, Minneapolis; Mark Swenson, interviews by author, 3 March 2010 and 10 June 2010, Minneapolis.

6. David Haymes, interview by author, 30 June 2010, Chicago.

7. Andrés Duany, interview by author, 26 July 2010, Miami.

8. Allan Shulman, interview by author, 26 July 2010, Miami.

9. Jeff Hamilton, interview by author, 21 July 2010, Portland, Oregon.

10. Stewart Ankrom, interview by author, 21 July 2010, Portland, Oregon.

11. Ed McNamara, interview by author, 22 July 2010, Portland, Oregon.

12. David Haymes, interview by author, 30 June 2010, Chicago.

Chapter 5

1. Alain de Botton, *The Architecture of Happiness* (New York: Pantheon, 2006), 183.

2. Kimberly Devlin and Jack L. Nasar, "The Beauty and the Beast: Some Preliminary Comparisons of 'High' Versus 'Popular' Residential Architecture and Public Versus Architect Judgments of Same," *Journal of Environmental Psychology* 9 (1989): 333–344.

3. Robert Gifford, Donald W. Hine, Werner Muller-Clemm, and Kelly T. Shaw, "Why Architects and Laypersons Judge Buildings Different: Cognitive Properties and Physical Bases," *Journal of Architectural and Planning Research* 19, no. 2 (Summer 2002): 131–148.

4. Phil Hubbard, "Conflicting Interpretations of Architecture: An Empirical Investigation," *Journal of Environmental Psychology* 16 (1996): 75–92.

5. Robert G. Hershberger, "A Study of Meaning and Architecture," in *Environmental Aesthetics: Theory, Research and Applications*, ed. Jack L. Nasar (Cambridge: Cambridge University Press, 1988), 175–194; Linda Groat, "Meaning in Post-modern Architecture: An Examination Using the Multiple Sorting Task," *Journal of Environmental Psychology* 2 (1982): 3–22; Kimberly Devlin, "An Examination of Architectural Interpretation: Architects Versus Non-architects," *Journal of Architectural Planning and Research* 7 (1990): 235–244; Gifford et al., "Why Architects and Laypersons Judge Buildings Different."

6. Margaret A. Wilson and David V. Canter, "The Development of Concepts During Architectural Education: An Example of a Multivariate Model of the Concept of Architectural Style," *Applied Psychology: An International Review* 39 (1990): 431–455; Hubbard, "Conflicting Interpretations of Architecture," 81; Gifford et al., "Why Architects and Laypersons Judge Buildings Different," 145–146.

7. Ann Forsyth and Katherine Crewe, "New Visions for Suburbia: Reassessing Aesthetics and Place-making in Modernism, Imageability, and New Urbanism," *Journal of Urban Design* 14, no. 4 (2009): 415–438.

8. Ibid., 418; Herbert J. Gans, *Popular Culture and High Culture: An Analysis and Evaluation of Taste*, 2nd ed. (New York: Basic Books, 1999).

9. Gail Lissner, interview by author, 1 July 2010, Chicago.

10. James Loewenberg, interview by author, 29 June 2010.

11. Blair Kamin, *Terror and Wonder: Architecture in a Tumultuous Age* (Chicago: University of Chicago Press, 2010), 59–64.

12. Blair Kamin, "Waves of Creativity: Aqua, the World's Tallest Building Designed by a Woman-owned Firm, Is One of Chicago's Boldest—and Best—New Skyscrapers," *Chicago Tribune*, 4 November 2009.

13. Jorge Pérez, interview by author, 28 July 2010, Miami.

14. "Builder 100, 2007," *Builder*, available from http://www.builderonline.com/builder100/2007.aspx (accessed 17 August 2012); "Builder 100, 2012," *Builder*, available from and http://www.builderonline.com/builder100/2012.aspx (accessed 17 August 2012); Joel Russell, "The Billion-Dollar Club," *Hispanic Business Magazine*, June 2004, available from http://www.hispanicbusiness.com/2004/5/26/the_billiondollar_club.htm (accessed 17 August 2012); Siobhan Morrissey, "25 Most Influential Hispanics in America," *Time*, 22 August 2005, http://content.time.com/time/specials/packages/article/0,28804,2008201_2008200_2008208

,00.html; "The 400 Richest Americans," *Forbes*, 17 September 2008, available from http://www.forbes.com/lists/2008/54/400list08_Jorge-Perez_RGG7.html (accessed 17 August 2012); Jorge Pérez, *Powerhouse Principles: The Ultimate Blueprint for Real Estate Success in an Ever-Changing Market* (New York: Penguin, 2008).

 15. "Matthew Haggman, "Miami Condo King Battles to Survive Real Estate Slump," *Miami Herald*, 28 February 2009, available from http://www.mcclatchydc.com/2009/03/01/63030/miami-condo-king-batt les-to-surviv e.html (accessed 17 August 2012).

 16. "School of Architecture Dedicates a Building Apart: The New Jorge M. Pérez Architecture Center Is a Symbol of the School's Mission," *VERITAS* 48, no. 3 (November 2005).

 17. Pérez, interview by author.

 18. Ibid.; Pérez, *Powerhouse Principles*.

 19. Robbie Whelan, "Miami Condos on Upswing," *Wall Street Journal*, 2 November 2011.

 20. Martha Brannigan, "Related Says My Brickell Units Are Selling Strong," *Miami Herald*, 14 June 2012.

Chapter 6

 1. Herb Emmerman, interview by author, 30 June 2010, Chicago.

 2. Harvey Molotch, *Where Stuff Comes From: How Toasters, Toilets, Cars, Computers, and Many Other Things Come to Be as They Are* (New York: Routledge, 2003), 131, 152–153.

 3. Ibid., 132–133.

 4. Ibid., 133–135; Herbert Blumer, "Fashion: From Class Differentiation to Collective Selection," *Sociological Quarterly* 10 (1969): 275–291; Ray Oldenburg, *The Good Great Place* (New York: Paragon, 1989).

 5. Molotch, *Where Stuff Comes From*, 133–135, 157.

 6. Herb Emmerman, interview by author, 30 June 2010, Chicago.

 7. Jim Losik, telephone interview by author, 24 June 2010.

 8. Cathy Tinker, interview by author, 30 June 2010, Chicago.

 9. Gregg Covin, interview by author, 26 July 2010, Miami; telephone interview by author, February 4, 2014.

 10. David Villano, "Residential Development: Condo Power—Miami-Dade—June 2004," *Florida Trend*, 1 June 2004, available from http://www.floridatrend.com/article/12049/residential-development-condo-power-miami-dade-june-2004 (accessed 2 February 2014).

Chapter 7

 1. Sun Tzu, *The Art of War*, trans. Samuel B. Griffith (New York: Oxford University Press, 1963), 73.

 2. Markets turn down fast, catching not only inexperienced developers. These comments are representative of what many very experienced developers had to say after the bust in 2008. The words and figures have been modified to ensure anonymity.

 3. Anthony Downs, *Real Estate and the Financial Crisis: How Turmoil in the Capital Markets Is Restructuring Real Estate Finance* (Washington, DC: Urban Land Institute, 2009), 103.

 4. Ibid., 103–104.

 5. Ibid., 107–108.

 6. Ibid.

7. Ibid., 108–109.

8. Ibid., 109–111; Nassim Nicholas Taleb, *The Black Swan: The Impact of the Highly Improbable*, 2nd ed. (New York: Random House, 2010).

9. Tanya Bell, interview by author, 13 April 2010, Minneapolis.

10. Warren E. Buffett, Chairman of the Board of Berkshire Hathaway, Inc., in a letter to shareholders for the year 2001, 28 February 2002, available from http://www.berkshirehathaway .com/2001ar/2001letter.html.

11. Anthony Downs, "Perverse Incentives: A History of Economic and Financial Practices from the Late 1980s to 2006 That Have Resulted in the Mortgage and Credit Crises of 2007 and Beyond," *Urban Land* 67, no. 3 (March 2008): 117–123.

12. David "Buzz" Ruttenberg, interview by author, 1 July 2010, Chicago.

13. Sandon J. Goldberg and Sharon A. Meyers, "Oversupply in the Office Market: The Legacy of the 1980s," Solomon Brothers Real Estate, Bond Market Research (New York: Solomon Brothers, 16 May 1989).

14. Ruttenberg interview; Warren E. Buffett, "Buy American. I Am," *New York Times*, 16 October 2008, available from http://www.nytimes.com/2008/10/17/opinion/17buffett .html?_r = 0 (accessed 1 March 2014).

15. John Carroll, interview by author, 21 July 2010, Portland, Oregon.

16. Steve Rosenberg, interview by author, 21 July 2010, Portland, Oregon.

17. Andrés Duany, interview by author, 26 July 2010, Miami.

18. Tibor Hollo, interview by author, 27 July 2010, Miami.

Chapter 8

1. James C. Collins and Jerry I. Porras, *Built to Last: Successful Habits of Visionary Companies* (New York: HarperCollins, 1997), 8.

2. Francesco Guerrera, "Welch Condemns Share Price Focus," *Financial Times*, 12 March 2009, available from http://www.ft.com/cms/s/0/294ff1f2-0f27-11de-ba10-0000779fd 2ac.html#axzz1YiPM2TIg (accessed 16 December 2010).

3. Corey Ryan, "Officials Implode South Padre Tower," *The Monitor*, 13 December 2009, available from http://m.themonitor.com/news/local/video-officials-implode-south -padre-tower/article_1352fa1f-a2d9-5959-a883-641a9a4a9b65.html?mode = jqm (accessed 16 December 2010); Lynn Brezosky, "Leaning South Padre Tower Turned into 55,000 Tons of Debris," available from http://www.mysanantonio.com/news/79169072.html?showFull Article = y (accessed 16 December 2010).

4. Ryan, "Officials Implode South Padre Tower"; Brezosky, "Leaning South Padre Tower."

5. "Ocean Tower, LP, a Texas Limited Partnership, Plaintiff, vs. Raba-Kistner Consultants, Inc., a Texas Corporation; Datum Engineering, Inc., a Texas Corporation; and Zachry Construction Corporation, a Delaware Corporation, Defendants," 26 June 2008, in "Ocean Tower Lawsuit, Full Text," Texas Supreme Court, available from http://www.supreme.courts .state.tx.us/ebriefs/10/10088801Rec.pdf (accessed 16 December 2010).

6. John Kay, *Obliquity: Why Our Goals Are Best Achieved Indirectly* (London: Profile, 2010), 1–9.

7. Ibid., 39–44.

8. Ibid., 60–67, 171–179.

9. Ibid., 4–5, 73, 92.

10. Ibid., 59–67, 88–97.

11. Ibid., 173.

12. Ibid., 175–177.

13. Ibid.

14. Collins and Porras, *Built to Last*, 9, 214.

15. Kay, *Obliquity*, 21–23.

16. Ibid., 172.

17. Charles Lindblom, "The Science of 'Muddling Through,'" *Public Administration Review* 19 (1959): 79–88; Gary Klein, *Sources of Power: How People Make Decisions* (Cambridge, MA: MIT Press, 1999); Malcolm Gladwell, *Blink: The Power of Thinking Without Thinking* (New York: Little, Brown, 2007).

18. David "Buzz" Ruttenberg, interview by author, 1 July 2010, Chicago; Gerald W. Fogelson, interview by author, 1 July 2010, Chicago; Jorge Pérez, interview by author, 28 July 2010, Miami; John Carroll, interview by author, 21 July 2010, Portland, Oregon.

19. Collin Barr, interview by author, 7 May 2010, Minneapolis.

20. Robert Engstrom, interview by author, 4 June 2010, Minneapolis.

21. Ardyth Hall, telephone interview by author, 15 June 2010.

22. Craig Robins, interview by author, 22 July 2010, Miami.

23. Kyle Munzenrieder, "Design District Taking on Bal Harbour in Battle of the High-End Boutiques," *Miami New Times*, 22 February 2012, available from http://blogs.miaminew times.com/riptide/2012/02/design_district_taking_on _bal.php (accessed 19 February 2014).

24. Ina Paiva Cordle, "Miami Design District's Transformation into a Luxury Shopping Destination Is Underway," *Miami Herald*, 23 September 2013, available from http://www .miamiherald.com/2013/09/23/3644911/miami-design-districts-transformation.html (accessed 19 February 2014).

25. "Interview with Craig Robins, CEO and President of Dacra," *The Collector Tribune*, 14 February 2012, available from http://www.collectortribune.com/2012/02/14/interview -with-craig-robins-ceo-and-president-of-dacra/ (accessed 19 February 2014).

Chapter 9

1. Herb Emmerman, interview by author, 30 June 2010, Chicago.

2. Joseph A. Schumpeter, *Capitalism, Socialism, and Democracy*, 5th ed. (1942; London: George Allen and Unwin, 1976), 131–134.

3. Robert C. Solomon, *Ethics and Excellence: Cooperation and Integrity in Business* (New York: Oxford University Press, 1993), 246–251.

4. Ibid., 249.

5. Ibid., 250–251.

6. Ibid., 251.

7. Lewis Hyde, *Trickster Makes This World: Mischief, Myth, and Art* (New York: Farrar, Straus, and Giroux, 1998).

8. Ibid., 45, 52, 276.

9. Ibid., 62, 76, 78.

10. Ibid., 45, 284.

11. Ibid., 46–47, 62.

12. Ibid., 139–140.

13. Beth Broome called 1111 Lincoln Road "a robust house of cards." Beth Broome, "Herzog and de Meuron Strips Down in Miami Beach with a Revealing New Parking Garage," *Architectural Record* (June 2010), avaliable from http://archrecord.construction.com/projects/ portfolio/archives/10061111Lincoln_Road-1.asp (accessed 28 August 2014).

14. Edwin Heathcote, "1111 Lincoln Road by Herzog and de Meuron," *IconEye*, 29 March 2010, available from http://www.iconeye.com/architecture/features/item/4336-1111 -lincoln-road-by-herzog-de-meuron (accessed 28 August 2014).

15. Rowan Moore, "1111 Lincoln Road, Miami, Florida; Leighton House, London," in *The Observer*, 28 March 2010, available from http://www.guardian.co.uk/artanddesign/2010/ mar/28/1111-lincoln-miami-herzog-meuron (accessed 19 February 2011).

16. Robert Wennett, interview by author, 26 July 2010, Miami.

17. In 2010, Federal Realty's portfolio contained approximately 18.2 million square feet in major metropolitan areas on the East and West Coasts, and the company's market value was about $5 billion.

18. John Holusha, "Commercial Property/430 West 14th Street; A Developer Puts a Bet on the Meatpacking District," *New York Times*, 16 July 2000, available from http://www.ny times.com/2000/07/16/realestate/commercial-property-430-west-14th-street-developer-puts -bet-meatpacking-district.html?pagewanted = 2 (accessed 19 February 2011).

19. Paul Goldberger, "Wheelhouse: Herzog and de Meuron Reinvent the Parking Garage," *The New Yorker*, 9 August 2010, available from http://www.newyorker.com/arts/ critics/skyline/2010/08/09/100809crsk_skyline_goldberger (accessed 19 February 2011).

20. Heathcote, "1111 Lincoln Road."

21. Fred A. Bernstein, "Come to Park; Stay for the Architecture," *New York Times*, 1 December 2009, available from http://www.nytimes.com/2009/12/02/business/02parking .html?pagewanted = all&_r = 0 (accessed 19 February 2011).

22. Ibid.

23. Madeleine Marr, "Miami's on Benedikt Taschen's Map," *Miami Herald*, 20 May 2010, available from http://www.miamiherald.com/2010/05/20/v-print/1638289/miam . . . (accessed 19 February 2011); Elaine Walker, "High-end Coffee Exec Focuses on Quality, Experience," *Miami Herald*, 21 June 2010, available from http://www.miamiherald.com/2010/06/ 21/v-print/1688457/high. . . . (accessed 19 February 2011).

24. Goldberger, "Wheelhouse"; Moore, "1111 Lincoln Road."

25. Hyde, *Trickster Makes This World*, 47.

Chapter 10

1. David "Buzz" Ruttenberg, interview by author, 1 July 2010, Chicago.

2. John Logan and Harvey Molotch, *Urban Fortunes: The Political Economy of Place* (Berkeley: University of California Press, 1988). See also Allan Altshuler and David Luberoff, *Mega-Projects: The Changing Politics of Urban Public Investment* (Washington, DC: Brookings Institution Press, 2003); and Peter Hendee Brown, *America's Waterfront Revival: Port Authorities and Urban Redevelopment* (Philadelphia: University of Pennsylvania Press, 2009).

3. See, for example, the classic text on negotiating and conflict resolution by Roger Fisher, William L. Ury, and Bruce Patton, *Getting to Yes: Negotiating Agreement Without Giving In* (New York: Penguin, 2011).

4. Ruttenberg interview.

Index

Page references in italics refer to illustrations

Acknowledgments

I would first like to thank Ross Fefercorn and Bob Lux, two Minneapolis developers who gave me my first two opportunities to work in the real estate development business. They each taught me an extraordinary amount while allowing me to see the world through their eyes—the eyes of the developer—and I owe my enlightened perspective to them.

I owe an enormous debt of gratitude to the many other developers, architects, planners, public officials, investors, lenders, and others in the real estate business who allowed me to interview them and who continued to take my phone calls and correspond with me long afterward. They all gave generously of their time, memories, and personal philosophies, and some of their life stories serve as the backbone of the book. Every one of them taught me something and influenced my thinking, and my greatest regret is that I was not able to include all of their very interesting and relevant stories. My thanks to Stuart Ankrom, Chris Carley, John Carroll, Kevin Cavanaugh, Gregg Covin, Frank Delvecchio, Ken DeMuth, Andrés Duany, Herb Emmerman, Erin Flynn, Jerry Fogelson, Bob Haddon, Harvey Haddon, Jeff Hamilton, David Haymes, Tibor Hollo, Ben Kaiser, Gail Lissner, Jim Loewenberg, Jim Losik, Corey Martin, Ed McNamara, Jorge Pérez, Gerald Posner, Pat Prendergast, Craig Robbins, Steve Rosenberg, Buzz Ruttenberg, Kelly Saito, Ethan Seltzer, Ron Shipka Sr., Allan Shulman, Charles Sieger, Tiffany Sweitzer, Cathy Tinker, Robert Wennett, Dennis Wilde, Homer Williams, and Bernard Zyscovich.

I owe another enormous debt of gratitude to the many friends and colleagues in the Twin Cities whom I spoke to early on. They helped me to clarify my questions and frame up my ideas. Each of them, too, taught me something new so thanks to Collin Barr, Cecile Bedor, Tanya Bell, Barry Berg, Colleen Carey, Al Carlson, Paul Carlson, Rick Collins, Susan Diamond, Karen Dubrosky, Beth Elliott, Bob Engstrom, Susan Evans, Dan Farley, Bob Feyereisen, Becky Finnegan, Spencer Finseth, Patricia Fitzgerald,

Margo Geffen, Don Gerberding, Andy Gittleman, Lisa Goodman, David Graham, Tim Griffin, Curt Gunsbury, Ardyth Hall, Brett Hildreth, Scott Hoffman, Nick Koch, Murray Kornberg, Lori Larson, Chuck Leer, Chuck Lutz, Jeremy Mayberg, David Motzenbecker, Gretchen Nicholls, Merrie Sjogren, John Slack, Dan Smith, Bob Spaulding, Mark Swenson, Lucy Thompson, Missy Thompson, Kit Richardson, Mark Rutzick, Jim Rutzick, Sherman Rutzick, Jay Walljasper, and Ellison Yahner. Indeed, since 2010 I have spoken with anyone and everyone who has shown even the faintest interest in the subject so for those of you whose ears I have bent but I have forgotten to mention, my thanks to each of you as well.

In 2008 I began teaching a course in private-sector real estate development at the University of Minnesota's Humphrey School of Public Affairs, where every week I asked my students to put themselves in the developer's shoes. I would like to thank all of those students for allowing me to develop and try out in class many of the ideas that appear in this book. Thanks in particular to those who read the draft chapters and offered comments and to Barrett Steenrod, who helped me over a hurdle with a thoughtful suggestion in class one night on how to better organize and tell the stories. Finally, thanks to my two excellent teaching assistants and former students, Ian Baebenroth and Amanda Janzen, and to John Adams, who first hired me to teach at the Humphrey School.

Five friends who are also colleagues in the development business in the Twin Cities have been particularly generous to me over the past several years, reading and marking up multiple versions of the manuscript and then meeting with me as a group over Indian food to offer their thoughts and suggestions. My most profound and sincere thanks go to Peter Berrie, Noah Bly, Michael Byrd, David Frank, and Brian Gorecki for responding to my calls and for helping me to write a more readable book for a broad audience. Amanda Johnson Ashley, David Benning, Spencer Finseth, and Gustav Larsson also read early drafts and offered invaluable insights as did two anonymous reviewers: one who read and commented on the manuscript twice, and an anonymous member of the press's editorial board who tactfully pointed out a huge blind spot in my argument. The book is far better for all of their comments and observations.

At the University of Pennsylvania Press my gratitude and thanks go to Genie Birch and Susan Wachter, codirectors of the Penn Institute for Urban Research and coeditors of The City in the Twenty-First Century series, for publishing my first and now, this, my second book. Thanks also to Peter

Agree, editor-in-chief, who once told me to consider him a personal cheer-leader. I have, and he, Erica Ginsburg, Amanda Ruffner, and Jennifer Konieczny have all cheerfully worked to make the production of this book as smooth a process as possible and to make the final product as good as it can be.

Finally, I offer my deepest thanks to my indulgent and supportive family. To my daughter, Astrid, who was born while I typed away on the first draft of the manuscript for this book, and to my son, Magnus, for allowing me to complete a second book in his lifetime. Most important, I thank my loving wife, Anna, who patiently listened to me talk about real estate development for seven years, all the while offering insightful suggestions. I also thank Anna for supporting all of my creative endeavors throughout our marriage and our time together. She has given me the freedom to thrive in my career and my life, and I am very fortunate to have found her.

Printed and bound by CPI Group (UK) Ltd, Croydon, CR0 4YY

16/04/2025

14658414-0001